DATE DUE

s

*The Routle   one of the most
comprehen   second edition,
it contains:

- A nev
- Upda
- Name
- A sur   ture
- An ex
- Illust
- A ma

Presenting   ery of Egyptian
mythology   useums and all
those inte

**George H   collections in the
Education   cturer and writer.

D0824819

You may also be interested in the following Routledge Student Reference titles:

Archaeology: The Key Concepts
Edited by Colin Renfrew and Paul Bahn

Ancient History: Key Themes and Approaches
Neville Morley

Fifty Key Classical Authors
Alison Sharrock and Rhiannon Ash

Who's Who in Classical Mythology
Michael Grant and John Hazel

Who's Who in Non-Classical Mythology
Egerton Sykes, revised by Allen Kendall

Who's Who in the Greek World
John Hazel

Who's Who in the Roman World
John Hazel

The Routledge Dictionary of Egyptian Gods and Goddesses

George Hart

Second edition

Routledge
Taylor & Francis Group

LONDON AND NEW YORK

First published 2005
by Routledge
2 Park Square, Milton Park, Abingdon, Oxon OX14 4RN

Simultaneously published in the USA and Canada
by Routledge
270 Madison Ave, New York, NY 10016

Routledge is an imprint of the Taylor & Francis Group

Typeset in Times New Roman by
Newgen Imaging Systems (P) Ltd, Chennai, India
Printed and bound in Great Britain by
TJ International Ltd, Padstow, Cornwall

British Library Cataloguing in Publication Data
A catalogue record for this book is available
from the British Library

Library of Congress Cataloging in Publication Data
Hart, George, 1945–
    The Routledge dictionary of Egyptian gods and
goddesses / George Hart. – 2nd ed.
        p. cm.
    Rev. ed. of: Dictionary of Egyptian gods and goddesses. 1986.
    Includes bibliographical references.
    1. Gods, Egyptian – Dictionaries. 2. Mythology, Egyptian –
Dictionaries. I. Title.

BL2450.G6H37 2005
299′.31211–dc22   2004030797

ISBN 0–415–36116–8 (hbk)
ISBN 0–415–34495–6 (pbk)

To my mother and in memory of my father

Contents

Preface

This revision of the original Dictionary published in 1986 includes a completely new Introduction in which I have tried to provide some crucial historical data and a chronological framework of the visual and textual sources for the individual entries. Also I have taken the opportunity to add four new deities and expand the information on a number of others. There is now a more comprehensive time chart and the Select further reading has been updated to reflect the significant number of salient books now available on Egyptian religion.

I would initially like to thank Vivian Davies, Keeper of the British Museum Department of Ancient Egypt and Sudan, for having given me the opportunity to write the first edition of this Dictionary. This new edition is enhanced by the addition of hieroglyphs for most of the gods' names and my thanks go to Dr Nigel Strudwick, British Museum Department of Ancient Egypt and Sudan for producing these. Also I am grateful to Garth Denning who has used his skills as an archaeological illustrator to add a new map and some additional drawings. Obviously I would like to express my gratitude to the editorial staff at Routledge for enabling this new edition to be produced.

Those entries in small capitals refer to gods/goddesses who have a separate entry in the text; a list of concordance of the names of Egyptian gods and goddesses will be found on page 169.

Outline time chart

Modern Names	Dynasties/Rulers	Dates
Predynastic period		
Nagada II		3500–3200 BC
Nagada III	*King Scorpion*	3200–3000 BC
Early Dynastic Period	I–II	3000–2686 BC
	I	
	Narmer	
	Aha	
	Den	
	Anedjib	
	II	2890 BC
	Raneb	
	Seth Peribsen	
	Khasekhemwy	
Old Kingdom/Pyramid Age	III–VI	2686–2181 BC
	III	
	Djoser Netjerikhet	
	Sekhemkhet	
	IV	2613 BC
	Sneferu	
	Khufu	
	Khafra	
	Menkaura	
	V	2494 BC
	Userkaf	
	Sahura	
	Neferirkara	
	Nyuserra	
	Djedkara Izezi	
	Unas	
	VI	2345 BC
	Teti	

(*continued*)

Continued

Modern Names	Dynasties/Rulers	Dates
First Intermediate Period	IX–X	2181–2055 BC
Middle Kingdom	XI–XII	2055–1773 BC
	XI	
	Mentuhotep II	
	Mentuhotep IV	
	XII	1985 BC
	Amenemhat I	
	Senwosret I	
	Amenemhat II	
	Senwosret III	
	Amenemhat III	
Second Intermediate Period	XIII–XVII	1773–1550 BC
HYKSOS KINGS	XV	1650 BC
	Khyan	
	Apepi	
THEBAN KINGS	XVII	1580 BC
	Seqenenra Taa	
	Kamose	
New Kingdom	XVIII–XX	1550–1069 BC
	XVIII	
	Iahmose	
	Amenhotep I	1545–1504 BC
	Queen Hatshepsut	
	Thutmose III	1479–1425 BC
	Amenhotep II	
	Thutmose IV	
	Amenhotep III (and Tiye)	1390–1352 BC
	Akhenaten (and Nefertiti)	1352–1336 BC
	Tutankhamun	1336–1327 BC
	Ay	
	Horemheb	
	XIX	1295 BC
	Sety I	
	Ramesses II	1279–1213 BC
	Merenptah	
	XX	1186 BC
	Sethnakht	
	Ramesses III	1184–1153 BC
	Ramesses V	
	Ramesses VI	1143–1136 BC
	Ramesses XI	

Continued

Modern Names	Dynasties/Rulers	Dates
Third Intermediate Period	XXI–XXV	1069–664 BC
	Psusennes I	
	XXII	945 BC
	Sheshonq I	
	Osorkon I	
	Osorkon II	
SUDANESE KINGS	XXV	747 BC
	Piye	
	Shabaqo	716–702 BC
	Taharqo	
Late Period	XXVI–XXXI	664–332 BC
	Psamtek I	
	XXVII	525 BC
	Cambyses of Persia	
	Darius I of Persia	
	XXX	380 BC
	Nectanebo I	
	Nectanebo II	
	XXXI	343 BC
	Artaxerxes III of Persia	
Macedonian Kings		332–305 BC
	Alexander the Great	332–323 BC
	Philip Arrhidaeus	
Ptolemaic period		305–30 BC
	Ptolemy I Soter	
	Ptolemy IV Philopater	221–205 BC
	Ptolemy XII Auletes	
	Cleopatra VII	51–30 BC
	Ptolemy XV Caesarion	
Roman period		30 BC–AD 395
	Augustus	30 BC–AD 14
	Tiberius	
	Hadrian	AD 117–138
	Diocletian	AD 284–305
	Constantine I	AD 324–337
	Theodosius	
Byzantine period		AD 395–642
	Justinian	AD 527–565
Arab Conquest of Egypt		AH 21/AD 642

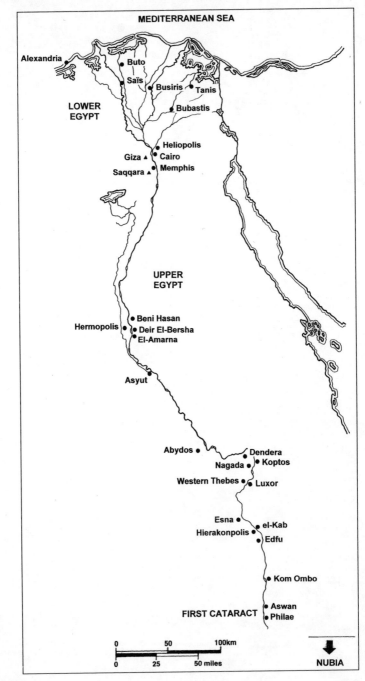

Map of Egypt.

Introduction

Ancient Egyptian sources

1 *Early Egypt*

The chronology of Egyptian civilisation in the period before the first rulers governed a united country is complex and liable to re-interpretations based on the results of contemporary rigorous archaeological excavations and surveys throughout the northern Nile Valley. Before confining this synopsis to evidence concerning Egyptian deities, it might be helpful to mention the general parameters of this formative era. Currently there is a strong indication that Southern or Upper Egypt had gained a cultural ascendancy over Northern or Lower Egypt by *c.*3500 BC. In archaeological terms this southern culture is described as Naqada II – the name deriving from a site, just north of modern Luxor, where the early cemeteries provided pottery and artefacts which together with comparative material from other locations enabled experts to devise a relative chronology for Egypt during the fourth millenium BC. Among the most significant sites that are likely to reveal radical new evidence for this period are Abydos and Hierakonpolis in Upper Egypt and Buto in the northern Nile Delta. The political domination by the south over the north, involving military campaigns and a final conquest, was achieved during the Naqada III period, by *c.*3000 BC. From this time on Egyptologists work within a chronological framework based on the grouping of rulers into 'dynasties' – a system of reference first employed by an Egyptian priest called Manetho who wrote a history of Egypt in Greek in the third century BC. Manetho's Dynasty I begins with a ruler called Menes, who is usually taken to equate with the archaeologically attested King Narmer, and his Dynasty XXXI ends with the reign of the Persian King Darius III in 332 BC. In modern scholarship these dynasties are frequently arranged into larger entities to form 'Kingdoms' and 'Intermediate Periods'.

THE INTERPRETATION OF IMAGES FROM PREDYNASTIC EGYPT

From the Naqada period there are a number of artefacts that concern Egyptian gods and goddesses. The most informative category are the siltstone ceremonial palettes, the surfaces of which are carved with diverse images. Originally palettes were totally utilitarian in purpose, being used to grind up pigments for eye cosmetics, but they developed into early examples of relief carving of which about twenty survive in either complete or fragmentary condition. Some of them are the borderline between the end of the Naqada III period and the beginning of Dynasty I. On a number of them the scenes include the NOME GODS (representing the different administrative districts of Egypt) or gods on royal standards such as the emblem of the god MIN or the ibis of the god THOTH. On the fragment of the 'Towns' Palette in Cairo Museum the hawks, scorpion and lion hacking at battlements could portray symbols of divine kingship. Some interpretations are more speculative. For example, on the 'Lion Hunt' Palette (fragments in The British Museum and the Louvre Museum) there is an image of the joined foreparts of two bulls, possibly writing the name of a god, next to a structure that could be his sanctuary.

The pale beige marl clay vases of Naqada II are painted with red-ochre scenes that tantalise us in trying to decipher images perhaps relating to religious rituals. Are the many-oared boats conveying shrines in festival along the Nile? Are the prominent female figures with their arms raised like curving horns above their heads performing a dance in honour of a cow-goddess such as BAT or HATHOR? With the advent of hieroglyphs in the late Predynastic period – ivory labels discovered in the tomb of a ruler buried at Abydos date from *c.*3400 BC – many problems of identification are solved.

EVIDENCE FROM EARLY DYNASTIC EGYPT

During the first two dynasties the information on gods and goddesses increases through a number of artefacts. Royal cylinder seals carved from stones like steatite can be incised with the names of rulers which might be formed with the name of a deity such as HORUS or NEITH. One seal impression – the cylinder seals were rolled across clay stoppers of jars – from Abydos is actually a Kinglist of Dynasty I and includes the writing of KHENTAMENTIU – the ancient jackal god of Abydos – whose name, meaning 'Foremost of the Westerners', the more powerful god OSIRIS came to share.

The ivory or ebony labels attached to equipment buried in the royal necropolis at Abydos also illuminate relevant features of early Egyptian beliefs. Two such labels in the British Museum date to the reign of King Den of Dynasty I – one showing the monarch clubbing an enemy to death preceded by the standard of the god WEPWAWET and the other depicting the king in the ceremony of rejuvenation in the jubilee festival ('Heb Sed'). The ceremony of the 'Running of the APIS Bull' is also recorded on sealings and labels from the first two dynasties.

The Narmer Palette, found at Hierakonpolis and now in Cairo Museum, is carved on both sides with scenes that conventionally are interpreted as the conquest of Lower Egypt. A more recent, though not necessarily more convincing, interpretation, would see the violent imagery, such as King Narmer about to slay the principal enemy leader with a blow of his mace and the inspection by the monarch of the decapitated bodies of ten other opponents, as commemorating an already existing political situation through an image of triumph. On this important monument there are also some notable religious images. The designs on both sides are surmounted by a frontal face with bovine ears and horns – surely the image of the cow-goddess BAT (or HATHOR) in whose sanctuary the palette was originally dedicated. On the obverse a hawk with a human arm coming from its breast holding a rope that goes through the nostrils of an enemy's head is part of a rebus that can be straightforwardly interpreted as the god Horus, with whom Narmer is identified, capturing the Delta. On the reverse Horus sails in a ceremonial boat while below is another powerful image of divine kingship where the king takes the form of a raging bull destroying a town's walls with his horns. Similarly, on the 'Battlefield' Palette in the British Museum the ruler is portrayed as a magnificently maned lion biting at the mangled body of an enemy, perhaps a prototype for the concept of the king in the form of the sun-god's sacred animal eventually evolving into the iconography of the sphinx.

2 *Old Kingdom Egypt*

Following the construction (*c.*2650 BC) of the Step Pyramid of King Djoser Netjerikhet of Dynasty III at Saqqara, the first large-scale stone edifice in the world, the documentation on gods and goddesses proliferates at an incredible pace in the tombs of royalty and the upper echelons of ancient Egyptian society. The Old Kingdom comprises Dynasties III–VI, a time-span of over 500 years in which we witness the zenith of Pyramid Age architecture and its decline and during which we marvel at some of the finest examples of sculpture and reliefs.

In the mastabas and rock-cut sepulchres of the officials, who lived at Memphis and who were buried predominantly at Saqqara and Giza, there are funerary formulae which indicate the importance of gods like ANUBIS and OSIRIS in sanctioning and guarding the tombs and providing all basic and luxury requisites for eternity. Full epithets for these deities now appear in the hieroglyphic inscriptions which give a deeper insight into their roles vis-à-vis the human race and also references to their major cult centres. From the myriad of titles boasted by the highest courtiers we can isolate many which emphasize, for example, the flourishing cults and festivals of RA, the sun-god, THOTH, god of wisdom, PTAH, creator-god of Memphis and MIN, god of procreativity. In inscriptions specifically for the wives of officials there are clear indications of the devotion of women to the cults of the goddesses HATHOR, goddess of sexual allure and the creator-goddess NEITH.

THE ROYAL HEREAFTER IN THE PYRAMID TEXTS

It is probable that in the imposing dimensions and angles of the pyramids there is inherently the symbol of primeval mound which arose from the waters of NUN at the beginning of time and on which the sun-god creator stood to bring the universe into being. More excitingly for comprehending the richness of Egyptian religion are the hieroglyphic inscriptions carved in and around the burial chambers of the pyramids. The earliest inscriptions, many still showing the lapis lazuli colour of the original paint, are found in the Pyramid of King Wenis of Dynasty V at Saqqara which can be dated to c.2350 BC. Known as 'Pyramid Texts' they really form the world's first elaborate compendium of religious literature. Some texts reflect offering rituals that occurred at the time of the king's burial, covering a wide variety of commodities such as loaves, cakes, onions, beer, wine, weapons, sceptres, incense and linen clothing. The remainder of the texts (divided in modern editions into over 700 'Utterances') confront us with a complex theology and a legion of divine names. So there are texts mentioning a sun-god creator with different manifestations as the anthropomorphic RA-ATUM, the hawk RA-HARAKHTI and the scarab beetle KHEPRI. The ascension of the king to the sun-god's realm of eternity in the sky is paramount in the theology of the Pyramid Texts. There are allusions to the ancient astral cult in which the king becomes one of the STAR-GODS and many references to the crucial role of the sky-goddess NUT in protecting the monarch. A skeletal form of the myth of the struggle between OSIRIS and SETH emphasises the victory of the king as HORUS. One of the most intriguing of the Pyramid Texts depicts the king, with the help of blood-thirsty gods like SHEZMU, hunting, slaughtering, cooking and eating gods in order to absorb their supernatural powers. Obscure and contradictory as many of the Utterances can be, the Pyramid Texts are the starting point in understanding the development of the solar cult, the concept of divine kingship and ancient speculations on the Afterlife.

Crucial information, particularly for rituals and festivals, can be extracted from the royal annals carved on basalt, the fragments of which are now in museums in

Palermo, Cairo and London. Although much of the inscription is lost or worn, these annals provide details on the major events of the reigns of rulers from the first five dynasties. Monarchs dedicate statues of the deities on specific dates, such as King Shepseskaf, last ruler of Dynasty IV, consecrating an effigy of WEPWAWET in the first year of his reign. The annals list offerings of food, drink and land to major gods and goddesses in specified sanctuaries while the reigns of the kings of Dynasty V, staunch promoters of the cult of RA, are marked by the emphasis on rituals in sun temples.

3 *Middle Kingdom Egypt*

After the end of the Pyramid era, there was about a century of rivalry for the throne of Egypt, until King Mentuhotep II brought the whole country under his control in 2055 BC. The first two dynasties of the Middle Kingdom indicate a vigorous government and fortification of Egypt's eastern and southern borders. But surviving monuments concerning Egyptian deities are not as extensive as those of the Old Kingdom. In terms of state cults one reason for the lack of temples is that the building projects of New Kingdom pharaohs often required the dismantling of earlier edifices. However, enough evidence survives to evaluate the importance of the god MONTU in the Theban temples and to trace the rise to prominence of the god AMUN at the temple of Karnak.

The rock-cut tombs of regional governors in Middle Egypt at Beni Hasan and El-Bersha and at Qubbet el-Hawa at Aswan are lively and of great interest but do not leave visual representations of deities except in the hieroglyphs of their names in inscriptions, e.g. KHNUM and SATIS, pre-eminent at the Nile Cataracts. However, stelae of officials – particularly that of Ikhernofret now in Berlin Museum

and that of Sehetepibre now in Cairo Museum – originally set up at tombs or cenotaphs at Abydos, give valuable insights into the rituals of the festival of OSIRIS.

THE AFTERLIFE FOR OFFICIALS FROM THE COFFIN TEXTS

Middle Kingdom wooden rectangular coffins found in the tombs of governors of districts in Middle Egypt are universally agreed to provide the finest examples of draughtsmanship in the exquisitely detailed painted hieroglyphs. An outstanding example is the Coffin of Djeheuty-nakht from his tomb at El-Bersha dating to Dynasty XII, now in the Boston Museum. Below the hieroglyphic funerary formulae, he is seated in front of a panoply of food and drink – geese with entwined necks, a dove flapping its wings, heads of bull and oryx, onions and figs and jars of wine. In addition, a frieze of objects of daily life have been depicted to ensure his well-being forever, including a bed, headrests, jewellery and weapons. This display of artistry and colour can distract attention from vertical rows of less detailed hieroglyphs in black around the lower walls of the coffin. These are spells, taken from a corpus of over 1,000, known as the Coffin Texts, concerning the Afterlife, which supply a mine of information about Egyptian deities. While there are some similarities with the Pyramid Texts, the general thrust is towards the survival, through the magical power of the words, of the individual against the hazards imagined to exist in the realm of the dead. Spells were included to enable the transformation of the deceased into a god. There is also a prominent role given to the god SHU, associated with air and sunlight which of course Egyptians would hope to continue to enjoy in the next world. One important aid to survival in the Afterlife was painted on the floor of Middle Kingdom coffins and is known as the 'Book of the Two Ways' – basically a map giving the safe land and river routes to follow avoiding perils like walls of fire.

4 *New Kingdom Egypt*

Following the expulsion, in 1550 BC, of the Hyksos, foreign rulers from the Levant, who had occupied the Delta at the end of the Middle Kingdom, and controlled strategic regions of the Nile Valley for about 100 years, pharaohs of Dynasties XVIII–XX, expanded Egypt's frontiers into Syria and the Sudan, and enhanced the landscape with vast temples and prosperous cities. From the five centuries of the New Kingdom there is an abundant legacy of architecture, reliefs and papyri to inform us about traditional deities, new arrivals imported from the Near East such as BAAL or ASTARTE, and the myriad of gods and goddesses in the Underworld.

In this period Hymns to AMUN-RA impress us with their eloquence and elevated thought. They convince us that the ancient Egyptians, fully at ease with their polytheism, were viewing the cosmos as a continual proof that a transcendental sun-god was behind the manifestation of every other deity. The British Museum stela of the brothers Suty and Hor, directors of building projects in the reign of King Amenhotep III of Dynasty XVIII, extols the splendour of the sun-god that dazzles all creation and describes the god's supremacy by using different images of the forms he can take. From the reign of Ramesses II of Dynasty XIX, a papyrus in Leiden Museum is considered to be the most lyrical and inspired analysis of the nature of the creator god – omnipresent yet hidden, the One God revealed through the trinity of AMUN of

Thebes, RA of Heliopolis and PTAH of Memphis.

The pharaoh Akhenaten ascended the throne of Egypt in 1352 BC and for 16 years Egypt witnessed traumatic religious and political decisions. The supremacy of Thebes gave way to the new capital Akhetaten – Horizon of the Sun-Disk – (known usually under the modern name of Amarna) built on the edge of the eastern desert in Middle Egypt. Here Akhenaten promulgated the worship of the sun-god under the austere iconography of ATEN which was simply the disk of the sun adorned with the ROYAL URAEUS with rays emanating from it, their tips shaped like hands reaching from the sky to the royal family. Because of the destruction wreaked on the temples, tombs and palaces of this city after Akhenaten's death, the visual imagery and inscriptions concerning the cult, the prominent feature in the decoration of the tombs of the courtiers cut in the eastern cliffs, are often exceedingly fragmentary or entirely lost. The reliefs from the temples at Amarna which depicted the royal family officiating in the cult of the Aten, were taken off to the western bank of the Nile to be used as filling material in the Temple of THOTH at Hermopolis, a similar fate befell Akhenaten's temple at east Karnak, although in this case many reliefs have been recovered by archaeologists from the structures in which they were hidden, so that some of the original scenes are now extensively reconstructed. Fortunately, the Great Hymn to the Aten, in which Akhenaten's own beliefs are synthesised into a rapturous celebration of the sun-god, survives in the tomb of the courtier Ay.

Osiris is prominent in tombs and on stelae in his role as the god who will universally guarantee eternal happiness to the deserving in the Afterlife. In contrast, the Great Hymn carved on the stela of

Amenmose in the Louvre Museum describes in veiled references the murder of OSIRIS and, via the powers of his consort ISIS and the approval of the tribunal of gods, the transmission of the kingship of Egypt to his son HORUS. Adding a spicy touch to our sources on mythology the Papyrus Chester Beatty I, written in Dynasty XX, is a tale full of sexual and violent episodes in the struggle between Horus and SETH for the throne of Egypt.

THE ROYAL HEREAFTER FROM THE VALLEY OF THE KINGS

The pharaohs of the New Kingdom intended – with the exception of Akhenaten – to be buried at Thebes beyond the western cliffs in the remote and secluded Valley of the Kings. Their tombs varied in dimensions and in the style of decoration but the inclusion of scenes and texts from various Books of the Netherworld were crucial to the survival of the pharaoh beyond death. The earliest source for names and functions of UNDERWORLD DEITIES is the 'Book of the Hidden Chamber' (frequently referred to as the 'Amduat'), first found on the walls of the tomb of the pharaoh Thutmose III (c.1425 BC). The essential leitmotif is the journey of the sun-god through the 12 hours of the night, defeating APOPHIS the snake-god of chaos and emerging unscathed on the eastern horizon at dawn. Other major compositions similar in purpose to the Amduat, which are particularly lavishly painted in the tombs of the Ramesside kings (Dynasties XIX–XX) are the 'Book of Gates' (GATE DEITIES) and the 'Book of Caverns' (CAVERN DEITIES). In addition, a further eight 'Books' have been identified in the Valley of the Kings. In the 'Litany of RA' the seventy-five manifestations of the sun-god are shown while on the ceiling of the sarcophagus chamber in the tomb of Ramesses VI

(c.1140 BC) there are two 'Books' consisting of dramatic depictions of the sky-goddess NUT through whose body the sun-god travels during the night and, following his birth at dawn, along whose body he sails in daytime. Nowhere more than in these royal tombs can we understand the ancient Egyptian complexity of thought, richness of imagination and anxieties about eternity.

BOOKS OF THE DEAD

The tombs of the elite hierarchy below the pharaoh contain religious scenes of worshipping OSIRIS, RA and other deities but most emphasis is placed on representations of the career and pleasures of the deceased and images of daily life along the Nile about 3,500 years ago. The most valuable source on deities of concern to this echelon of society are papyrus scrolls, commonly called by the modern designation 'Books of the Dead'. The scroll was placed in the burial chamber either in the coffin with the mummified body or in cases shaped in the image of the composite god PTAH-SOKAR-OSIRIS. This papyrus was vital to existence beyond the tomb in Duat or the Underworld in the realm of Osiris but still enjoying the light of the sun – hence the ancient Egyptian title for it was the 'Spells for Coming Out by Day'. The collection of spells, added to and modified, down to Roman Egypt, originated shortly before the New Kingdom and had become an essential item of funerary equipment by 1480 BC. It formed a manual of pragmatic instructions mixed with magical incantations aiming to get an individual into an idyllic world mirrored on Egypt. From our point of view the vignettes illustrating various spells are a mine of information on the iconography of Underworld deities. To understand the precious legacy of these scrolls, one only has to glance at one of the most famous scrolls, the Book of the Dead of the Royal Scribe Ani which is now in the British Museum. For example, there is the vignette of the Weighing of the Heart (ASSESSOR GODS) with a rare representation of the childbirth goddess MESKHENET as well as a splendid depiction of AMMUT, her crocodile head amalgamated onto a leopard torso and hippopotamus hind legs. Also the draughtsman has rendered a variety of animal heads of the dangerous guardians of the Seven Gateways (GATE DEITIES) in Duat which Ani and his wife Tutu are shown approaching.

Like the Books of the Netherworld in the Royal Tombs these papyri scrolls give us an insight into the aspirations and fears in the minds of ancient Egyptians as they attempted to draw up a kind of 'insurance-policy' for the Afterlife.

5 Evidence from the major temples

Sanctuaries of Egyptian deities can be shown to have existed in the Predynastic times with conclusive archaeological evidence from Hierakonpolis proving that there was a temple there as early as the Naqada II period c.3500 BC. In terms of decorated superstructures of the Old Kingdom giving inscriptions and images of deities, we have a few hints on how much information has been lost from the few surviving reliefs and statues. Examples, now in the Cairo and Berlin Museums, include the relief of the lioness-goddess SAKHMET discovered in Valley Temple of King Sneferu at Dahshur, the goddess HATHOR and NOME GODS flanking King Menkaure on triad statues from Giza, and the gods Seth, SOPEDU and WADJ WER on the superb reliefs from the Pyramid Temple of King Sahura at Abusir. For the Middle Kingdom there is also limited documentation available such as the fragmentary

reliefs from the Temple of King Mentuhotep II at Deir el-Bahari on which it is possible to identity Hathor and MONTU and the reconstructed peripteral temple of Senwosret I at Karnak with fine reliefs of the monarch in rituals before AMUN.

In the New Kingdom there is a quantum leap in the architectural and iconographic evidence about deities, myths and sanctuaries. The following temples, listed here in a north–south order, are especially important:

The temple of Sety I at Abydos   Dedicated to seven deities, its major purpose is to magnify the cult of OSIRIS. Through outstanding low-reliefs, often still with bright paint surviving on them, all the crucial temple rituals, shown as being performed by the pharaoh himself, are revealed to us. Furthermore, in the Room of SOKAR we can witness the mystery of the conception of HORUS through the magical power of ISIS.

The temple of AMUN at Karnak   This temple is in magnitude the most impressive in Egypt. Out of the plethora of New Kingdom reliefs we can isolate as of special interest the scenes on the interior of the walls of the Northern Hypostyle Hall dating to the reign of King Sety I where there are outstanding depictions not only of Amun but also of MONTU, THOTH and WERET-HEKAU as well as the pharaoh himself reading his name written on the leaves of the sacred 'ished' tree of Heliopolis.

The temple of Luxor   In the First Court and Colonnade are reliefs showing the land and river processions of the New Year Festival of Opet. In the southern section of the temple, predominantly decorated in the reign of King Amenhotep III, scenes show AMUN in the 'Theban Theogamy' impregnating the pharaoh's mother and also the ithyphallic AMUN KAMUTEF.

The mortuary temples of western Thebes On the desert edge the monarchs erected temples to perpetuate their name and stress their closeness to the major deities. Queen Hatshepsut's Temple at Deir el-Bahari incorporates a chapel HATHOR and one to ANUBIS as well as reliefs showing her divine birth as the child of AMUN. In Ramesses II's temple known as the Ramesseum the king kneels before Amun, MUT and KHONSU to receive the scimitar of war while the ceiling of the Hyptostyle Hall depicts the STAR-GODS. The fullest panorama of deities as well as a detailed rendering of the Festival of MIN is found in the Temple of King Ramesses III (Dynasty XX) at Medinet Habu.

Of the rescued temples of Nubia, south of the First Cataract of the Nile on the edges of Lake Nasser, the salient religious scenes are found in the Temple of Amada begun under King Thutmose III and Ramesses II's temples at Derr and Abu Simbel (particularly in the temple dedicated to his queen Nefertari).

In Graeco-Roman Egypt there was a sustained momentum of building temples particularly in Upper Egypt and Nubia even though the Greek Ptolemies and the Roman emperors did not for the most part subscribe to Egyptian religious beliefs – except perhaps by supporting the Hellenistic cults of ISIS and SARAPIS in the Mediterranean world and beyond. It was a perceptive policy for these rulers to let themselves be portrayed on temple walls as pharaohs thereby maintaining the illusion of a traditional god-king on the Egyptian throne. The temples were often excessively decorated, almost as if the priests were reluctant to leave any surface uncarved.

The temple of HATHOR *at Dendera* In the crypts of the temple are depictions of the most precious cultic objects originally stored there while on the roof is the kiosk to which the statue of the goddess would be taken daily to receive the rays of the sun-god. The exterior rear wall of the temple shows Cleopatra VII in the role of the goddess Hathor. On the walls of the 'mammisi' or 'birth-house' where the cult of IHY, child of Hathor and HORUS was celebrated the officiating pharaoh is the Roman Emperor Trajan.

The temple of KHNUM *at Esna* Although only the Hypostyle Hall dating to the Roman era survives, there are good reliefs of the ram-god fashioning mankind on the potters wheel, and some of the extremely difficult hieroglyphic texts give vital information about the creator-goddess NEITH.

The temple of HORUS *at Edfu* This temple, constructed under the Ptolemies, is architecturally the best preserved in Egypt. Consequently, we get a good idea of the limited light in which Egyptian priests performed the daily rituals. In the First Court scenes show the flotilla of bringing the statue of HATHOR from Dendera while reliefs on the western ambulatory wall vividly illustrate the drama enacted on the now-vanished Sacred Lake where Horus spears to death his enemy SETH depicted in the form of a hippopotamus.

The temple of SOBEK *and* HAROERIS This is an intriguing dual temple in whose ruined sanctuaries it is still possible to see the subterranean hiding places used by the priests to deliver oracles. The temple calendar survives in hieroglyphs on the extant wall of a small chapel, whereas the outer northern wall, where the surgical instruments are depicted, shows 'ears' and 'sacred eyes' connected to the function of the temple as a place of healing.

The temple of ISIS *at Philae* In the last temple to hold out against the advent of Christianity, the main scenes concern the myth of OSIRIS, Isis and HORUS – including the representation of marshes in the mammisi alluding to the Delta where Isis hid her son for protection against SETH. In the Gateway of Hadrian a crocodile carries Osiris to his sanctuary on the neighbouring island of Biga and there is a depiction of HAPY, god of the Nile flood, in his cavern below the cataract.

Classical sources

Until the decipherment of Egyptian Hieroglyphs in 1822, the only extensive accounts of pharaonic religion that could be understood existed in Greek or Roman Literature. Each author has to be evaluated carefully today in the light of knowledge from the primary Egyptian sources but there is every reason not to neglect this body of evidence.

1 *The histories of Herodotos*

Herodotos wrote his 'Investigations' into the wars of the Greeks and Persians by *c.*425 BC. Despite his modem detractors, there is every reason to believe that he travelled to those countries where he gives 'eye-witness' descriptions, even if his interpretation of phenomena or events is incorrect. Book Two is a thorough exposition of geographical, historical, architectural, social and religious topics which he noted down during his journey in Egypt – which incidentally he visited when it was under Persian occupation (Dynasty XXVII). From the point of view of religion, Herodotos' observations cover priests, festivals, sacred animals, Egyptian deities – under Greek names – and mummification.

2 *The library of history of Diodorus Siculus*

In Book One of this vast work Diodorus gives an account of Egypt which he visited sometime in the first century BC. He writes extensively about OSIRIS and ISIS

and also discusses sacred animals such as the APIS and MNEVIS bulls.

3 *Plutarch on* ISIS *and* OSIRIS

This book is the most valuable classical source on Egyptian mythology. Plutarch completed it *c.* AD 120. His book is rich in detail about Isis, Osiris and the role played by Typhon, as the god Seth is called. Understandably Plutarch's account is occasionally coloured by Hellenistic scholarship.

4 *The Golden Ass of Apuleius*

This racy novel written in Latin in the second century AD gives the best description of the ceremonies which a person had to undergo to become an initiate of the mysteries of ISIS and OSIRIS.

From antiquity to today

From the reign of the emperor Constantine onwards, Christianity spread through Egypt and Nubia. Temples became Christian basilicas, the last sanctuary to fall to the new religion being the Temple of ISIS on the island of Philae in the reign of Justinian in the sixth century AD. By AD 642 the Arab army of Amr ibn al-Asi had defeated Byzantine forces and Islam began to transform the religious landscape of Egypt into the predominantly Muslim country of today.

In some ways the concepts and names of Egyptian deities survived official suppression of their cults. The Gnosticism in the codices discovered in a cave at Nag Hammadi in Upper Egypt and the collections of Coptic spells of ritual power clearly derive some of their explanations and terminology from ancient Egyptian religion. From the Corpus Hermeticum, texts written in Alexandria in the early centuries AD, there is a coalescence of Greek and Egyptian thought so that THOTH becomes Hermes Trismegistos, even being represented in churches such as in the fifteenth century pavement of Siena Cathedral. The Rosicrucian movement (dating from the early seventeenth century), has a tradition rooted in alchemy and Hermeticism. In Freemasonry, whose official origins begin in the early eighteenth century, strong links were soon forged with the Egyptian initiation rituals preserved in Apuleius – famously Mozart's 'The Magic Flute' is resonant with the mysteries of ISIS and OSIRIS. Ancient Egyptian religion, mostly in a highly idiosyncratic form, figures significantly in the development of the 'Theosophical Society' from the end of the nineteenth century onwards, especially through Helena Blavatsky's book 'Isis Unveiled' and Rudolph Steiner's lectures in Leipzig in 1908 on Egyptian myths and mysteries. Notions on Egyptian deities in anything written by Aleister Crowley can be totally disregarded. There have also been fashions for interpreting Egyptian architecture in esoteric terms completely out of keeping with the intentions of the ancient architects. The most quoted example of such an esoteric approach is the attempt by Piazzi Smythe in the 1860s to prove that the measurements of the Great Pyramid at Giza contained hidden astronomical and historical information. Equally misguided is the interpretation of the Temple of Luxor in terms of human anatomy in Schwaller de Lubicz' book 'The Temple in Man' published in 1957. Ancient Egypt has no need of a modern veneer of mysticism or esotericism to keep, like Shakespeare's Cleopatra, its 'infinite variety' – and certainly we can enjoy an exciting dialogue with its gods and goddesses through the wealth of surviving hieroglyphs and images to be found on the banks of the Nile and in museums across the world.

A

Aken The custodian of the ferryboat in the Underworld. Rather amusingly he has to be woken from slumber by the ferryman MAHAF to provide the boat for travel on celestial waters.

Aker

 An earth-god also presiding over the juncture of the western and eastern horizons in the Underworld.

The motif of Aker consists of the foreparts of two lions, or two human heads, juxtaposed so that they face away from each other.

Aker opens the earth's gate for the king to pass into the Underworld. He absorbs the poison from the body of anyone bitten by a snake and neutralises the venom in the belly of a person who has swallowed an obnoxious fly. More importantly he imprisons the coils of the snake APOPHIS after being hacked to pieces by ISIS. This idea of enclosure accounts for the socket holding the mast of the Underworld ferryboat being identified with Aker.

In the Egyptian notion of the Underworld Aker could provide along his back a secure passage for the sun-god's boat travelling from west to east during the hours of night. From the tomb of Ramesses VI (Dynasty XX) in the Valley of the Kings, the massive tomb of Pedamenopet (Dynasty XXVI) in el-Asasif necropolis at Thebes, and mythological papyri of the priesthood of AMUN in Dynasty XXI, it is possible to reconstruct a 'Book of Aker', concerned with the solar journey from sunset to sunrise. Scenes include the Double Sphinx of Aker above a body symbolising both OSIRIS and RA in one form and the decapitation and burning of their Underworld enemies.

A more threatening side to Aker can be detected when he pluralises into the Akeru or earth-gods. In apotropaic passages in the Pyramid Texts the Akeru are said not to seize the monarch; later there is a general hope for everyone to escape the grasp of the earth-gods. The Akeru appear to be primeval deities more ancient than GEB, earth-god of the cosmogony of Heliopolis.

Amaunet

A goddess whose name means 'hidden one' and whose shadow, among the primeval gods, is a symbol of protection. A deity at Karnak temple at least since the reign of Senwosret I (Dynasty XII), she is predominantly the consort of AMUN playing, however, a less prolific role than his other wife MUT. A statue datable to Tutankhamun's reign which was set up in the Record Hall of Thutmose III (Dynasty XVIII) at Karnak shows the goddess in human form wearing the Red Crown of the Delta.

Reliefs at Karnak clearly mark her as prominent in rituals closely associated with the monarch's accession and jubilee festival. For instance, in the monument of Thutmose III, known as the Akh-menu, Amaunet and MIN lead a row of deities to watch the king and sacred bull in the jubilee celebration. Much later in the Greek domination of Egypt she is carved on the exterior wall of the sanctuary suckling the pharaoh Philip Arrhidaeus

(Macedonian Kings) who is playing the role of the divine child immediately following the scene depicting his enthronement.

A late equation at Karnak identifies her with NEITH of the Delta – comparable to the analogy made between Mut and SAKHMET – but she retains her own identity well into the Ptolemaic period. Amaunet is also one of the eight creator deities or OGDOAD worshipped at Hermopolis.

Amenhotep-Son-of-Hapu   Courtier who was royal scribe and 'overseer of all the work of the king' in the reign of Amenhotep III (Dynasty XVIII), deified in the Ptolemaic period from his reputation as a man of wisdom.

Amenhotep came from Athribis in the Delta and rose to prominence in the Theban court. He was responsible for recruiting military personnel and labourers for state building projects. As chief architect of the pharaoh he must have been involved in the lavish programme of temple construction – not only at Thebes but also in Nubia at the temple of Soleb. He was Amenhotep III's most trusted and privileged official, being given management of the vast estates of Sitamun, the eldest royal daughter, and, exclusively for a commoner, awarded a mortuary temple in western Thebes. Granite statues show him in the position of a corpulent seated scribe, and he is also represented in a beautifully carved relief on a wall of the tomb of his relative the vizier Ramose. A statue of him as an elderly official states that he lived to be 80 years old; his tomb is in the Qurnet Murai sector of the Theban necropolis.

His revered status of royal scribe, of which among all his titles he seems the most proud, seems to be the reason for his deification in Ptolemaic times. His cult, however, seems to be confined to Thebes (contrast IMHOTEP) where he is

worshipped as a benefactor and healing genius. At Deir el-Medina, Deir el-Bahari and in the temple of PTAH at Karnak he shares his cult centres with Imhotep of whom he is claimed to be the inseparable brother.

The scribal statues of him dedicated in his lifetime in the main temple at Karnak became cult intermediaries, in the Ptolemaic period, for supplicants anxious to gain the ear of the greater deity, AMUN.

Am-Heh

   A threatening Underworld god whose name means 'Devourer of Millions'. He dwells in a Lake of Fire. His ferocity is heightened by having the face of a hunting dog and an appetite for sacrifices. Only ATUM can fend off Am-Heh.

Ammut

   Underworld goddess whose name, 'Devouress of the

Papyrus of Hunefer, Dyn. XIX, British Museum.

Dead', aptly conveys her grim role as annihilator of those who have led wicked lives on earth. In funerary papyri she is frequently depicted in the vignette showing the weighing of the dead person's heart in the Hall of the Two Truths. The iconography of this goddess incorporates dangerous creatures of river and land, emphasising no escape for anyone found guilty of heinous crimes in the tribunal. Her head is mainly a crocodile, her front legs and middle represent a lion or leopard and her back legs become the ample rear of a hippopotamus. Called the 'Great of Death' in some papyri, her task is to swallow the heart of anyone judged unfit to survive in the realm of OSIRIS.

Amun

Primeval deity and supreme god of the Egyptian pantheon.

Amun is depicted anthropomorphically, often enthroned like a pharaoh. His flesh is coloured blue suggesting lapis lazuli, an imported, highly prized stone considered worthy of a god. His crown symbolises a sky-god, consisting of a modius surmounted by two high plumes. Each feather is divided vertically into two sections – the 'dualism' in the iconography reflects the Egyptian world-view of balanced opposites, e.g. the Two Lands (North and South Egypt). In each plume the horizontal segments add up to seven, a highly charged number in Egyptian religion. In addition to the linen-kilted form of the god, many representations exist of Amun boasting a hugely erected phallus.

The god Amun. The Great Harris Papyrus, Dyn. XX, British Museum.

1 *His sacred animals*

The Nile Goose is sacred to Amun probably on account of its association with the act of creation (see GENGEN WER).

The pre-eminent sacred creature of Amun is the ram with curved horns (ovis platyra aegyptiaca). This image of the god was probably suggested by the ram's procreative energy. 'Woserhat', the splendid, gilded, wooden festival boat of Amun 'lord of the two horns', had a ram's head at its prow and stern, and the processional roads to his temple were flanked with crio-sphinxes (ram-headed lions) each one guarding between its front legs a statue of the pharaoh. The Greek historian Herodotus quotes an unlikely tale for the origin of the ram of Amun: the hero Herakles, eager to see the true form of Zeus (= Amun), was finally given the opportunity; Zeus, however, deceived Herakles by disguising himself with a ram's fleece – hence the iconography of a ram-headed deity.

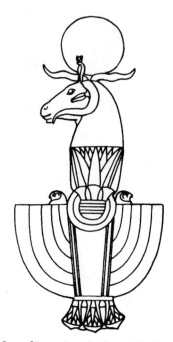

The Ram of Amun. Temple of Sety I, Abydos, Dyn. XIX.

2 *His name and true form*

Amun's name seems to be connected with the word meaning 'to conceal' and it is indicative of the Egyptians' own ideas on the god's nature to interpret it as the 'hidden one'. Thus the Greek writer Plutarch appears on target when he quotes from the Egyptian priest–chronicler Manetho the name Amun as meaning 'what is concealed' or 'invisible'. Another possibility is that the god's name comes from the ancient Libyan word 'aman' meaning 'water'. But except for vague references to the Nile or Mediterranean Sea this is not a prominent facet of the god's nature. For the Egyptians Amun could only be understood as permeating the cosmos, occasionally illuminated by an epithet that attempts to conceptualise his universality.

Since they were unable to pin the god down to one explanatory 'nomen', the Egyptians stressed his complexity by calling him 'asha renu' or 'rich in names'.

Similarly the human iconography of the god is really an admission by the Egyptians that his true shape eludes visual representation – 'hidden of aspect, mysterious of form' is one description of the god. According to hymns even other deities are unaware of his true appearance, none of them being in existence before him. It is also stated that his image is absent from the hieroglyphs which only give the phonetic signs comprising his name; other gods often have their names involving a major manifestation, e.g. an ibis or crocodile, but the stark consonantal structure of Amun's name offers no such visual clue. The concept of the god's invisibility admirably suits his association with the 'breeze' or the notion of Amun as an unseen demiurge.

3 *The earliest occurrence of Amun*

The god is first mentioned in the Pyramid Texts (from the end of Dynasty V). Ascending to the sky, the king as the son of GEB will sit 'upon the throne of Amun'. The god has status among the primeval deities and protects the gods with his shadow. Perhaps these thoughts are the embryo of Amun's universal kingship.

4 *Amun-Ra, King of the gods*

In the New Kingdom the divinity of Amun was enhanced by interpreting him as a mysterious manifestation of the ancient sun-god of Heliopolis. The name of the god is given the additional symbol of the solar disk. The solar connection is found in imagery of Amun and the lion, the sun-god's creature: Amun is called 'a fierce red-eyed lion'. Amun as sun-god is the meaning of a description applied to him in

'Lord of the Thrones of the Two Lands'. Hathor shrine of Thutmose III, Dyn. XVIII, Cairo Museum.

prestigious and it led to Amun being regarded as the pre-eminent deity of the pantheon. His title 'king of the gods' (first occurrence in the White Chapel of Senwosret I of Dynasty XII) illustrates his supreme status. The Egyptian title for 'Amun-Ra king of the gods' was 'Amon-Ra nesu netjeru' which lies behind the Greek version of 'Amonrasonther'. This sovereignty is also conveyed by an epithet first found in the Middle Kingdom, 'Lord of the Thrones of the Two Lands' (i.e. Upper and Lower Egypt are under his sway). Later it was natural for the Greek writers like Herodotus and Plutarch to 'rationalise' Amun by observing that he was Olympian Zeus among the Egyptians. This identification with the Greek god is maintained into the Roman period. Excavations at Tell el-Farama south-east of Port Said revealed evidence of a temple to the chief deity Zeus Casius. The site is to be equated with ancient Pelusium, a name deriving from the Egyptian description meaning 'house (i.e. temple) of Amun'.

the Book of the Dead as 'eldest of the gods of the eastern sky'. During the reign of Amenhotep III in Dynasty XVIII two brothers, Suti and Hor, were architects involved in the monument of Amun now called Luxor temple. On a granite stela in the British Museum they illustrate the

5 *Amun and the pharaoh*

Since the Middle Kingdom certain Egyptian rulers had been given names incorporating that of the god.

Royal Name	Meaning	Greek Version	Dynasty
Amenemhat	Amun is pre-eminent	Ammenemes	XII
Amenhotep	Amun is content	Amenophis	XVIII
Hatshepsut Khenemet-Amun	United with Amun		XVIII

equation between Amun and the sun-god by beginning the hymn 'Amun when he rises as HARAKHTI' (see HORUS, section titled 'Harakhti'). It was a conscious development to make the god even more

Pharaohs repeatedly called themselves 'Mery-Amun' or 'beloved of Amun'. Also, since the assertion that the ruler was 'son of RA' had been upheld from the Pyramid Age in the royal titulary, it followed that Amun was father of the monarch. There is one occasion when the god has to be reminded of this paternal protection for the pharaoh. On the battlefield at Kadesh by the river Orontes Ramesses II (Dynasty XIX) finds himself alone surrounded by 2,500 enemy chariots. He proceeds to chide Amun for abandoning 'his son' in this apparently hopeless situation. Does Amun favour the Middle Easterners? What about the monuments, war-spoils and endowments of lands and cattle that Ramesses II has already given to Amun from previous campaigns? Are these to count for nothing? The god answers these rebukes by giving the pharaoh's hand strength equivalent to that of 100,000 soldiers and Ramesses II cuts his way out of the hostile chariotry. The surprise arrival of Egyptian reinforcements will have been the more likely reason for Ramesses's narrow escape from death but the pharaoh prefers to stress the father–son bond.

THE THEBAN THEOGAMY

Two rulers of Dynasty XVIII have left inscriptional and pictorial evidence of the

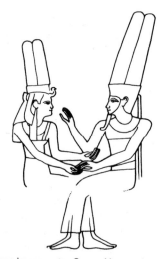

Amun impregnates Queen Mutemwiya. Temple of Amenhotep III, Luxor, Dyn. XVIII.

'divine marriage' between their mothers and the god Amun.

Queen Hatshepsut's temple at Deir el-Bahari shows a relief of her mother visibly pregnant by the god. On a wall south of the sanctuary in the temple of Luxor, Amenhotep III is the offspring of the union between Queen Mutemwiya and Amun. There is a discreet symbolism portraying the act of intercourse between the couple seated closely opposite one another on a couch supported by two goddesses. Of course the earthly husbands of these queens had been buried in the Valley of the Kings well before the liaisons with Amun were promulgated on the temples.

CAMPAIGNS AND VICTORIES

Scenes of Amun holding out the scimitar of war to a conquering pharaoh are visual statements that the Egyptian imperium in the Middle East and Nubia derives from the god's strength and inclination. A synopsis of a campaign beyond the Egyptian frontier illustrating the military role of Amun is given in the table.

To let Amun savour his son's victory, Thutmose III had the names of the vanquished enemy commanders written on leather (for durability) and deposited in the god's temple at Karnak. A eulogy on the king's triumphs during his reign survives on the 'poetical stela' in Cairo Museum. Amun addresses the king in high prose and rhythmic stanzas emphasising how he has brought states as far away as Naharin on the river Euphrates under Egyptian control. The god causes the enemies of Thutmose III to become terror-stricken at seeing the manifestation of the pharaoh not only as a fully armed warrior but also as a 'shooting-star', 'invincible bull' or a 'crocodile'. The gift of Amun to the king has been nothing less than world dominion.

Dynasty XVIII c.1456 BC

The god instigates war	Amun commands Thutmose III to extend the borders of Egypt by conquest of the Middle East.
The god advises on policy	Generals at the pharaoh's war council abandon their cautious route-suggestions to the enemy camp in favour of Thutmose's plan of a bold frontal assault – attributing the strategy to Amun.
The god fights for Egypt	In the battle of Megiddo in Palestine, Thutmose wins the field, invulnerable through Amun's protection.
The god is thanked	The rich booty (including horses and gilded chariots), left on the field by the enemy in their flight to reach the walled city of Megiddo, becomes the property of the pharaoh's army. They praise Amun for the victory.
The god's new foreign domains	After the successful siege of the town, the defeated army do obeisance to the king and acknowledge the sovereignty of Amun.

6 *Amun at Thebes*

On the eastern bank of the Nile at modern Luxor stand two temples dedicated to Amun:

IPET-SUT = 'THE ONE WHICH COUNTS OFF PLACES', i.e. AS THEY BRING IN TRIBUTE

Modern Karnak whose ancient name indicates the temple's superiority over all other sites in Egypt is a vast enclosure containing the Great Temple of Amun aligned along an east–west axis. To the north is an area sacred to the god MONTU, 'lord of Thebes', indicating peaceful coexistence with Amun who surpassed him in importance at Thebes from the end of Dynasty XI onwards. Archaeology has revealed that structures existed on the site of the temple in its present form from at least the reign of Senwosret I of Dynasty XII. The monument, however, is really best regarded as a witness to pharaonic piety towards Amun from the beginning of the New Kingdom to the Ptolemaic period. Its perfection as the god's residence was conveyed in Egyptian terms by calling it 'Akhet' or the 'horizon', the region where light emerges at dawn. A good example of how the temple was seen as an architectural expression of the relationship between the monarch and the god can be seen from three elements given here chronologically.

The obelisk of queen Hatshepsut (Dynasty XVIII) This solar symbol, made of red Aswan granite, 27.5 m high and weighing 320 tons, was one of two obelisks set up by the queen in front of the pylon (IV), called 'Amun great in majesty', which marked the entrance to the temple in the early eighteenth dynasty. Both the hieroglyphs on the shaft of the obelisk and those on its supporting base emphasise that Hatshepsut erected the obelisks for her 'father' Amun and that he personally directed the scheme. They were originally tipped with electrum to glitter in the sun. She claims the office of monarch which she holds was given to her by the king of the gods, all part of the propaganda to justify her usurpation of the throne. For the same reason, on part of the upper shaft of her fallen obelisk now near the sacred lake at Karnak, Hatshepsut is shown kneeling before Amun whose hands extend to her blue crown acknowledging her as rightful ruler.

Akh-menu of Thutmose III (Dynasty XVIII)   This is the hall of columns in the style of tentpoles, and its environs to the east of the sanctuary of the temple, celebrating the jubilee festival of the king. The name means 'glorious are the monuments'. In this festival hall a ruined chapel of the king commemorates Amun 'lord of the sky residing in Akh-menu' by a series of reliefs whose source must have been the notes and sketches made by scribes on his campaigns abroad. The scenes consist of birds, plants and animals unfamiliar to the Egyptians in their own environment. It is Amun as a universal god who is being highlighted by the depiction of Middle Eastern flora and fauna. From the Akh-menu also comes the king list carved during the reign of Thutmose III (now in the Louvre Museum) which suggests that there were possibly monuments at Karnak before those archaeologically attested of Middle Kingdom date – the list of royal ancestors as it survives begins with the name of King Sneferu of Dynasty IV.

The Great Hypostyle Hall   The 6,000 m^2 with 134 columns and a myriad of ritual scenes and inscriptions is perhaps the most grandiose statement of royal piety to the god. For the most part the hall was the work of Sety I and his son Ramesses II of Dynasty XIX. Religious processions in honour of Amun, carried in state in a shrine on his sacred boat, or personal confrontations between the pharaoh and the god meet the eye on every column and inch of wallspace. The size of the Great Hypostyle Hall alone is evidence of the readiness of the pharaoh to apportion vast resources of men and materials to a strategically unimportant site in Upper Egypt. Some idea of this overwhelming preference for projects in honour of Amun at Thebes can be found in a lengthy document of Dynasty XX (in the British Museum and known as the Great Harris Papyrus), which in one section lists the prisoners-of-war assigned as labour to the Egyptian temples by Ramesses III. It is the relative proportions given in the figures rather than their historical accuracy which is significant:

Temples at	*Prisoners*
Thebes (Amun)	86,486
Heliopolis (RA)	12,364
Memphis (PTAH)	3,079

From the same source it is known that Amun (i.e. the priesthood on behalf of the god) had the personal possession of 160 towns in Egypt and nine in the Middle East.

In the southern vicinity of Karnak temple were separate monuments to the goddess MUT, major consort of Amun, and their child KHONSU. Also Amun's feminine counterpart AMAUNET occurs in statuary and reliefs in the god's main temple.

AMUN EM IPET RESYT = 'AMUN WHO IS IN HIS SOUTHERN SANCTUARY'

The 'sanctuary' is today known as Luxor temple, 3 km south of Karnak, representing the cult apartments of the ithyphallic form of Amun. The extant temple is mainly from the reigns of Amenhotep III (Dynasty XVIII) and Ramesses II (Dynasty XIX). A stela discovered in the mortuary temple of Amenhotep III on the western bank describes Ipet as consisting of broad halls of fine sandstone with gold embellishing its gates, and massive pylons with flagstaves stretching into the sky. The major festival of Amun at Thebes involved his cult image being transported from Karnak to Ipet with scenes of jubilation, evocatively rendered on the walls of Amenhotep III's colonnade in Luxor temple. Shrines of Amun, MUT and KHONSU are carried on sacred boats on the priests' shoulders to the splendid temple barges which are then towed to the quay at Ipet Resyt. The land procession includes soldiers, chariots, musicians and acrobatic dancers. The celebrations for this New Year festival included the feasts of 'night of Ipet' and of 'abiding in Thebes'. The complicated sanctuary at Ipet possesses one of the few edifices surviving in Egypt carrying cartouches of Alexander the Great (Macedonian Kings) – depicted here as an Egyptian pharaoh offering to ithyphallic Amun.

Amun on the western bank This is really the procreative form of Amun worshipped predominantly in the mortuary temples of the pharaohs on the desert edge. The underlying idea is that the fertility powers of Amun can activate the renewal of life in the necropolis – death in Egyptian terminology is 'wehem ankh' or 'repeating life'. It is possible to see this aspect of Amun in two localities in particular in western Thebes:

(i) Amun of djeser-menu This is part of the temple complex known today as Deir el-Bahari, the site of Queen Hatshepsut's terraced temple (Dynasty XVIII). It has already been shown that this monarch claimed a special relationship with Amun – the theogamy of her mother Ahmose and Amun, and her obelisks to Amun at Karnak. There are two further assertions of the royal link with the god to be seen at Deir el-Bahari. First, the architectural layout is consciously bringing the queen into proximity with Amun – the temple sanctuary and its processional way to the cultivated area and Nile lines up directly with the east–west axis of

Karnak temple. Second, the series of reliefs in the southern colonnade at Deir el-Bahari, commemorating the expedition of five ships sent by the queen down the Red Sea to the land of Punt (= probably modern Eritrea and Ethiopia) has as its goal the trade of Egyptian goods for frankincense. This fragrant gum resin was of great importance in the temple rituals celebrating Amun, the 'tear drops' of incense being regarded as the sweat of the god.

(ii) Amun of djeme This is in the southern district of western Thebes embracing Deir el-Medina (a village of workers on the royal tombs) and Medinet Habu (Thutmosid temple and mortuary temple of Ramesses III of Dynasty XX). It was to Medinet Habu, the eighteenth-dynasty temple, that Amun of Ipet Resyt was ferried across the Nile every 10 days. A stela of Amenhotep III (Dynasty XVIII) creates for us a picture of the splendid boat used for transporting the god's statue: the craft was constructed of cedar of Lebanon overlaid with silver and gold and supporting a huge golden shrine with flagpoles and obelisks. Clearly the wealth and splendour of the monarchy hides behind the pageantry surrounding Amun.

7 *Amun beyond the first cataract of the Nile*

In Nubia temples were built in honour of Egypt's sovereign god as part of a deliberate policy of creating an extended imperium in the south, developed primarily to secure routes to the gold deposits. So ingrained did the worship of Amun become in Nubia that even when the pharaohs lost control of their southern province, local dynasts continued to uphold the god's cult. Consequently, in the eighth century BC the march of conquest northwards from just below the fourth cataract of the Nile into Egypt, by the Sudanese King Piye (Dynasty XXV), brought to the throne pharaohs who were staunch supporters of Amun, ready to enrich his monuments. Indeed, from the victory stela of Piye, the granaries of the defeated Egyptian princes were handed over to the priests of Amun at Karnak. A further sign of the adherence of these rulers of Kush to the god is not only the epithet 'beloved of Amun' added to their names, but also the substitution of the royal title 'son of Amun' for that of the 'son of RA' to introduce their cartouches. The following is a list giving some of Amun's temples in chronological order.

of the north wind upstream derive from Amun's nature – as elusive to define as the air, which, like all the other gods, is but a manifestation of the mysterious Amun. Speculation on Amun as a universal supreme god brought the Egyptian theologians very close to the concept of monotheism, although they never took the steps that would exclude all other deities from the temples. The worship of Amun in this aspect was henotheism in Egyptian terms – turning one's concentration onto the supreme god while not denying that he has provided a myriad of other divinities to be honoured as evidence of his procreative power.

Inaugurating Ruler	Site	Remarks
Thutmose III	Amada, mid-first to second cataracts	Reliefs of the temple's foundation ceremonies. Name and form of Amun hacked out under the pharaoh Akhenaten, restored under Sety I
Amenhotep III	Soleb, towards third cataract	Built in the style of Luxor temple
Horemheb	Gebel Barkal, towards fourth cataract	Great temple of Amun 'who is upon the pure mountain', counterpart to Karnak
Ramesses II	Abu Simbel, towards second cataract	Great temple, with four 20 m high seated colossi of king carved into façade, shared between Amun, HARAKHTI, PTAH and deified Ramesses II

8 *Amun as creator*

The god's temple Ipet-Sut is called by Hatshepsut on her obelisk 'mound of the beginning', indicating that it was the place where Amun brought the cosmos into existence. Hymns from the late New Kingdom emphasise the role of Amun as a primeval deity, creating sky and earth by his thoughts. The phenomenon of the annual Nile inundation, and the blowing

AMUN KEM-ATEF

This is the form of Amun as an ancient snake deity whose name translated is 'he who has completed his moment'. It can be elucidated as the god, having come swiftly to the end of one lifetime (the snake shedding its skin), renews himself in another cycle of living. In this form Amun is the ancestor of the eight primeval deities of OGDOAD worshipped in Middle Egypt at el-Ashmunein (ancient Hermopolis). Although preexisting the eight, Amun circulates as one of them to bring about creation. Amun Kem-Atef is the origin of Kneph, a self-engendered immortal, mentioned by Plutarch as the only divinity the inhabitants of the Theban region worship. The cult of Amun as a serpent seems to be attested by Herodotus at Thebes, where he states the snake with two horns (horned viper) was sacred, and buried in the temple. As a possible archaeological proof, it has been pointed out that a mummified snake called the 'lord of life' is in the Berlin Museum.

AMUN KAMUTEF

This is the ithyphallic form of Amun. The epithet 'kamutef' means 'bull of his mother'. Probably two major concepts lie behind the phrase. One is that, since the god is 'self-begotten' or 'creator of his own egg', he cannot have a father and so must perform the act of impregnating his own mother. The goddess envisaged is the sky-cow, so the analogy of a bull can be readily adopted. The second notion is tied up with the respect the Egyptians had for the bull's sexual prowess and strength – it had been a royal symbol since the Predynastic period. The representations of ithyphallic Amun Kamutef in Luxor temple leave one in no doubt of the god's ability as a sexual 'athlete' although it is his fertility, resulting in a never-ending cycle of successful pregnancies, that is really prognosticated by the iconography.

9 *Amun as magician*

In the Book of the Dead Amun provides a potent spell for preserving the corpse and for preventing any injury to the eyes. He is also regarded as a curer of eye ailments in non-funerary texts. In magical medicine in Ancient Egypt, spells evolved that might effect a cure by the power of a god's name. Amun seems to be a god to call upon if anyone has suffered a scorpion bite. He can even be evoked with other gods if a cat has been bitten and poisoned – Amun's responsibility will be to heal the feline limbs. Life could frequently be endangered in Ancient Egypt by lions, crocodiles and snakes. Against the crocodile, named as Maga son of SETH, a spell was devised which, to be effectual, had to be recited over a picture of Amun standing on a crocodile and being adored by the Ogdoad. The charm by virtue of Amun 'bull of his mother' will conjure up flames to burn up the crocodile.

10 *Amun as protector of commoners*

Outside of the state temples Amun is envisaged as being an advocate of the humbler echelons in Egyptian society. In papyri containing hymns to Amun during the Ramesside period, the god ensures fair play for the poor in the law courts – he is called 'vizier of the humble'. He is not open to bribery nor will he try to extort the poor man's belongings as, the text says, is done by court clerks and attendants. Among the community of workmen on the royal tombs living at Deir el-Medina in western Thebes, the draughtsman Nebra had a friend Nakhtamun who fell seriously ill. With a remarkable frankness the cause of the illness is attributed to some past misdeed. Nebra prays to Amun to be compassionate to his friend. Amun who 'comes at the voice of the poor' saves the man from death, manifest in his form of the north wind. On a votive stela, Nebra's original anxious request for Nakhtamun's recovery is incorporated into the paeon to praise Amun, the 'listening god', for his mercy.

A papyrus in Moscow dated to the reign of Ramesses XI, last ruler of

Dynasty XX, contains the report of the difficulties encountered by an official of Karnak temple called Wenamun, sent by the high priest Herihor to obtain cedarwood from Lebanon. In one passage, mention is made of a statuette of 'Amun of the road' which Wenamun carries with him and guards carefully. It is likely then that Egyptians at all levels of society, forced to undertake long journeys from home, put a certain amount of trust in the god as a protector of travellers.

Anat

Warrior-goddess of Ugarit on the Syrian coast and attested in Egypt from the end of the Middle Kingdom.

The Hyksos rulers seem to have promoted her cult and in the Ramesside Era Anat was a prominent goddess in the Delta. Wearing a high crown flanked with plumes, her martial nature is emphasised by the shield, lance and battle axe. The fact that Anat can be shown under the iconography of HATHOR is not surprising since Hathor can closely relate to foreign deities (e.g. BAALAT at Byblos or in the Sinai peninsula) as well as possessing a bloodthirsty, albeit usually subdued, side to her nature.

Anat is called 'mistress of the sky' and 'mother of all the gods' but it is her warlike character that predominates in both Egyptian and Near Eastern references to her. Anat's introduction into the Egyptian pantheon was on account of her protecting the monarch in combat. For example, Ramesses III (Dynasty XX) uses Anat and ASTARTE as his shield on the battlefield and in Dynasty XIX, and even Ramesses II's dog, shown rushing onto a vanquished Libyan in a carving in Beit el Wali temple, has the name 'Anat in vigour'.

Her acceptability to the Egyptians is reflected by the large precinct dedicated to her at Tanis as well as in the theophorous name Anat-em-Heb, i.e. 'Anat in (her) festival' (on the model of Hor-em-heb or the more frequent Amen-em-heb). Occasionally the goddess is found in a direct phonetic rendering of a Syrian name as in the case of Ramesses II's daughter Bint-Anat or 'daughter of Anat'. In the Egyptian view she, along with Astarte, was a daughter of the sun-god RA. The intervention of NEITH of Sais in the struggle for the throne of Egypt resulted in Anat and Astarte becoming wives of the god SETH – a consolation prize for his loss of the kingship to HORUS.

From cuneiform texts found in Ugarit on the Syrian coast the picture of Anat is one of a ruthless goddess with a strong sexual element to her. Covetous of a splendid bow belonging to a youth called Aqhat she sends an eagle to slay him when he refuses to part with it. In another mythological cycle she avenges the murder of her brother BAAL by slaying Mot his killer – in fact she cleaves him with her sword, shovels him onto a fire, grinds his bones and scatters them in the fields for birds and beasts. Her relationship with her brother Baal seems to be more analogous to the concept of 'sister' meaning 'beloved'. There is evidence of a sexual union between Anat and Baal, the offspring of which seems to have been in the form of a wild bull. This aspect of Anat as a fertility goddess can be seen on non-royal Egyptian monuments where Anat can figure in the company of the ithyphallic MIN.

Andjety

God in anthropomorphic form originally worshipped in the

mid-Delta in Lower Egyptian nome 9 (see NOME GODS).

Andjety (meaning 'he of Andjet', i.e. the town of Busiris) was the precursor of OSIRIS at the cult centre of Busiris. The iconography of this god persuasively argues for his being the forerunner of Osiris. Andjety holds the two sceptres in the shape of a 'crook' and a 'flail', insignia which are Osiris's symbols of dominion. Also his high conical crown decorated with two feathers is clearly related to the 'atef' crown of Osiris. As early as the beginning of Dynasty IV King Sneferu, the builder of the first true pyramid tomb, is carved wearing this crown of Andjety. The close relationship of the god to the monarch is also evident from the earliest references in the Pyramid Texts, where the king's power as a universal ruler is enhanced by his being equated to Andjety 'presiding over the eastern districts'. Perhaps Andjety is an embodiment of sovereignty and its attendant regalia. As such he would readily be absorbed into the nature of Osiris and by extension into the pharaoh himself. The most likely explanation of his epithet, 'bull of vultures', found in the Middle Kingdom Coffin Texts, is that it emphasises his role as a procreative consort of major goddesses.

Andjety figures in a funerary context as well. The notion that he is responsible for rebirth in the Afterlife is probably the reason for the substitution for the two feathers of a bicornate uterus in early writings of his name in the Pyramid Texts. In the Underworld too there is an obvious identification between Andjety and Osiris, as ruler. Hence in the Temple of Sety I (Dynasty XIX) at Abydos, the king is depicted burning incense to the god Osiris-Andjety who holds a 'crook' sceptre, wears two feathers in his headband and is accompanied by ISIS.

Anti

Hawk-god of particular importance in nomes 12 and 18 of Upper Egypt (see NOME GODS). His cult is attested in the Early Dynastic Period. There are cogent reasons to read his name as Nemty meaning 'Wanderer' as an alternative to Anti meaning 'Claw'.

Anti is represented standing on a crescent-shaped boat and in the Middle Kingdom Coffin Texts is described as supervising the sailing of the 'henu' boat of another falcon deity SOKAR.

A natural assimilation is made as early as Dynasty VI between Anti and HORUS in his form of a falcon of gold. Both are called Lords of the East, protecting the region where the sun-god rises, and soaring with him at dawn into the firmament. In the Pyramid Texts there are two hawk-gods who equate with Anti:

(i)   Dunawy 'He who extends the arms (i.e. wings)'.
(ii) Dunanwy 'He who extends the claws'.

A complicated late Egyptian document (known as the Papyrus Jumilhac) relates an interesting myth involving Anti in which provincial theologians localise gods of universal import for the 'home market'. The essence of this legend consists of an explanation for three ritual images: a bovine statue worshipped in the northernmost nome (22) of Upper Egypt, whose most prominent deity was HATHOR, the fetish of an animal carcass on a pole (the 'Imyut' symbol), and a statue of Anti made of silver belonging to his temple in nome 12 of Upper Egypt.

The following is a synopsis of the cause-and-effect factors in this myth.

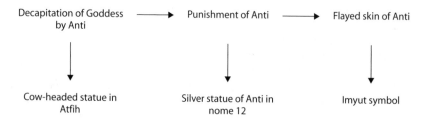

The papyrus states two occurrences which we can relate to each other:

(i) Anti is wrapped up in linen bandages, his skin having been flayed off because of a crime committed in nome 22 of Upper Egypt at Atfih.

(ii) THOTH restores the head of a cow-goddess in Atfih after a crime has been committed.

From this it can be assumed that the head of the cow-goddess had been cut off by Anti – an act reminiscent of Horus's decapitation of ISIS because she prevented him from slaughtering SETH, mentioned in Papyrus Chester Beatty I concerned with the struggle for the throne of Egypt. In Atfih the cow-goddess of most prominence and victim of Anti was Hathor, who by the time that the Papyrus Jumilhac was written had become closely assimilated to Isis. The restoration of the cow-head of the goddess mirrors once more the Horus-Seth papyrus where decapitated Isis is given a head which bears the crown of Hathor, i.e. cow horns enclosing a sun disk. It is possible to see this legend of Anti committing the criminal act – decapitation of the goddess – alluded to in the description of the priest of the temple of Hathor at Atfih: 'he who makes firm the foremost part', i.e. adfixes the head to the body. RA and the ENNEAD learn with outrage of Anti's crime and order the terrifying punishment that the skin should be stripped from him: 'as to his flesh and his skin, his mother created them; as to his bones, they exist through the semen of his father. He will be flayed of his flesh and skin.' Because of this fate, adherents of Anti in nome 12 made his cult image of silver since that metal was symbolic of a god's bones and they held in horror gold which constituted divine flesh, and symbolised to them the flaying of their deity. The flayed-skin motif or Imyut is usually associated with ANUBIS, but it can be seen how it was adopted into the Anti myth. At Atfih, where Anti cut off Hathor's head, there was another goddess called HESAT, the White Cow. In the Pyramid Era she is called the mother of the flayed-skin fetish and forms part of a sacred triad with MNEVIS, as her consort, and Anubis, as her son. Accordingly, by identifying her as the cow-goddess decapitated by Anti, the Anubis emblem can be brought into the legend. Hesat sees the skin of Anti and anoints it with an unguent containing her milk. The flesh of Anti is restored to a state of healthiness and is tied upon a supporting pole which in terms of Egyptian ritual imagery is analogous to the Imyut symbol of Anubis.

Anubis

Canine god of cemeteries and embalming. His most usual form is that of a crouching desert dog, ears pricked up and tail hanging, wearing a collar of magical force and sporting the flagellum of OSIRIS from the centre of his body.

The Anubis dog is probably the jackal and is thus referred to under the name 'sab' in early texts. But other dogs, e.g. the rust-coloured pariah, could have been prototypes. Anubis is perhaps a quintessence of these desert hounds. Certainly the black coat of Anubis is not true to nature but symbolic. It represents the discolouration of the corpse after its treatment in natron and the smearing of the wrappings with a resinous substance during mummification. This leads on to the idea of rebirth in the Afterlife. Also black suggests fertility to the Egyptian mind because it is the colour of the Nile silt which produced rich harvests – hence the notion of springing to life after bodily death is inherent in the dark fur of Anubis. Anubis can appear as anthropomorphic

Tomb of Tutankhamun, Dyn. XVIII, Cairo Museum.

up to his shoulders with the jackal head then superimposed. Very rarely indeed, as in a chapel in the temple of Ramesses II (Dynasty XVIII) at Abydos, is Anubis totally human in shape.

One Egyptian papyrus derives Anubis's name from the verb 'putrefy' linking him with the decomposition of the corpse. However, whatever the etymology of his name Anubis's power probably originated from the observation of desert dogs scavenging bodies in the shallow graves of the late Predynastic period. To prevent such dismemberment Anubis in his canine manifestation was taken as a protector.

In the Pyramid Era Anubis is closely allied to the monarch who is described as having ATUM's body but the face of Anubis. This connection with royalty perhaps led to the attempt to link Anubis's name with the similar word for 'prince'. When the king joins the sun-god in the Afterlife he takes Anubis with him on his neck – presumably the image being similar to that of HORUS protecting the head of Khafra (Dynasty IV) on the diorite statue in Cairo Museum. Further, the king enters his pyramid like Anubis 'on his belly' meaning in the crouching posture of Anubis – a vivid word-picture of the agility required by the monarch to negotiate some of the narrower corridors in a pyramid. From the Palermo Stone, a fragment of royal annals carved in the Old Kingdom, we learn that statues (called 'births') of Anubis were used to designate the year in which they were ceremonially dedicated.

The nature of Anubis is best revealed by the epithets used alongside his name.

1 *Khenty-Imentiu*

This describes Anubis as 'foremost of the westerners' indicating his leadership over those buried in the cemeteries of Egypt, the majority of which were on the west bank of the Nile where the sun-god sank into the Underworld at night. Anubis is pictured in one text as burying the deceased in a sturdy mound of sand in the west.

2 *Khenty-Seh-Netjer*

Here Anubis is the one 'presiding over the god's pavilion'. The wooden effigy of Anubis found in the tomb of Tutankhamun represents the god crouching on a shrine or pavilion gilded and decorated with amuletic signs. Symbolically the pavilion can be both the tent where the ritual of embalmment is carried out and the secure burial chamber which, in the case of royalty, was the 'Golden Hall' where a series of gilded wooden shrines encased the sarcophagus. The structure for embalming is also known as the 'Per Wabet' or House of Purification. It was a special one of these which Anubis, with assistance from THOTH, constructed for the god OSIRIS.

3 *Tepy-Dju-Ef*

This means Anubis 'who is upon his mountain'. The imagery is that of the god watching from the heights of the desert cliffs overlooking the cemeteries.

4 *Neb-Ta-Djeser*

'Lord of the sacred land' referring to the desert in which the necropoleis were situated. Like the previous title this emphasises the geographical environment in which Anubis moves as god of burials. There is a title in the Pyramid Texts, 'Jackal ruler of the bows', which amplifies this aspect of Anubis as a necropolis guardian since it is the forerunner of the motif on the seal used on royal tombs in the Valley of the Kings at Thebes consisting of a recumbent jackal over nine bows.

Historically these bows signify enemies of the pharaoh in the Middle East and Nubia which he has subdued; here they seem to indicate Anubis's triumph over hostile Underworld forces.

5 *Imy-Ut*

This epithet stresses Anubis's role in mummification by calling him 'he who is in the place of embalming'. His association with embalming is recognised in the Pyramid Age where the putrefaction of the king's flesh is prevented in the name of Anubis. Archaeological evidence shows that evisceration was part of the royal mummification process from at least the beginning of Dynasty IV – Cairo Museum has the jars containing the residue of the internal organs of Queen Hetepheres, mother of Khufu, builder of the Great Pyramid at Giza. Anubis washes the royal entrails, just as he guards the chest containing the viscera of OSIRIS. Crouching Anubis can be seen surmounting the chest dragged on a sledge to the tomb in many burial scenes. Anubis physically embalms the body of the king, purifying it with unguent from the eight 'nemset' jars and the eight 'aabet' jars. It is Anubis who brings the 'hekenu' oil to anoint the body of Osiris. He makes the savour of corpses sweet with incense and wraps them with linen bandages made by the goddess TAYET. In the Book of Caverns found in some tombs in the Valley of the Kings, RA instructs Anubis to bind the head of the monarch to prevent its loss and to mould linen strips to the face thus halting decomposition and preserving the features. In an address to the Ferryman of the Celestial waters, the bow-warp of the boat is called the 'tresses of ISIS', attached by Anubis using his skill as an embalmer – phraseology which anticipates some of the techniques used for thickening the hair on mummies of royal ladies in the New Kingdom.

Priest wearing jackal mask in Opening the Mouth ceremony. Book of the Dead of Hunefer, British Museum.

Anubis has a special emblem symbolising his role as an embalmer. It is a headless animal skin (occasionally clearly feline) sometimes dripping blood, tied to a pole. This emblem can also be jackal-headed, as in the Litany of Ra describing the sun-god's journey through the Underworld.

Anubis's presence in the funerary ceremony of Opening the Mouth, performed on the mummy and statues of the deceased in order to vivify them in the tomb, is symbolised by a priest wearing a jackal mask. Anubis originally provided iron from the sky for the magical adze required in this ritual. Anubis's protection extends to the tomb chapel as well as to the burial chamber since the spirit of the deceased can ascend to it to partake of food offerings or employ the magical forces in the hieroglyphs or reliefs. Usually, special formulae are given in the hieroglyphs to protect the burial of the deceased and ensure the food supply in the Afterlife. At the beginning of the Pyramid Age these invocation formulae are addressed to Anubis alone; later Osiris is incorporated and gradually supplants Anubis. Here is a typical example:

> A gift which Anubis presiding over the sacred land gives, namely a burial in the western necropolis for the king's acquaintance and scribe of the treasury . . . Ankh-haf. (A limestone architrave from his tomb at Giza now in the British Museum)

In the Underworld Anubis appears in vignettes of the Book of the Dead, in the Hall of the Two Truths, where the weighing of the heart ceremony takes place. He stands by the scales, sometimes adjusting the plumb of the balance, and is described as 'he who counts the hearts'. We find this idea already present in the Pyramid Texts where Anubis, as 'claimer of hearts', frees the king from restrictions on earth in order for him to join the gods in the sky. Anubis guides those who have passed the rigorous test and whose hearts have been vindicated as honest towards the throne of Osiris.

Anubis is credited with various parents. According to one tradition he is the son of NEPHTHYS and Ra. The Greek writer Plutarch also makes Nephthys his mother but attributes this to her adultery with Osiris the husband of her sister Isis. A benign Isis then adopts Anubis as her own son. Clearly this is an attempt to incorporate the independent deity Anubis into the Osirion pantheon. In an Egyptian papyrus of a later date we find the same tradition when Anubis is called 'son of Isis'. In the earlier tradition of the Coffin Texts the cow HESAT gives birth to Anubis and from the same source BASTET is Anubis's mother. This latter affiliation is quite likely to derive from the writing of Bastet's name which uses an unguent jar, whose importance in the mummification process we have already seen. This link is intensified by the presence in the necropolis at Memphis of cult focal points for Bastet and Anubis known as the Bubasteion and Anubeion. In the Pyramid Texts there are references to a daughter of Anubis in the form of a celestial serpent called Kebehwet who refreshes and purifies the monarch.

Papyri and reliefs of the Graeco-Roman period show a transformation of the pharaonic Anubis into new roles. He becomes a cosmic deity ruling over the sky and the earth. In a rather Promethean aspect he brings light to the human race and furthers its prospects by manufacturing effective love philtres. On the walls of the catacombs at Alexandria Anubis is dressed in armour like a warrior as a guard of Osiris. Strangely his lower body is in the shape of a snake. Outwardly this seems divorced from Egyptian tradition, but it is

worth bearing in mind that 2,500 years earlier in the Pyramid Age Anubis accompanies the monarch as a serpent ruling over Heliopolis.

Anukis

Goddess of the cataracts of the Lower Nile whose name in Egyptian is Anket. She is shown as a lady wearing on her head a modius from which stem ostrich feathers.

Her cult can be traced back to the Old Kingdom in Upper Egypt, especially at Elephantine, and Seheil (an island south of Aswan). Although strongly associated with Lower Nubia, she is not an imported goddess but has her origins in Egyptian

Anukis suckling the pharaoh. Temple of Ramesses II, Beit el-Wali, Dyn. XIX.

speculation on the nature of a deity beyond their southern frontier. Her name could mean the 'embracer', either benignly as a nurse or lethally as a strangler. If this is so, she would possess a dual temperament similar to HATHOR, with whom she is closely connected in Thebes.

She is called the daughter of RA and it is not until the New Kingdom that she takes the role of the divine child of KHNUM and SATIS.

Her sacred animal is the gazelle.

Apedemak   Lion-god of war indigenous to the Sudanese culture of Meroe. The Meroitic civilisation displays many Egyptian influences and incorporates gods from the pharaonic pantheon but Apedemak is likely to be a totally African deity. He is represented as anthropomorphic to the shoulders with leonine head and holding a sceptre surmounted by a seated lion. His association with battles is admirably captured in the lion imagery – in pharaonic Egypt too the lion-motif can represent a killer-deity in a southern environment (see TEFNUT). Mention of Apedemak is rare in Lower Nubia although in a chapel dedicated to ISIS at Dabod, just above the first cataract of the Nile, Meroitic ruler Adikhalamani (*c*.200 BC) calls himself 'beloved of Apedemak'. The main sanctuary of Apedemak was at Musawwarat es-Sufra in the sands of the Butana, north of the sixth Nile cataract. For about 800 years from 300 BC this vast temple complex, which included a major temple to Apedemak (as well as chapels to him and another Meroitic deity SEBIUMEKER), was the destination of sacred pilgrimages. From reliefs in his monuments Apedemak's cult involves specially bred temple cattle and an important regard for the African elephant.

Apis

Bull-god, manifestation or living image of PTAH of Memphis. Apis can be called the 'son of Ptah' or his 'herald', acting as an intermediary for mankind to communicate with the creator-god of Memphis through oracles.

Dedicatory bronzes and a description by the Greek writer Herodotus give the special qualities marking out this bull from the herd as sacred. The bull's mother, known as ISIS, conceives Apis through a flash of lightning. The opportunity of witnessing the mystery of the birth of Apis is a privilege held out to the deceased in the Afterlife. The Apis bull is black except for a small white triangular patch on its forehead. Between its horns it carries the emblem of the sun disk and Uraeus (see WADJET) – sometimes it is the moon disk in later iconography of the bull. On its back are the protective wings of a vulture-goddess (the 'eagle' in Herodotus's account). A minor feature is that the hairs of its tail divide into two

Late Period statuette, British Museum.

strands; dualism of this sort pervades Ancient Egyptian thinking and can often be interpreted as representing the original two kingdoms of north and south. The scarab beetle, which the priests find under the tongue of Apis according to Herodotus, is drawn from solar imagery.

At Memphis Apis lived in palatial quarters near the temple of Ptah where Herodotus mentions statues of the bull-god (surely anthropomorphic to the shoulders with bovine head superimposed) which supported the roof and were nearly 7 m high. The Pyramid Texts and Book of the Dead suggest that the cult of the living Apis was celebrated to the north of Memphis in the Delta towns of Sais and Athribis.

The Palermo Stone which contains annals of early Egyptian kings gives evidence of Apis being worshipped shortly after the founding of the Egyptian state (c.3000 BC) in the reign of Den. The antiquity of the cult is also attested by the surviving fragments of the Egyptian priest Manetho (who wrote a history of pharaohs in the Greek languages for the benefit of the Ptolemaic ruler early in the third century BC): the worship of Apis is stated to have been inaugurated during Dynasty II in the reign of King Kaiechos (Kakau in Egyptian Kinglists or Raneb in archaeological sources).

The pharaoh identifies closely with Apis – bull imagery (with its inherent notion of strength and fertility) being an ancient characteristic in the propaganda of the god–king, as can be seen from carved slate palettes and in one of the names used in the royal protocol 'victorious bull'. Celebrating his jubilee festival, a ceremony concerned with the rejuvenation of the monarch's powers, the pharaoh strides briskly alongside the galloping Apis bull. This ritual which took place at Memphis is vividly portrayed in a relief on a block from a dismantled chapel in the Temple of

Karnak at Thebes where Queen Hatshepsut (Dynasty XVIII), dressed in the regalia of a pharaoh, renews her vital strength to govern by striding with Apis.

In the funerary cult this royal link with Apis continues. The king ascending to the sun-god in the Afterlife claims he will not be harmed enroute by murderous apes because his power is such that he was responsible for restoring the head of Apis, presumably cut off by these assassins. However, it is the bull-god that is usually the protector. The might of the phallus of Apis is a means by which the king can climb into the realm of the sun-god. It is the vigour of Apis which gives a person control over the four winds in the next world. Transformation into Apis, 'high of horns, beautiful of names, far-seer and wideranger', will enable a person to avoid the abomination of possible reversal of natural phenomena in the Afterlife and the forced consumption of obnoxious substances.

An average lifespan for Apis was 14 years. During this time festivals would be held at Memphis where Apis could be seen by the higher echelons of society at the window of appearances in the temple, a procedure borrowed directly from royal ceremonial. On the death of Apis Egypt mourned as if for the loss of the monarch himself.

The bull was mummified on lion-headed alabaster tables some of which survive at Memphis. The funeral was an occasion of display and pomp, with men dragging to the tomb the sledge on which the embalmed and bejewelled bull had been placed in a couchant position. The burial place was in the northern quarter of the desert plateau of Saqqara, the necropolis overlooking the capital Memphis where Apis had lived. Vast underground catacombs, discovered in 1851 by Mariette and popularly known as the Serapeum, were cut for the successive bull burials. In some vaults were huge sarcophagi of granite weighing up to 70 tons, to protect the bull and its burial valuables – all systematically plundered. Some burials date to the New Kingdom but the majority of tombs were cut from the mid-seventh century BC onwards. No archaeological or inscriptional evidence shows that the Persian ruler Cambyses (Dynasty XXVII) sought revenge for calamities incurred on his conquest of Egypt by killing Apis during a festival to show that the bull was not a god but flesh and blood. Indeed there appears to be no break of Apis burials under the Persian domination of Egypt and this story in Herodotus is part of his intent to discredit Cambyses.

This later subterranean gallery of tombs stretches for 198 m. Evocative of the demise of the Apis cult is the massive granite sarcophagus lying empty in a corridor, abandoned by the workmen of the last priestly officiants of the bull's worship.

When Isis, mother of Apis, who had been brought to Memphis with her illustrious offspring, died she was given the honour of burial in the Saqqara necropolis in the vaults known as the Iseum, as yet not fully explored. But from here an interesting stela commemorates the burial of an Isis cow while the ruler Cleopatra VII (Ptolemaic Period) was out of Egypt, probably meeting Mark Antony in Syria.

Occasionally, in funerary texts, Apis is given the task of threshing grain in the Underworld, an obvious reflection of the role of oxen in Egyptian agriculture, as seen, e.g. in paintings like that in the tomb of Menna at Thebes. However, a more elevated existence in the Hereafter is usually attributed to Apis. Following concepts about the rank of the dead pharaoh in the Underworld, Apis, upon dying, becomes the god OSIRIS. It is the sacred bull of Memphis in his form Osiris-Apis

that provides the Egyptian element in the nature of the hybrid god created under the early Ptolemaic rulers known as SARAPIS.

Apophis

Underworld snake-god whose lethal powers are directed against the sun-god. Eternal and persistently hostile, Apophis symbolises primeval forces of chaos.

The gigantic body of Apophis, often a concertina of coils, represents a kind of void or 'black hole' forcing those he swallows into that non-existence which the Egyptians feared so greatly.

The name of Apophis was interpreted in the Roman period as 'he who was spat out' and linked to the saliva of the goddess NEITH.

All texts and depictions attempt to bring about the defeat and destruction of Apophis but his suppression is only momentary. Apophis becomes non-existent when the sun-god triumphs over him on

Apophis speared by Seth. Papyrus of Her-Weben, Dyn. XXI, Cairo Museum.

his journey in the solar boat through the Underworld. His indestructibility is such that he at once returns as a malevolent force trying to devour RA and his supporters. It is at the point when the sun-god subdues Apophis temporarily that the heads of his previous victims appear from his body. A scene in the tomb of Ramesses VI (Dynasty XX) in the Valley of the Kings shows the snake carried by gods, and with the twelve heads of those it has devoured emerging from its coils. Once Ra has passed by the heads are destined to return into the body of Apophis until freed again briefly on the next night.

In a papyrus in the British Museum, which dates to *c*.300 BC but contains linguistic styles of 2,000 years earlier, there is an account of the overthrow of Apophis and victory of Ra. Apophis is hacked up and burnt; this destruction is made more efficacious by practical instructions for magic including drawing a picture of Apophis in green on a new sheet of papyrus, sealing it in a box, setting it on fire and spitting on it four times.

Apophis is the serpent described as lying in wait to swallow Ra on Bakhu, the furthest mountain in the west. He is over 16 m long with his front consisting of flint. As the boat of the sun-god sinks into the western horizon Apophis hypnotises all its occupants with his stare except for the god SETH. The sun-god is in jeopardy but Seth charms the snake with a spell and Ra begins his journey through the Underworld.

Naturally, human beings require divine help against Apophis or can even transform themselves into powerful deities to counteract his onslaught. In order to board the sun-god's boat in the sky the Bull of Millions provides a ladder to escape from Apophis. As navigator of the solar boat the dead person claims to know how to repel Apophis and save Ra from becoming entangled in his coils. The deceased can assume the form of the god SHU to protect

the sun-god at the perilous entrance into the Underworld on the western horizon.

The overthrow and binding of Apophis is emphasised in violent statements or vivid pictures. There are references to seventy-seven papyri-rolls which are given to the dead person by means of a spell, containing formulae for bringing Apophis to his place of execution where he is cut up, crushed and consumed by fire. Apophis is represented with spearheads in his coils or, as at Gate 10 in the Underworld, chained by his neck. His symbolic annihilation is forcefully portrayed by the cat of Ra decapitating Apophis, blood spurting out as he cuts into the snake's vertebrae.

The fact that Apophis is a complete antithesis to the sun-god, i.e. the darkness of a chthonic deity opposed to the light of Ra, comes across in the imagery surrounding Gate 2 in the Underworld. There ATUM is condemning to destruction enemies of the sun-god and included among them is Apophis, the 'khefty' (opponent) of Ra, with his head to the ground awaiting slaughter.

Apophis is imagined as possessing a hideously loud roar which resounds throughout the Underworld. He is placed outside of the natural world requiring no nourishment except to 'breathe' his own shouts.

Arensnuphis   Anthropomorphic Nubian deity wearing a plumed crown who occurs in southern temples during the Graeco-Roman period, coeval with the Meroitic civilisation based around the mid-fifth to sixth cataract region.

The Egyptian rendering of his name 'Ari-hes-nefer' gives little clue to his nature, other than being a benign deity. A small kiosk-style temple was built in his honour on the island of Philae during the reign of Ptolemy IV Philopator (*c*.220 BC), the blocks from the southern enclosure wall showing that it was a joint enterprise with the Meroitic King Arqamani (Ergamenes II). However, only the fact that he is a 'companion' of the goddess ISIS, pre-eminent deity of Philae, can be elucidated from the inscriptions. He is also represented on a wall of Dendur temple (originally sited above the first cataract of the Nile, now re-erected at the Metropolitan Museum of Art, New York) where he accompanies the local deified heroes PETEESE and PIHOR being worshiped by the Roman emperor Augustus.

Ash

God of the western Desert (Sahara) including the fertile oases, and of 'Tehenu' or Libya, first attested on sealings from the Early Dynastic Period. Although his territory is in what the Ancient Egyptians called the Red Land (Deshret) as opposed to the crop-bearing silt of the Black Land (Kemet) bordering the Nile itself, Ash is not an outsider or a god of alien origins. He controls the produce of the oases in favour of the pharaoh – recent archaeology in the western Desert has shown how the Egyptian monarch enjoyed the prosperity of its major fertile depressions. Ash also had associations with vineyards in the western Nile Delta.

His shape is normally anthropomorphic as attested, e.g. in a relief from a temple of King Sahura (Dynasty V). He can also be shown with the head of a hawk. As lord of the desert an obvious identification was made between Ash and SETH as early as Dynasty II. This connexion was intensified because Ash, it would seem, was the original god of Ombos in Upper Egypt (not too far from modern Qena) before the arrival of Seth as its major deity – hence an epithet of Ash being 'nebuty' or 'he of Nebut (= Ombos)'.

Assessor gods

Forty-two Underworld deities who constitute the tribunal of jurors in the Broad Hall of the Two Truths.

They assess the earthly life of any new arrival in the Underworld, eagerly watching for evil doers whose blood they can drink. A just person whose heart in the balance against the goddess of Truth (MAAT) reflects an upright life will be declared 'true of voice' and fit for Paradise. Someone whose heart is weighed down with crime will be consigned to the Devourer of the Dead (AMMUT).

In the funerary papyri which we popularly term Book of the Dead, Spell 125 lists their names and places of origin, which can either be strictly geographical or atmospheric. In each instance there follows a denial made by the deceased of a specific sin that might have been committed – hence the expression 'negative confession' used modernly to describe this event. It was hoped that this protestation of innocence combined with the magic of knowing the deity's name would persuade the Assessors not to press with any accusations that might ruin the chance of eternal life in the Underworld. The following table gives a handful of these deities:

Number	Name of Assessor	Home Base	Crime-Concern
2	Flame-Embracer	Kheraha	Robbery
3	Beaky	Hermopolis	Greed
5	Terrifying of Face	Rosetau	Murder
9	Bone-Breaker	Herakleopolis	Lying
13	Consumer of Blood	Slaughter block	Butchery of temple cattle
27	His-Face-Behind-Him	Tomb	Sexual deviation

Astarte

A warrior-goddess of Canaan and Syria who is a Western Semitic counterpart of the Akkadian ISHTAR worshipped in Mesopotamia.

In the Egyptian pantheon to which she was officially admitted in Dynasty XVIII her prime association is with horses and chariots. On the stela set up near the sphinx by Amenhotep II celebrating his prowess, Astarte is described as delighting in the impressive equestrian skill of the monarch when he was still only crown-prince. In her iconography her aggression can be seen in the bull horns she sometimes wears as a symbol of domination. Similarly, in her Levantine homelands, Astarte is a battle-field-goddess; e.g. when the Peleset (Philistines) killed Saul and his three sons on Mount Gilboa, they deposited the enemy armour as spoils in the temple of 'Ashtoreth' (= Astarte).

Like ANAT she is the daughter of RA and the wife of the god SETH but also has a relationship with the god of the sea. From the woefully fragmentary papyrus giving the legend of Astarte and the sea the following information can be gleaned: the sea-god YAMM demands tribute from the gods which involves the goddess of harvest RENENUTET. Her place is then taken by Astarte called here 'daughter of PTAH'. The story is lost from this point on but one assumes this liaison results in the goddess tempering the arrogance of Yamm.

Astarte. Gold pendant, Ugarit, Syria, c.1500 BC, Louvre Museum.

Aten

Sun-god who in his zenith under the pharaoh Akhenaten (Dynasty XVIII) became the universal and almost exclusive deity.

The unmistakable iconography of Aten consists of a disk with the Uraeus (see WADJET) on its lower arc. Rays emanate from it which terminate in hands, holding the hieroglyph of 'life' if they shoot towards the nose of the king or queen. Thereby, Aten transmits his 'beauty' (neferu) to the monarch who is the intercessor between mankind and the god.

Aten's elevation to the unrivalled solar and creator god of Egypt occurred in the fourteenth century BC. Although the supremacy of Aten lasted only for a few decades, it was one of the most traumatic religious experiences through which the intellectual scribe, priest or courtier had to live. Atenism is also of major importance for any world-wide survey of man's religious beliefs. The worship of Aten was not a sudden innovation on the part of one king, but the climax of a religious quest among Egyptians for a benign god limitless in power and manifest in all countries and natural phenomena.

1 The cult before the reign of Akhenaten

The word 'aten' itself carries the literal meaning of a disk, not always in a solar context, e.g. the surface of a mirror or the moon. But it is in its sun-imagery that we can trace its progression to godhead. It is the sun as an astronomical concept that is conveyed by 'aten' in the inscription of Queen Hatshepsut's standing obelisk in the temple of Karnak – the electrum covering the shaft illuminates Egypt like the sun ('aten'). The sun disk is a symbol in which major gods can appear, e.g. 'ATUM who is in his disk ('aten')'. It is only a small step from this link with divine power for the 'aten' itself to become a god. It is in an inscription of the pharaoh Thutmose I (Dynasty XVIII) found at Tombos in Nubia that the word 'aten' occurs for the first time with the god symbol following it in the form of a deity bearing a sun disk on his head. But nearly 500 years earlier, even without this symbol, the word 'aten' carried the

idea of divinity. In the narrative of the adventures of a harem official, Sinuhe, the pharaoh Amenemhat I (Dynasty XII) assassinated in 1956 BC is described as soaring into the sky and uniting with Aten his creator.

Thus the connection between Aten as a manifestation of the sun-god and the ruler of Egypt is formulated in texts by the Middle Kingdom. Later Iahmose (Dynasty XVIII), the Theban ruler who finally drove the last foreign Hyksos monarch out of Egypt into Palestine, is flattered on a stela by being likened to 'Aten when he shines'. His successor, Amenhotep I (Dynasty XVIII), becomes on death 'united with Aten, coalescing with the one from whom he had come'.

The earliest iconography of Aten appears on a monument at Giza dedicated to Amenhotep II (Dynasty XVIII). It is a winged sun disk with outstretched arms grasping the cartouche of the pharaoh. By the reign of Thutmose IV (Dynasty XVIII) Aten is by royal assent a prominent deity still rising in the state pantheon. During his rule a historical text on the underside of a scarab mentions Aten in the vanguard of the pharaoh's army in battle – a role commonly given to AMUN.

The pharaoh Amenhotep III, father of Akhenaten, furthered the fortunes of Aten. From his reign comes the earliest evidence of a priesthood and temple to Aten at Heliopolis. Several of his courtiers bore titles connecting them with the Aten cult, e.g. Hatiay, 'scribe of the two granaries of the Temple of Aten in Memphis', and Ramose (not the vizier but the owner of tomb 46 in the Theban necropolis), 'steward of the mansion of the Aten', depicted with his wife going to view the sun disk. The palace of Amenhotep III at Malkata on the west bank at Thebes was called 'splendour of Aten'. From the latter years of this king it was also known as the

The rays of Aten. El-Amarna, Dyn. XVIII, Berlin Museum.

'Per Hay' or 'home of rejoicing' – a description we shall meet again applied to part of the Great Temple of the Aten at el-Amarna. Here also, at Malkata, Amenhotep III ordered the construction within 16 days of a lake over a mile in length for the pleasure of his principal wife Queen Tiye – inaugurating it by sailing its waters on a boat called 'Aten glitters'.

2   *The cult after the accession of Akhenaten*

Throughout previous reigns in Dynasty XVIII adherents of Aten had gradually consolidated for him a position of power in the state, coexisting nevertheless with a number of other major deities in whom Egyptians could see a manifestation of the sun. When Akhenaten became sole ruler on the throne of Egypt in 1352 BC Aten was rarefied into supreme god of the kingdom almost totally absorbing, supplanting or eliminating rival divinities.

At the outset of his reign Akhenaten kept Thebes as the religious capital of

The pharaoh Akhenaten, Temple of Aten at Thebes, Dyn. XVIII, Cairo Museum.

Egypt, audaciously building a temple to Aten outside the eastern perimeter wall of the rival temple of AMUN at Karnak. This temple was torn down after Akhenaten's reign but over 35,000 blocks (or 'talatat') survive, having been reused during the reign of Horemheb (Dynasty XVIII) as filling material for Pylon IX on the southern axis of Karnak temple. From these 'talatat' it is possible to retrieve an idea of the scope of the decoration of the walls in the Aten temple. This supplements information gleaned from the excavation of the foundations of the dismantled temple. The structure was called the 'house of Aten' ('Per Aten') and possessed pillared courts with striking colossal statues of Akhenaten and at least three sanctuaries. The relationship between Aten and the sun-cult of Heliopolis is emphasised by calling one of these sanctuaries 'mansion of the Benben' symbolising the primeval mound on which the sun-god emerged from NUN to create the universe – 'Benben' is the name used for the sanctuary at Heliopolis and is written at Karnak with an obelisk symbol following it, another borrowing from Heliopolitan imagery, possibly indicating that an actual obelisk was once situated in east Karnak. Parts of Aten's Theban temple were pre-eminently the domain of Nefertiti, Akhenaten's principal queen. She obviously aided Akhenaten in the task of promulgating the Aten cult and like the pharaoh had a special relationship with the sun-god. This is evident from the writing of her cartouche where the name of Aten is reversed against the normal orientation of the hieroglyphs to face the symbol of Nefertiti as queen. In the section of the Karnak Aten temple called 'meeting the Aten' ('Gem-pa-Aten'), Nefertiti and two daughters worship below the sun disk to the exclusion of the pharaoh himself.

This first blossoming of Aten worship on the pro-Amun ground of Thebes can be seen as well from the tomb of Akhenaten's vizier Ramose on the west bank of the Nile. Most of its decoration consists of exquisite low relief carved while Ramose was vizier during the last years of Amenhotep III and a painted funerary procession in conventional Theban style. But on the rear wall of the pillared tomb-chapel is a mixture of traditional design and startling developments in art made by Akhenaten to achieve the propagation of his cult. Although mutilated by enemies of Akhenaten's ideas after his death (the rays of Aten being sliced through to prevent his 'beauty' reaching the king), the wall reflects unequivocally that the adherence to Atenism was a prerequisite for any courtier holding a high political appointment.

Naturally the priests of Amun-RA, for so long the supreme god of the Egyptian state, were rankled by their loss of influence. But they could only grumble. Akhenaten mentions on two stelae that the priests were saying more evil things about him than they did about his father and grandfather. Thus we learn about the conflict between royalty and the Theban priesthood that can be traced back at least to the reign of Thutmose IV. More explicit is the fact that no member of the priestly hierarchy at Thebes had any power to curb a pharaoh's inclination – hence no suppression of Atenism as soon as it was clearly a political threat.

By the sixth year of his reign Akhenaten desired a major sanctuary for Aten on land uncontaminated by other deities. Sailing north from Thebes into Middle Egypt with its imposing limestone cliffs he discovered a natural amphitheatre on the east bank of the Nile which he called 'Akhet-Aten' or 'Horizon of Aten'. It is commonly known today by a conflation of Arabic designations as 'el-Amarna'. This was to be the centre of the Egyptian empire for the rest of Akhenaten's reign. He marked out the taxable area of Aten on both banks with fourteen boundary stelae on which he emphasised his allegiance to Aten by changing his titulary of the Five Great Names that he had assumed on his coronation – a new era had dawned.

Title	Year 5 at Thebes	Year 6 at el-Amarna
HORUS	Strong Bull Lofty of Plumes	Strong Bull Beloved of Aten
He of NEKHBET and WADJET	Great in Kingship in Karnak (Ipet-swt)	Great in his Kingship in Akhetaten
Horus of Gold	Crowned in Heliopolis of the south (i.e. Thebes)	Raising high the Name of Aten
King of Upper and Lower Egypt	Ruler of the Nine Bows, Lord of Crowns, Seizer of the Crown of Upper Egypt, Neferkheperura Waenra	Living by Truth (MAAT) Lord of the Two Lands Neferkheperura Waenra
Son of Ra	His beloved Amenhotep, god-ruler of Thebes	Living by Truth (Maat) Lord of Crowns Akhenaten Great in his Lifetime

From the new protocol taken by the pharaoh it can be seen that the seat of government has moved from the palace at Thebes to the royal residence at el-Amarna. His original name Amenhotep ('Amun is content') becomes Akhenaten or 'Beneficial to Aten' indicating his piety. Regarding the theology of Aten it is interesting to note that Akhenaten retains in his new titulary all references to the sun-god Ra. In his prenomen there is 'Neferkheperura' ('Beautiful are the manifestations of Ra') and 'Waenra' ('Sole one of Ra'). Aten is really the god Ra absorbed under the iconography of the sun disk. The eminence of Aten is a renewal of the kingship of Ra as it had been during its apogee over a thousand years earlier under the monarchs of Dynasty V.

This significant correlation between Aten and Ra (or RA-HARAKHTI) can be observed in various ways. In an inscription from the sandstone quarries of Gebel el-Silsila which provided the hardcore for the Karnak temple of Akhenaten, Ra-Harakhti is called the 'light which is in Aten at Ipet-swt (Karnak)'. Four of Nefertiti's daughters have names compounded with Aten – Merytaten, Meketaten, Ankhesenpaaten, Nefernefruaten-ta-shery – but the last two children are given the names Nefernefrura and Setepenra. In a rock-cut tomb in the desert cliffs at el-Amarna the investiture of its owner as the high priest of Aten covers a wall. His name is Meryra. In fact the title of the Aten's chief officiant is borrowed directly from the hierarchy of Heliopolis – the high priest in both cults is the 'Great Seer'. The link is intensified in the evidence of the boundary stelae where Akhenaten regards Aten as being manifest in MNEVIS, the sacred bull of Ra, directing a tomb

to be cut for it in the eastern cliffs at el-Amarna.

Aten's temples at Amarna suffered the same fate as his Theban sanctuaries – torn down with the blocks removed for bolstering up monuments at nearby Hermopolis. But the temple foundations have been surveyed and the elevation can be ascertained from carvings in the tombs of Akhenaten's courtiers. The great temple was called the 'House of Aten in Akhetaten' and was well under way by the ninth year. It was a vast complex of courts and offering tables open to the rays of Aten – unlike the roofed sanctuaries of Amun at Karnak. There were two introductory sections in the temple. The forepart known as the 'House of Rejoicing' ('Per Hay') where in the inaugural light at dawn the knowledge that Aten will rise becomes beyond doubt. Then followed the 'Gem-Aten' ('Meeting Aten') consisting of courts where the full celebration of the rays of the god at sunrise took place. Beyond this to the east was the main sanctuary where Akhenaten and Nefertiti officiated as the intermediaries between the populace and the god. The ceremony involved consecrating offerings on the altar by a sweep of the royal sceptre and by burning incense. In addition to the royal dais it has been calculated that there were 772 offering tables in the temple proper with up to 900 in the areas immediately to the north and south of the temenos wall. It is impossible that each day every table received a quota of perfume pomades, fruit, flowers, meat and drink – even reducing the offerings to just one item such as lettuce is out of the question. But doubtless in the daily cult within the temple one offering table on each side of the east–west axis received full offerings for the Aten's rays. The colossal statues of Akhenaten in the temple probably received offerings from priests and courtiers to urge the pharaoh to pass on their prayers to Aten since direct access to the god was prohibited to all except for him and Nefertiti.

Aten's nature as seen through the eyes of pharaoh is really all that survives in the theology of el-Amarna. We can understand all the essential elements of Atenism from a study of the two forms of titulary which Akhenaten gave the god – these names of Aten are often called 'Didactic'. Cartouches are used to emphasise the overall kingship of Aten – eliminating the claim of Amun-Ra to be king of the gods. Aten is also thought to celebrate jubilee festivals like the pharaoh himself. The earlier protocol is clearly henotheistic – indeed it would be difficult to prove that Akhenaten ever really formulated a concept of true monotheism – incorporating several different manifestations of the one sun-god:

Live the beautiful god who delights in Truth (Maat depicted as a goddess with a feather on her head), Lord of all which his disk encircles, Lord of the Sky, Lord of the Earth, Aten, living and great, illuminating the Two Lands. May my father live!
    First cartouche = Live Ra-Harakhti rejoicing on the Horizon.
    Second cartouche = In his name as SHU who is in Aten. Given life forever eternally, Aten, living and great, who is in jubilee dwelling in the Temple of Aten in Akhetaten.

The later, more refined, titulary reads:
    First cartouche = Ra lives, ruler of the Horizon rejoicing in the Horizon.
    Second cartouche = In his name as Ra, the father, who has returned as Aten.

Here the direct equation of Aten with the more ancient sun-god of Heliopolis is at its most cogent.

Other temples to the Aten were constructed beyond the confines of el-Amarna. At Memphis, always the political and administrative nucleus of pharaonic Egypt, blocks have survived from Akhenaten's reign giving evidence of the cult being celebrated in some structure. In Nubia beyond the third Nile cataract the cult of Aten was celebrated in the temple of Sesebi.

Following the death of Akhenaten and the subsequent attempt under the early Ramesside rulers to consign him to oblivion as an anathema, Aten dwindled to a minor deity. It would be tempting to see Akhenaten's vision of a sole creator-god carried after his death beyond the borders of Egypt by the ancestors of the writers of parts of the Old Testament where similar attitudes to a unique divinity are found. (For example, in Psalm 104 whose resemblance to the Great Hymn to the Aten has often been remarked upon.) However, much more historical evidence and proof of transmission are required even to begin to formulate a theory of interconnection. As yet such suggestions are purely speculative and nowhere near approaching the obvious relationship between the Egyptian Instruction of Amenemope and the Hebrew Book of Proverbs.

It is worth remembering the advanced religious thinking that took place when Aten was paramount. Ideas about an overall creator-god were already in existence before Akhenaten's reign as is evident on the stelae of the brother architects Suti and Hor in the British Museum where the sun-god is adulated as a supreme deity dwelling in different gods such as Amun, Ra or Horus. But it is under Akhenaten that those ideas are most elaborately conceptualised. Hymns to Aten, which certainly received royal scrutiny, if not actually composed by the pharaoh, survive in the rock tombs to the courtiers at el-Amarna. The following epitome of the Great Hymn to the Aten from the tomb of the vizier Ay tries to stress the ways in which Aten is unique:

1 Aten is the sole creator-god whose immaculate beauty is transmitted to earth from a great distance in the form of rays.
2 Night is the negation of Aten and a time to fear – lions and snakes abound threatening death. The only release is the dawn of Aten on the horizon.
3 The structured order of daily life prospers under Aten – work is done in the fields and river traffic sails unhindered.
4 Aten is responsible for the miracle of human life, nurturing the seed in the womb until birth when his protection extends to the child. No life form is too insignificant for his care – Aten looks after even the chick inside the egg.
5 Nature thrives below the rays of Aten – trees blossom, cattle, birds and fish are healthy. (This is, surely, the textual imagery equivalent of the painted wall and pavement scenes of calves, ducks and foliage that enhanced the palaces at Malkata and el-Amarna.)
6 Aten is invisible to man, performing a myriad of benefits in this world of his making. In the limited world-view of the ancient Egyptian Aten extends his ingenuity to providing a Nile in the sky (i.e. rain) for the Syrians who lack the Egyptian Nile from the Underworld with its annual flood.
7 Aten divided mankind into races of different colour and speech – a concept of respect for foreigners as creations of Aten more striking when we realise the vilification which Egyptian state propaganda usually meted out to Syrians and Nubians.

However, this outward-looking, perceptive hymn ends on a note that conjures up the jealousy of a despot towards the god he has installed as head of the state religion – attention is drawn to the fact that Akhenaten alone has knowledge of Aten. Accordingly the god's will for all other Egyptians is made clear via the orders of Akhenaten and Nefertiti. Individual contemplation of Aten or personal interpretation of his designs is absent from the prayers in the tombs of Akhenaten's courtiers.

Atum

Sun-god and creator of the universe.

The name 'Atum', carries the idea of 'totality' in the sense of an ultimate and unalterable state of perfection. Atum is frequently called 'Lord of Heliopolis' ('Iunu' in Egyptian), the major centre of sun worship. The presence of another solar deity on this site leads to a coalescence of the two gods into Ra-Atum.

Temple of Sety I, Abydos, Dyn. XIX.

Illustrations of Atum normally show him in anthropomorphic form sometimes wearing the combined crowns of Upper and Lower Egypt, sometimes the royal headcloth. He can appear upright and stately or in the stance of a respected official leaning on his staff of office. The notion of an elderly Atum symbolises the setting sun.

A number of creatures are sacred to Atum including the lion, bull, ichneumon and lizard. Also Atum as a snake is very significant because it represents a concept not as a rule mentioned by the Egyptians – namely a cosmic collapse and a 'Gotterdämmerung' from which only Atum and OSIRIS survive. In a dialogue between these two deities in the Book of the Dead Atum states that he will eventually destroy the world, submerging gods, men and Egypt in the primal waters (NUN) which were all that existed at the beginning of time. In this holocaust Atum and Osiris will live on in the form of serpents. A similar idea occurs in a rock inscription at Hatnub in Middle Egypt where, in mythological time, an earlier cycle of catastrophe resulted in the only survivor being the 'kerhet' snake. The imagery is taken from the snake shedding its skin (i.e. destruction) and emerging in a new form (i.e. survival).

As early as the Pyramid Era there are references to the creation of gods of the elements by Atum. Arising self-engendered out of the primeval water, Atum took his phallus in his hand and brought it to orgasm. This hand performing the vital act of creation can figure in the hieroglyphs writing the god's name and is also the original source of the title 'God's Hand' adopted for the Theban priestess regarded as symbolically married to AMUN. The semen of Atum then produces the first two divinities in his cosmos, SHU and TEFNUT. These become the parents and grandparents of the remaining deities that form Atum's ENNEAD (or company of nine gods) at Heliopolis. A coeval but variant explanation of the means by which Atum created his offspring is based on the similarity of the sound of the names of Shu and Tefnut to the words for to spit and expectorate, the two deities being envisaged as arising from Atum's mucus.

Atum is called the father of the king of Egypt, intensifying the link between the sun-god as Ra and the monarchy which is of paramount importance from at least Dynasty IV. Thus the paternal protection of Atum is sought for the pyramid in which the king is buried. In the Afterlife Atum embraces his son, the dead monarch, raising him into the sky as head of the star-gods. By using magic formulae the king might even hope to surpass the power of Atum, becoming himself the supreme deity and rule as Atum over every god. Through this solarisation of the king the royal flesh itself becomes a manifestation of Atum.

In the political sphere it is essential for Atum to be seen participating in the coronation ritual of the pharaoh. For instance, in the temple of Amun at Karnak reliefs show Atum together with MONTU, two great gods of North and South Egypt respectively, conducting the king into the sacred precinct. The underlying message is that Atum as creator-god is the ultimate source of pharaonic power: it was after all to HORUS (of whom the king of Egypt is the living manifestation), belonging to the fifth generation of Atum's family, that the throne of Egypt was awarded.

Atum's omnipotence quells hostile forces in the Underworld. He overcomes the dangerous snake NEHEBU-KAU by pressing his fingernail on its spine. Before Gate 9 of the Underworld Atum stands confronting the coiled serpent APOPHIS condemning him to be overthrown and annihilated. Also in tombs of all periods of the

New Kingdom in the Valley of the Kings at Thebes, e.g. (Amenhotep II) Dynasty XVIII, Sety I (Dynasty XIX) and Ramesses VI (Dynasty XX), the walls depict Atum resting on his staff supervising the punishment of the enemies of the sun which is usually drowning or beheading. It is Atum who offers protection to the deceased on his journey through the Underworld to paradise, ensuring a safe passage past the Lake of Fire where there lurks a deadly dog-headed god who lives by swallowing souls and snatching hearts. Despite Atum's invincibility one would like to know more about a tantalising reference in the Coffin Texts to Atum losing his beard on the 'day of rebellion' – an inestimable trophy for the sun-god's opponents.

B

Baal

⚱ \\ ⌐⊃| Prominent god of the sky and storms whose cult spread from Ugarit in Syria into Egypt, where he possessed a priesthood by Dynasty XVIII.

Aliyan Baal, son of a less well-attested god Dagan, dwelt on Mount Sapan (hence Baal-Zaphon) in north Syria but also became associated as a local deity of other sites such as Baal-Hazor in Palestine, and Baal-Sidon and Baal of Tyre (Melkart) in Lebanon. Although the name Baal can mean 'lord' or 'owner' it was being used as a proper name for a specific god by the sixteenth century BC.

Baal wielding thunderbolt. Stela from Ugarit, Syria, c.1700–1500 BC, Louvre Museum.

Baal has a pointed beard, a horned helmet and wields a cedar tree, club or spear. His epithet in the cuneiform texts, 'he who rides on the clouds', is admirable for a god of tempests and thunder – relating thereby to the Mesopotamian thunder-god Adad and in Egypt to the god SETH. Ramesses II (Dynasty XIX) in his almost fatal struggle against the Hittite confederation at the battle of Kadesh is called 'Seth great of strength and Baal himself'. The war cry of Ramesses III (Dynasty XX) is like Baal in the sky, i.e. Baal's voice (the thunder) which makes the mountains shake. His relationship to the warrior–pharaoh image may account for the popularity of his cult at Memphis, capital of Egypt, and the theophorous name Baal-Khepeshef or 'Baal-is-upon-his-sword'.

In the Middle East Baal's dominion was greatly enhanced when he became the vanquisher of YAMM god of the sea. But Baal was killed in a struggle with Mot (possibly a personification of death) and descended into the Underworld. He returns to life by the intervention of his sister–lover ANAT, who also slays his murderer. It is curious that the Egyptians did not, in extant texts at any rate, relate this myth symbolising the continual cycle of vegetation to their own OSIRIS legend.

Baalat

⚱ ⌐⊃|◊\\◊🕊 A Canaanite goddess connected probably via her responsibility for products valued by the Egyptians with HATHOR. Her name means 'mistress' and she is clearly the feminine counterpart to BAAL. In her role as Baalat Gebal 'mistress of Byblos' she protects the cedar-wood trade between Lebanon and Egypt which goes back to the reign of King Sneferu (Dynasty IV). Her significance parallels that of Hathor of Dendera who is described as dwelling at Byblos. In the Sinai peninsula the turquoise mines at Serabit el-Khadim were protected by Hathor. In Hathor's temple there is a small sandstone sphinx inscribed by the dedicator both with the name of the Egyptian deity, in hieroglyphs, and with the name of Baalat, in an early alphabetic script.

Babi

A fierce, blood-thirsty baboon-god.

As early as the Old Kingdom Babi 'bull (i.e. dominant male) of the baboons' represents supernatural aggression to which the monarch aspires. He controls the darkness and will open up the sky for the king since his phallus is the bolt on the doors of heaven. This virility symbol is carried over into a later spell where in order to ensure successful sexual intercourse in the Afterlife a man identifies his phallus with Babi. Perhaps it is not entirely fortuitous that the Underworld ferryboat uses Babi's phallus as its mast.

This dangerous god lives on human entrails and murders on sight. Hence spells are needed to protect oneself against him, particularly during the weighing the heart ceremony in the Hall of the Two Truths where a person's fitness for paradise is determined. Naturally this hostile aspect of Babi leads to an identification with SETH. Conversely Babi can use his immense power to ward off dangers like snakes and control turbulent waters. Understandably in the Book of the Dead the deceased makes the magical

progression to become Babi who in turn transforms into the 'eldest son of OSIRIS'.

Banebdjedet

Ram-god whose name means 'ba (or 'soul') lord of Mendes', his cult centre in the north-east Delta. He was worshipped there together with his consort HATMEHYT (a local fish-goddess whom he had supplanted in importance) and his son HARPOKRATES (see HORUS section titled 'Horus The Child'). This site, known today as Tell el-Ruba, has revealed a cemetery with sarcophagi for the burial of the sacred rams.

The strong sexual urges displayed by rams are the probable reason for the interesting relationship between Banebdjedet and the mother of the pharaoh Ramesses III (Dynasty XX) who left an account of it on a stela in his mortuary temple at Medinet Habu in western Thebes. The god TATENEN (called here PTAH-Tanen) states to the king, whom he regards as his son, that he transformed himself into Banebdjedet in order to copulate with the queen. But it could also be that the inscription is attempting to identify the chthonic deity Ptah-Tanen with the sun-god, traditional father of the Egyptian pharaoh, since the ram-god in the religious text known as the Litany of RA is represented as 'lord of the sky' and 'life of Ra'.

In a papyrus (known as Chester Beatty I) dating from the reign of Ramesses V (Dynasty XX), Banebdjedet is brought into the litigation involving the struggle over the throne of Egypt between Horus and SETH. At the point where a stalemate occurs among the god–judges of the case, ATUM sends for Banebdjedet who is described as dwelling in Setit, i.e. the island of Seheil at the first cataract of the Nile at Aswan. The mention of this location neatly identifies Banebdjedet of

North Egypt with KHNUM, the southern ram-god. Banebdjedet (accompanied, incidentally, by Tatenen) urges the gods not to rush their decision but to consult the goddess NEITH. She counsels the award of the throne to Horus, which was the eventual outcome of the trial. However, in his immediate reaction to the goddess's advice Banebdjedet, like the sun-god himself, is reluctant to abandon the case of the god Seth, the elder brother, in favour of the younger, Horus.

Ba-Pef

The name of this god means 'That Soul' with an implication of dread or hostility contained in the demonstrative adjective 'pef'. In a reference in the Pyramid Texts the monarch passes by the House of Ba-Pef where there is pain or woe. From the mastaba-tomb of Meresankh III at Giza there is evidence that in the Old Kingdom at any rate Ba-Pef possessed a priesthood.

Bastet

Feline goddess, daughter of the sun-god.

Her earlier iconography employs lion imagery and it is not until *c.*1000 BC that the representation of Bastet as the cat becomes common. No real idea of her nature is contained in the writing of her name which is rendered phonetically, employing the hieroglyph of a sealed alabaster perfume jar possibly chosen to suggest the ritual purity involved in her cult.

As the daughter of RA she is associated with the rage inherent in the sun-god's eye, his instrument of vengeance. It was probably this ferocity that made the analogy so plausible between Bastet and the lioness. Her development into the cat-goddess par excellence, of the Late

Bastet with sacred rattle and kittens. Late Period bronze statuette, British Museum.

Period of Egyptian civilisation, retains the link with the sun-god (cf. the cat of Ra decapitating the Underworld snake APOPHIS) but in some ways softens the vicious side of her nature. She becomes a peaceful creature, destroying only vermin, and unlike her leonine form she can be approached fearlessly and stroked. It has been suggested that in one myth the Egyptians saw Bastet's return from Nubia, where she had been sent by Ra as a lioness and had raged in isolation, to Egypt in the form of the more placid cat as an explanation of the period of unapproachability in the cycle of menstruation. As tangential evidence the advocates of this theory cite the scenes in New Kingdom tomb paintings at Thebes where a cat is depicted under the lady's chair as a deliberate ploy to indicate that she will always be available for sexual intercourse with the tomb-owner in the Afterlife.

In her earliest appearances in the Pyramid Era Bastet is a goddess closely linked to the king. A magnificent example of precise engineering in the Old Kingdom, namely the valley temple of King Khafra at Giza, carries on its façade the names of two goddesses only – HATHOR of Southern Egypt and Bastet of Northen Egypt. The goddess is invoked as a benign royal protectress in the Pyramid Texts where, in a spell to enable him to reach the sky, the king proclaims that his mother and nurse is Bastet. Besides the king, Bastet has a son in the form of the lion-headed god MIHOS and is also the mother of a more artificial offspring combining the natures of NEFERTUM and the child HORUS, personifying her connection with perfume and royalty. With the dramatic extension of the roles of deities to assist Egyptian courtiers as well as the pharaoh that we find in the Coffin Texts of the Middle Kingdom, Bastet gives immense protection as first-born daughter of ATUM.

The aggressive side of Bastet can be seen in historical texts describing the pharaoh in battle. For example, in Dynasty XVIII Amenhotep II's enemies are slaughtered like the victims of Bastet along the road cut by the god AMUN. From her epithet 'lady of Asheru', the precinct of the goddess MUT at Karnak, it is clear that Bastet had a place on Theban soil where she could be equated with the consort of Amun – especially since the lioness and the cat were also claimed as sacred animals by Mut. Reliefs in the temple of Karnak show the pharaoh celebrating ritual races carrying either four sceptres and a bird or an oar in front of

Bastet who is called ruler of 'Sekhet-neter' or the 'Divine Field' – i.e. Egypt.

The goddess's most important cult centre was in the north-east Delta at Bubastis (a name ultimately deriving from the Egyptian 'per-Bastet' or 'house of Bastet'). Today the site is heavily ruined, the temple being so devastated that it does not even offer a skeletal image of its pristine splendour. Nearby are the tombs of some of the temple officiants including that of Iy, high priest of Bastet. In the fifth century BC the Greek historian Herodotus designates the festival of the goddess at Bubastis as the most elaborate

Mummified cat, sacred to Bastet. Roman period, British Museum.

in all Egypt. He gives Bastet the name of the Greek goddess Artemis (an identification still in use 500 years later when the Roman poet Ovid in his Metamorphoses states that the daughter of Phoebus (i.e. Artemis) can transform into a cat). Herodotus gives us an extremely vivid word-picture of the crowds congregating at Bubastis to celebrate the goddess's feast with music, licentious dancing and unrestrained wine-drinking. During the festival, shaking sacred rattles known as 'sistra' was a sign of jubilation to the goddess. The Greek writer Plutarch (*c.* AD 100) describes the 'sistrum' (primarily the cult instrument of Hathor) as having a representation of the cat-goddess on it and this is verified by examples of Ancient Egyptian bronze sistra with a supine cat on top as well as statuettes of Bastet holding the sacred rattle.

Cemeteries of cats have been excavated not only at Bubastis but also at other sites in the Nile Valley, e.g. Saqqara, the necropolis of Memphis, the capital city of Egypt, where Bastet played a tutelary role as 'lady of Ankhtawy' – the name given to this burial region, meaning 'life of the two lands' – and had a temple complex called the Bubasteion near the pyramid of King Teti (Dynasty VI). The stylish, well-wrapped mummies of the cats, often with the linen bandages forming geometrical patterns and faces painted to give a quizzical or humorous expression, reveal the universal affection in which the goddess's sacred creature was held by the Ancient Egyptians.

Bat

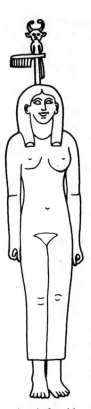

Bat emblem on head of goddess. Valley Temple of Menkaure, Dyn. IV, Cairo Museum.

Cow-goddess of Upper Egypt.

Bat is rarely depicted in Egyptian art, although as a jewellery-amulet she is more common. Her head is human but the ears are bovine and horns grow from her temples. Her body is in the shape of a necklace counterpoise. In fact the whole iconography suggests the sacred rattle or sistrum – fittingly, since her cult centre is in the district of Upper Egypt known as the 'Mansion of the sistrum'.

Without inscriptional evidence there must always be an element of caution but it does seem likely, on stylistic grounds, that the cow-goddess represented at the top corners of the Narmer Palette, a slate carving in Cairo Museum commemorating the unification of North and South Egypt into one state (*c.*3000 BC), is more likely to be Bat than HATHOR. Our earliest written evidence for the goddess, in the Pyramid Texts, would support this view: the king is Bat 'with her two faces', i.e. front and back of her sistrum emblem and similarly carved on each side of the palette. Even earlier, she might be the goddess on a palette on which stars are represented at the tips of her horns, indicating that, like most Egyptian cow-deities, she has celestial connections.

It is possible that Bat has a presence that maintains the unity of Egypt, both North with South and Nile Valley with deserts. In addition to her pre-eminent positioning on the Narmer Palette, she is represented in the centre of a pectoral of Dynasty XII flanked by the two protagonists in the struggle for the Egyptian throne, HORUS and SETH, in a state of reconciliation. However, her similarity to Hathor, the cow-goddess worshipped in the neighbouring southern district, was so close that Bat's personal identity was not strong enough to survive being totally assimilated into her by the New Kingdom.

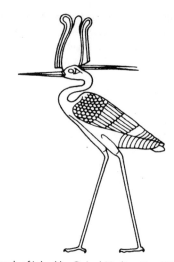

Tomb of Inherkha, Deir el-Medina, Dyn. XX.

Benu

Primeval bird sacred to the sun-god at Heliopolis.

The name Benu appears to be connected with the verb 'weben' meaning to 'rise in brilliance' or 'shine'. The bird itself in the Pyramid Age is the yellow wagtail, but later becomes represented as a heron with two long feathers growing from the back of its head.

The earliest mention of the Benu is the Pyramid Texts where it is described as one of the forms of the Heliopolitan sun-god ATUM. This link with the creator sun-god is maintained in the Middle Kingdom where the Benu of RA is said to be the means by which Atum came into being in the primeval water. Like that of the sun-god, the Benu's own birth is attributed to self-generation. Mythological papyri of Dynasty XXI provide a vignette of a heart-amulet and scarab beetle near to which stands the Benu described as 'the one who came into being by himself'. The Benu is also found as a symbol of anticipated rebirth in the Underworld, carved on the backs of heart-scarabs buried with the corpse to ensure the heart does not fail in the examination of past deeds in the Hall of the Two Truths (see ASSESSOR GODS). As the living manifestation of Ra (called his 'Ba' or 'soul') the Benu has a close association with the sun-god's temple at Heliopolis. On the sarcophagus of the Divine Adoratrice of AMUN, Ankhnesneferibra, in the British Museum the Benu is imagined as perched on a sacred willow tree in the temple.

Herodotus and the Phoenix

The Greek historian who visited Egypt in the fifth century BC writes that he learned about the sacred bird at Heliopolis from the mouths of priests of the sun-god. He calls it the Phoenix using a name which it has been shown could well derive from the Egyptian Benu. In Herodotus's sceptical account, every 500 years the Phoenix carries its dead predecessor from Arabia to Heliopolis for honours in the sun-god's temple. There is no evidence for the idea of a dying phoenix, the core of the later myth, in pharaonic Egypt. However, the classical phoenix of Greek tradition does have similarities with the Benu in the role of a sun-bird and the symbols of resurrection.

Bes

Dwarf-god, grotesque in appearance, benign in nature.

The Egyptians had a number of monstrously formed dwarf-deities for which the name Bes was employed. The god in a plumed crown was normally bearded with his broad face surrounded by a lion's mane and ears. His tongue often protruded in a playfully aggressive fashion. The body of Bes represented a bandy-legged dwarf wearing either a panther skin or a kilt, more Syrian than Egyptian, and a lion's tail. Imitating for magical purposes the solar iconography of the god HORUS of Behdet, Bes can be shown with his arms stretched out with a hawk's wings suspended from them. The 'sa' sign meaning 'protection' is frequently carried by Bes.

He has his most crucial contribution to make to Egyptian life in his role as protector of childbirth in partnership with TAWERET. A spell survives for reciting four times over a clay dwarf placed on the crown of the head of a woman in labour where complications have arisen. In it Bes is addressed as 'great dwarf with a large head and short thighs' and as 'a monkey in old age' – the notion of ugliness as a deterrent to evil spirits is as strong in Ancient Egypt as the swords which Bes often brandishes. Higher up in the echelons of Egyptian society Bes is present at the scenes of royal birth carved on the walls of Theban temples.

Cosmetic container in form of Bes, Late Period, British Museum.

Late Period limestone plaque. Private collection.

In Ptolemaic and Roman Egypt when the 'mammisi' or birth house became an integral unit in the whole temple structure, the image of Bes decorated the abaci above the columns, fittingly indicative of his protective role in the nativity of the son of the sanctuary's principal god and goddess.

It was thought that Bes brought good luck and prosperity to married couples and their children. Consequently, the god finds a place in the woefully few examples of decoration from secular dwellings: at Deir el-Medina on the west bank at Thebes where the community of artisans working on the royal tombs used to live Bes is painted dancing on the outer walls of the small bedroom. He is also present as part of the frieze on King Amenhotep III's bedroom wall in his palace at Malkata in western Thebes (Dynasty XVIII). Examples survive as well, showing Bes as a decorative element on the foot-board of the bed itself or on the head-rests used as pillows. If, as has been suggested, mirrors in Ancient Egypt possessed sexual symbolism, the presence of Bes on them could be seen as an encouragement to carnal fulfilment. Bes, furthermore, does have an association with cosmetic utensils in general, e.g. carved as a support for a tube to contain kohl, or on the handle of spoons that held other cosmetics.

The aggression of knife-carrying Bes is directed at any threat to the family. In this form he is incised on curved ivory batons in the Middle Kingdom which it seems had the prophylactic intent of warding off snakes and scorpions from the living quarters of a house. His head also frequently surmounts the figure of the child Horus carved on the 'cippi' or shield-shaped amuletic stelae of the Late Period. Although overwhelmingly a god of everyday life in Egypt, his fierceness is occasionally used as imagery in the Underworld, as, e.g. in the Mythological Papyrus of Dirpu where a deity guarding a doorway has the head of ANUBIS but the body of the knife-wielding, snake-strangling Bes.

His tutelary duties aside, Bes has a genial temperament which expresses itself through merrymaking and music. On furniture found in the tomb of Queen Tiye's parents (Dynasty XVIII) Bes strikes a tambourine, an instrument which he can also be seen shaking over 1,000 years later on the walls of the HATHOR temple on the island of Philae – there he plays the harp as well. In this latter instance Bes performs the task of placating the goddess Hathor with music on her initially reluctantly undertaken journey from Nubia to her sanctuary at Dendera. His popularity spread beyond the borders of Egypt: from Kition in Cyprus comes an ivory plaque of Bes (c.1200 BC). He was also used as a motif by Phoenician craftsmen in ivory-work which decorated the furniture and caskets of Nimrud in Assyria. Towards the end of Ancient Egyptian civilisation a new iconography reflected the adoption of Bes by the occupying Roman forces – statuettes of the god dressed as a legionary.

C

Cavern deities   In the Underworld there are at least twelve caverns of the west in which fierce gods and goddesses dwell. These deities are enumerated in the funerary papyri and on the walls of tombs in the Valley of the Kings. Their power seems to reach the world above since offerings are made to propitiate them by the living. They feed on the corpses and souls of those who have led criminal lives. The caverns are places for the punishment and extermination, usually by beheading, of the enemies of the sun-god RA.

Here is a selection of these deities from the tomb of Ramesses VI (Dynasty XX) and from the Book of the Dead.

Cavern	Resident Deities
1	Nine jackal-headed gods feeding on rottenness; snake guardians of the Silent Region
2	Flame-breathing snake called Sesy; primeval gods called Nariu who have the heads of catfish
3	NEHEBU-KAU encircling seven catfish-headed gods led by OSIRIS
4	Great one who is on his belly
5	NUT and ithyphallic Osiris
6	TATENEN
8	Those who raise their superiors to the sky
9	Gods of the Primeval Deep
10	Wailing goddesses brandishing axes dripping with blood
11	AMMUT

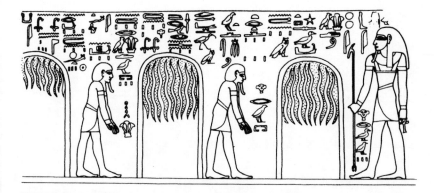

Caverns of Fire in the Underworld. Tomb of Sety I, Dyn. XIX.

D

Dedwen

Anthropomorphic god presiding over Nubia and its access to resources such as incense. In the Pyramid Texts the king is honoured as Dedwen lord of Nubia. The royal aroma is that of the incense brought by Dedwen for the gods. The connection with the monarch is also seen in the fact that Dedwen burns incense at royal births. Temples in Nubia were built for Dedwen by Thutmose III (Dynasty XVIII) at el-Lessiya (now relocated to Turin Museum) and in the fort on the island of Uronarti but there is no evidence for a cult centre of this god north of Aswan.

Denwen

Fiery serpent-god attested in the Pyramid Era who would have caused a conflagration destroying other deities but was thwarted by the king.

E

Ennead

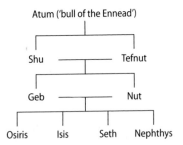 The company of Nine Gods originally at Heliopolis consisting of the sun-god creator and his descendants.

The word itself is from the Greek word for 'nine' – the Ancient Egyptians called these collective deities the 'Pesdjet'. Since the primeval matter (NUN) is not counted, the Heliopolitan Ennead comprises the following gods.

```
              Atum ('bull of the Ennead')
                       |
       ┌───────────────┴───────────────┐
      Shu ───────────────────────── Tefnut
       |
       ┌───────────────┴───────────────┐
      Geb ───────────────────────── Nut
   ┌────────┬──────────┬──────────┐
 Osiris    Isis      Seth      Nephthys
```

Other cult centres could also have an Ennead made up from their own major deities, the number of which did not always correspond to 'nine' and the gods of which were not always related in a genealogy such as given above. A good example of the versatility of an Ennead of gods can be found in an inscription in the temple of Redesiyeh cut in the rocks of the eastern desert during the reign of King Sety I (Dynasty XIX). The pharaoh dedicated the temple to AMUN and his Ennead.

Amun	OSIRIS	HORUS
RA	PTAH	ISIS

The remaining three members of the Ennead were deified statues of Sety I himself.

In the Pyramid Texts the 'Two Enneads' convey the concept of all the gods of the Egyptian pantheon. The Ennead are also envisaged as a judgement council both in mythology, where for instance they are in favour of truth over falsehood, and in historical inscriptions such as when they condemn the Libyan prince Merey to defeat at the hands of the pharaoh Merneptah (Dynasty XIX). Enneads can be referred to as 'great' or 'small' – the Great Ennead being responsible for 'nursing' Queen Hatshepsut (Dynasty XVIII) according to her obelisk-inscription at Karnak.

F

Fetket   Butler of the sun-god RA who provides the king with his drink supply.

G

Gate deities of the Underworld

Royal tombs at Thebes and funerary papyri of courtiers present a vivid picture of the Egyptian Underworld – known as 'Duat'. For pharaohs the illustration of the unhindered and safe passage of the sun-god through Duat was paramount since the monarch himself was envisaged as being among the deities in the solar entourage. In the case of officials the Underworld's perilous regions had to be traversed without injury to reach Paradise. For both sun-god and nobleman it was necessary to negotiate pylons or gates along the route. Ferocious guardian deities threatened to annihilate those approaching to enter the portals.

Gate deity with vulture head. Tomb of Queen Tawosret, Dyn. XIX.

Superiority, however, could be gained over these gods through the magical power concomitant with knowing their secret names. The following is a synopsis of how these hazardous gateways and their associated deities were imagined both for the sun-god and royalty, and for courtiers.

1 Underworld gates from walls of tombs in the Valley of the Kings

Each pylon consists of three elements – a flame-spitting serpent rising up before the gate, the gateway itself painted purely in architectural terms but labelled as if it were a goddess, and the resident guardian god. The sun-god's journey through these pylons can be summarised as follows.

Gate 1 The god SIA in the prow of the boat of the sun-god urges the snake called 'Desert-Protector' to open the gate. The sun-god under the form ATUM leans on his staff watching the destruction of his enemies.

Gate 2 The guardian god is 'Swallower of Sinners' and beyond the pylon is a lake of fire.

Gate 3 The serpent is called 'Stinger' and the gate itself called 'Mistress of Food'. Beyond it jackals guard the 'Lake of Life' forbidden of access to Underworld inhabitants because it is here that the god RA breathes.

Gate 4 Here there are gods carrying measuring-cords for fields in the Underworld, paralleling scenes found in courtiers' tombs which show the calculation by ropes of the corn crop for taxation. Also the Egyptian notion of the races of mankind is symbolised by illustrating four groups of figures representing the

Gate deities from the Papyrus of Ani, Dyn. XIX, British Museum.

'cattle of RA', i.e. mankind proper – the Egyptians); the Middle Easterners; Libyans and Nubians.

Gate 5   The gate is called 'Lady of Duration' and the serpent is 'Flame-Eyed'. Beyond is a dangerous stretch inhabited by the snake APOPHIS, 'Evil of Face' as he is described here. Twelve gods contain his deadly power by seizing him. The heads of those that Apophis has swallowed emerge from his coils as the sun-god passes through this region.

Gate 6   RA in his boat approaches seven jackal-headed poles with two enemies tied to each one ready for beheading.

Gate 7   The gate is called 'Shining One' and beyond it twelve gods hold a rope from which emanate four whips, four hawk heads and four human heads. The hieroglyphs relate this image to the mysterious appearance of RA, but not in sufficient detail for us to elucidate its subtleties.

Gate 8   Here exists a fire-breathing snake who burns up the enemies of OSIRIS.

Gate 9   On the back of a hawk-headed lion stand HORUS and SETH.

Gate 10   Beyond this gateway the snake APOPHIS is bound with chains so that RA can pass through without the snake attempting to swallow him.

Gate 11   The gate is called 'Mysterious of Approaches' and is guarded by a cat-headed god whose name is 'Meeyuty' – clearly a use of onomatopoeia to suggest a cat's 'mew'.

Gate 12   Beyond the gate ISIS and NEPHTHYS rear up in the form of serpents. Here the symbolism of the journey through the portals ends on the theme of the emergence of the sun once more into the sky as a sacred beetle.

2   *Underworld gates depicted in funerary Papyri*

GODS OF THE SEVEN GATES

The deceased is confronted by gateways in which dwell a god, his door keeper and a herald. These guardians are armed with knives but the deceased will pass by them unscathed through the recital of their names. The following tabulation gives the ritual naming taking place at each gate:

personified as a goddess and identifies her guardian god represented seated, armed with a knife and anthropomorphic to the shoulders but having normally the head of an animal (e.g. bull, hippopotamus) a bird (e.g. vulture) or a snake. The defied portal

Gate	God	Doorkeeper	Herald
1	Upside down of face Manifold of Forms	Secret Listener	Miserable of Voice
2	Stretched out of Forehead	'Seqed' (?)faced	Glowing
3	Eater of the Foulness from his Hindquarters	Watchful of Face	Curser
4	Hostile of Face Loquacious	Perceptive	Great of Face Crocodile-Repeller
5	Existing on Maggots	'Ashbu'	Hippopotamus Face Furious of Onslaught
6	Raging of Voice	Face-Eraser	Sharp of Face
7	Sharpest of Them	Strident of Voice	Rebuffing Insurgents

DEITIES OF THE TWENTY-ONE SECRET PORTALS OF THE MANSION OF OSIRIS IN THE FIELD OF RUSHES

To gain access through these portals the deceased recites the name of the gateway

is given a long string of epithets – in some cases numbering seven separate descriptions. Accordingly the following table selects just one or two of these in each instance:

Portal Number	Name of Portal as Goddess	Guardian God
1	Mistress of Trembling	Dreadful
2	Mistress of the Sky	Born of the Hindquarters
3	Mistress of the Altar	Cleanser
4	Powerful of Knives	Long-Horned Bull
5	Fiery One	Killer of Opponents
6	Mistress of Darkness	Destroyer
7	Veiler of the Weary One (i.e. Osiris)	'Ikenty'
8	Lighter of Flames, Extinguisher of Heat	Protector of his Body
9	Foremost	Fowler
10	Piercing of Voice (variant: High of Double Doors)	Great Embracer
11	Ceaseless in Knifing, Scorcher of Rebels	Cook of his Braziers

(*continued*)

Continued

Portal Number	Name of Portal as Goddess	Guardian God
12	Invoked by her Two Lands	Cat
13	She above whom Osiris (variants: Isis, ENNEAD) stretches his Arms	Destroyer of the Robber
14	Mistress of Anger, Dancing on Blood	Screecher
15	Great of Valour	Vigilant of Face
16	Dread	Clever in Bowing
17	Great on the Horizon	Spirit
18	Lover of Heat	Anointed
19	She who Foretells Mornings throughout her Lifespan, Possessor of the Writings of THOTH	Nameless
20	Dweller within the Cavern of her Lord	Nameless
21	Sharpener of Flint to Speak for her	Giraffe (in Egyptian 'Memy')

In the case of Portal 21, the guardian god 'Giraffe' has an interesting description following his name which places his birth in remotest time before pine and acacia trees existed and predating the origin of copper in the desert. Mostly, however, Underworld deities remain fairly obscure hiding behind epithets that are variously vivid or bland.

Geb

Earth-god and president of the divine tribunal on the kingship. Geb is well documented in the Pyramid Era where he is called the 'eldest of SHU'. His sister-consort is the sky-goddess NUT, their union producing the deities of the OSIRIS legend.

A description of the iconography of Geb occurs in a Pyramid Text where we read that he holds 'one arm to the sky and the other to the earth'. However, the best visual images of Geb are found much later in New Kingdom religious papyri. In these vignettes Geb reclines partly on his side, usually with one arm bent at the elbow. Being a chthonic deity he can be coloured green, indicating the vegetation which sprouts from him. On the Papyrus of Tentamun (Dynasty XXI) Geb's body is actually decorated with the symbols of the Nile reeds in flower. His phallus, when shown, can either be relaxed or stretching upwards towards the goddess Nut. He occasionally appears in the royal tombs in the Valley of the Kings wearing the hieroglyph which writes his name, the white-fronted goose, upon his head. For an obscure reason he is shown with the head of a hare in the solar boat painted on the ceiling of the sarcophagus chamber of the tomb of Ramesses VI (Dynasty XX).

As earth-god (more universal than AKER) he has an ominous side in the idea

Geb below the air-god and sky-goddess. Greenfield Papyrus, Dyn. XXI, British Museum.

that he might imprison the dead within him, preventing their free movement in the Afterlife. We meet this concept in the Pyramid Texts where it is asserted that the king does not enter or 'sleep' in (i.e. permanently in the state of death) the mansion of Geb upon earth. Also to be dreaded is the 'laughter' of Geb which figuratively evokes the devastating force of an earthquake. More benignly Geb provides the nourishments and fruits of the earth to everyone – barley being imagined as growing from the ribs of the god. This idea of fertility lies behind the Nile-god HAPY being addressed in a hymn as 'friend of Geb'. In magical texts for curing headaches great store is set by the 'khenem' plant of Geb over which HORUS and SETH fought in its form of the 'unique bush', probably a manifestation of the Eye of Horus. This notion of Geb as a god with an interest in healing is occasionally found in spells concerning scorpion stings; on one occasion the god gives ISIS his magical powers so that she can abate the poison in a child stung by scorpions.

In the myth of the transmission of the kingship to Horus, the culminating scenes take place in the 'Broad Hall of Geb'. Geb is the presiding judge in the dispute between Horus and Seth, a role which from the Pyramid Texts seems to have been handed over to him by ATUM the superior sun-god. Naturally Geb is sympathetic to his grandson Horus since originally Geb's heir to the kingship of Egypt was Osiris, the murdered father of Horus. That Osiris was preferred by Geb, as his eldest son, over Seth is quite clear: he fishes the body of the killed god out of the water for embalming. (For Geb's initial division of Egypt between the protagonists and its reversal, see Horus.) Once Horus has been vindicated in his claim, it is Geb's command that he be crowned as the lawful heir to the Egyptian throne. By extension Geb then becomes the staunch upholder of the ruling monarch. In the Pyramid Texts we read that Geb actively supports the king in the role of Horus victorious over Seth. The king performs a dance celebrating the belief that Geb will never allow harm to come to the rightful heir of the throne, the god putting his sandals on the heads of the sovereign's enemies.

Towards the end of pharaonic civilisation in Dynasty XXX there is papyrical evidence of a reinterpretation of Geb's connection with the throne. This document from Saft el-Hinneh in the Delta says that Geb usurped the kingship from Shu and, in addition, violated the body of his mother TEFNUT. Here, surely, the Egyptian tradition has become contaminated with the Greek myth of the usurpation of Ouranos by his son Kronos whom the classical writers in fact identify with Geb.

Gengen Wer   A primeval goose whose onomatopoeic name means Great Honker and who is a force of creative energy.

The imagery is that of the goose carrying the egg from which life emerges. In order to be part of this creation, a continuing cycle in the Egyptian mind, a person in the Underworld might be described as closely guarding or actually being the egg within the Great Honker.

This goose, also called the cackler ('Negeg' in Egyptian), is a form under which AMUN can appear as a creator-god.

H

Ha

God of the desert, particularly the regions of the west including the oases.

Ha is anthropomorphic and wears the symbol for desert hills on his head. As lord of the desert he wards off enemies from the west, probably referring to invading tribes from Libya.

Hapy

God of the annual Nile inundation.

Hapy lived in the caverns of the cataract of the Nile, presided over by KHNUM. He personifies the yearly flood rather than the Nile itself – hence references to a 'large' or 'small' Hapy.

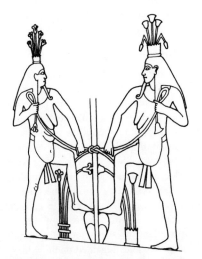

Hapy's fertility symbolised by the gods of Upper and Lower Egypt. Statue of Senwosret I, Dyn. XII, Cairo Museum.

The god is shown in human form with aquatic plants on his head. His body has emphasised pendulous breasts and a prominent paunch, an iconography whose message is abundance and fertility. The god holds before him an offering tray full of produce resulting from the Nile silt left by the receding waters of the river after the inundation. In the Middle Kingdom the god is 'master of the river bringing vegetation'. Other epithets for Hapy include 'lord of the fishes and birds of the marshes' which might explain the god being given a double-goose head in the temple of Abydos. Crocodile-gods are in his retinue and he possesses a harem of frog-goddesses with braided tresses.

Although the flood was the source of the country's prosperity, no temples or sanctuaries were built specifically in honour of Hapy. But his statues – including some where the pharaoh himself is carved as the god – and reliefs were included in the temples of other deities. The other side of the coin, as an Egyptian hymn to Hapy tells us, was that no temple priesthood could commandeer labourers to work on Hapy's building projects – demands often made in the names of other divinities.

Hathor

Universal cow-goddess, symbolic mother of the pharaoh.

The name of Hathor immediately suggests that the Egyptians themselves had great difficulty in defining the essence of this complex deity. It describes the goddess in relation to the god HORUS: 'mansion of Horus' is what her name means literally.

But it symbolises Hathor as the 'lady of the sky' whose womb protected the hawk-god. She is the daughter of the sun-god RA.

In art and architecture the goddess takes the following major forms:

(a) Lithe lady on whose wig is a crown of cow horns and a sun disk.

(b) Completely bovine as the 'Great Wild Cow'.

(c) As a pillar, the capital of which shows a human face, a wig (normally curling at the lappets on each side of her cheeks) but the ears of a cow.

Hathor can also be represented as a lioness, as a snake 'who laughs with

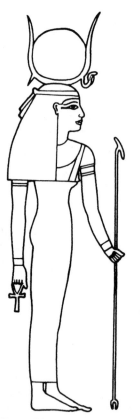

Tomb of Horemheb. Dyn. XVIII.

WADJET' or a sycamore. The papyrus was a plant sacred to her since the habitat of wild cattle was in the swamps by the Nile. A ritual of plucking up papyrus stalks was performed in her honour.

Her nature is predominantly benign but she does have a destructive streak which is best evidenced in the legend involving the narrowly avoided annihilation of the human race by Hathor as the 'Eye of Ra' (see under SAKHMET).

There was clearly a veneration of cow-goddesses in Predynastic Egypt but without hieroglyphs it is impossible to be certain if a cult belongs to Hathor or perhaps to BAT, the most likely candidate for the cow-heads on the Narmer Palette (c.3000 BC).

By the beginning of the Old Kingdom there is indisputable archaeological and textual proof of the worship of Hathor. The valley temple of King Khafra (Dynasty IV) at Giza was placed in its southern sector under the protection of Hathor. Her temples are mentioned on the Old Kingdom annals on the Palermo Stone and royal ladies from the early Pyramid Age onwards take the title 'priestess of Hathor'.

1 *Hathor and the pharaoh*

The king of Egypt is called 'son of Hathor'. This of course leads to a complication since the king as HORUS is the son of ISIS. It seems most probable that Hathor is the original mother of the hawk-god in the cycle of myth where Horus and SETH are brothers. She gave way to Isis when the legend was absorbed into the myth of OSIRIS, necessitating Horus to become the son of that goddess in order to gain the throne of Egypt. There is a further realignment in the relationship when Hathor becomes regarded as the wife of the sky-god Horus of Edfu.

The finest sculptural statement of the maternal concern that Hathor has for the

Hathor as cow protecting and suckling Amenhotep II. Hathor shrine of Tuthmosis III, Dyn. XVIII, Cairo Museum.

king can be seen on the triad from Menkaura's temple at Giza (Dynasty IV): the king is flanked by a local cow-goddess on one side while on the other his hand is protectively held by Hathor. In Dynasty XVIII on the west bank at Thebes at Deir el-Bahari, the Hathor chapel in Queen Hatshepsut's temple shows two reliefs emphasising the relationship between the goddess and the ruler of Egypt. In one the cow-goddess lovingly licks the hand of the enthroned monarch and in the other the Hathor-cow suckles the ruler. This latter motif occurs shortly after the reign of Queen Hatshepsut in a three-dimensional representation in a vaulted shrine originally at Deir el-Bahari but now in Cairo Museum: Hathor as a cow, papyrus stalks surrounding her head, provides her divine milk for Amenhotep II.

2 Hathor as a funerary goddess

This aspect of Hathor is especially prominent in western Thebes where the necropolis was under her safekeeping. As 'lady of the west' she is shown on stelae and funerary papyri as a cow leaving the desert in which the tombs have been cut to come down into the papyrus marshes.

Hathor as goddess of the west. Tomb of Horemheb, Dyn. XVIII.

This visually provides a link between the tomb and the life continuing in the Nile valley. In tombs in the Valley of the Kings Hathor's pre-eminence as a guardian of the western necropolis is left in no doubt since on decorated pillars around the sarcophagus chamber, such as those in the tomb of Amenhotep II, her figure outnumbers those of Osiris and ANUBIS. In the Book of the Dead the goddess as 'lady of the headland of Manu' (the western mountain) is said to be joined by the sun-god RA as he sinks below the horizon. Her protection extends to practical help for the deceased in the Underworld: her

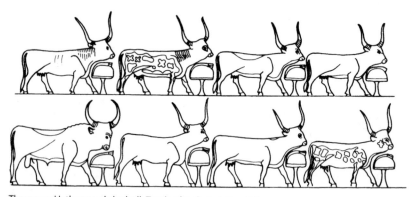

The seven Hathors and sky-bull. Tomb of Nefertari, Dyn. XIX.

outer garment, known as the 'tjesten', if possessed by someone in the Underworld, will give that person a safe path, particularly past enemies dwelling on the perilous Island of Fire.

3 *The seven Hathors*

Representations in tombs, such as that of Queen Nefertari (Dynasty XIX), and in the Book of the Dead show seven cows whose role is to determine the destiny of a child at birth. Each Hathor has her own name:

i   Lady of the universe
ii   Sky-storm
iii You from the land of silence
iv   You from Khemmis
v   Red-hair
vi   Bright red
vii Your name flourishes through skill.

Alternative names for the seven Hathors can be found in mythological papyri:

i   Lady of the House of Jubilation
ii + iii   Mistresses of the west
iv + v   Mistresses of the east
vi + vii   Ladies of the sacred land

These goddesses of fate are accompanied by the four rudders representing the cardinal points of the sky and are served by the 'bull of the west, lord of eternity'. Although not specified in the papyrus as 'seven', the Hathors who foretell the fate of the young prince (Papyrus Harris 500), threatened with doom (probably avoided – the end of the tale is missing) from a crocodile, snake and a dog, are the same goddesses. Occasionally in spells the seven Hathors protect the body from harm but it is usually the goddess Hathor in the singular who is connected with healing and childbirth. This role derives from her actions in the legend of the struggle between HORUS and SETH for the Egyptian throne, restoring sight to Horus after his eyes have been torn out. Archaeological evidence of this aspect of Hathor can be found in her temple precinct at Dendera: rows of mudbrick cubicles were built near the 'mammisi' for sick visitors to lie in while purified water from the sacred lake (previously run over an image of Hathor?) was poured over them to help effect a cure.

4 *Goddess of love, music and dance*

Hathor is the supreme goddess of sexual love in Ancient Egypt, immediately identified with Aphrodite by the Greeks when they came into contact with her cult. The turmoil or ecstasy which can result from physical desire are reflected in the conflicting forces of Hathor's personality as a goddess of destruction as 'Eye of RA' or a goddess of heavenly charm. In love poetry Hathor is called the 'golden' or 'lady of heaven'. Concomitant with her connection with love is her ability to encourage sensual joy by music and dancing. In fact the child of Hathor and HORUS at the temple of Dendera is the god IHY who really personifies musical jubilation. Dances in honour of Hathor are represented on the walls of courtiers' tombs, and in the story of the return of Sinuhe to the Egyptian court after years abroad, the princesses perform an Hathoric dance to celebrate the occasion. In the myth of the contest for power between Horus and SETH it is the goddess herself, 'lady of the southern sycamore', who cures her father Ra of a fit of sulking by dancing naked in front of him until he bursts into laughter.

Music in the cult of Hathor was immensely important and there were two ritual instruments carried by her priestesses to express their joy in worshipping the goddess.

SISTRUM

The bronze sacred rattle 'sesheshet' in Egyptian – popular into the Roman world – which was shaken in honour of Hathor, consisted of a column-handle with cow-eared Hathor at the top surmounted by a loop, across the width of which stretched three or four horizontal bars piercing small disks that would jangle. There was also the ceremonial sistrum made of glazed composition terminating in a naos or shrine, which was meant to be a votive offering to the goddess.

MENAT

This is a necklace, thick with beads and a counterpoise long enough to be grasped in the hand, which was not worn but shaken by Hathor's priestesses.

The crypts in the main cult centre of Hathor in Egypt at Dendera give, in superbly carved wall reliefs, an idea of the sacred musical instruments and ritual objects and statues of the goddess that were originally contained in them. Also at Dendera (Ancient Egyptian 'Iunet'), sacred to Hathor since at least the Old Kingdom, music accompanied the procession that brought the cult image of the goddess from the darkness of the sanctuary up onto the roof where a special chapel had been constructed for the ceremony of the union with the sun disk enabling Hathor to bathe in the rays of the sun-god.

5 *Goddess of foreign countries*

The best indication of Hathor's universality is the way in which foreign regions from which the Egyptians derived material benefit were regarded as personal domains of the goddess. In the Middle Kingdom she is called 'lady of Byblos' the long-established commercial centre for the timber trade. Excavations here have shown evidence of a cult to Hathor and her semitic counterpart ASTARTE. From the Old Kingdom another area beyond Egypt's frontier becomes the province of Hathor, namely Nubia. In the Dynasty VI the official Harkhuf came back from a southern expedition leading 300 donkeys laden with African produce such as panther skins, incense and ebony wood which are viewed as the gift of Hathor to the king. But the goddess's closest and most important links abroad lie in the turquoise mines of the Sinai peninsula. In Dynasty III Hathor is 'nebet mefkat', i.e. 'mistress of turquoise' in rock inscriptions near the mines at Wadi Maghara. Later from Dynasty XII through the New Kingdom a splendid temple was built and added to in her honour at Serabit el-Khadim.

Hatmehyt

 Fish-goddess worshipped in the Delta, particularly in the north-east at Mendes.

The fish as a divinity is comparatively rare in the Egyptian pantheon, but Hatmehyt's name means 'she who is in front of the fishes' referring to her pre-eminence in relation to the few rival fish cults. However, it could also be interpreted in a temporal sense to stress the goddess as the 'beginning' i.e. earliest fish-goddess to exist when Egypt emerged from the primeval waters.

She can be represented completely as a fish, the shape of which led to former suggestions that it was a dolphin. This has now been discarded in favour of an identification with the lepidotus fish, common in the Nile.

At Mendes, in a district for which the ancient standard was the fish symbol indicating that Hatmehyt was the senior deity in terms of residence there, her cult becomes subordinated to that of the ram-god BANEBDJEDET – interpreted after his arrival as her consort.

Haurun

An earth-god of Canaan identified most importantly in Egypt with the great sphinx at Giza.

Haurun is attested as a name in Egypt for over 1,200 years from 1900 BC when he occurs in the name of a foreign prince whom the Egyptians ceremonially curse.

It is likely that a settlement of Canaanite-Syrian workers near the sphinx in the New Kingdom made the initial analogy between the guardian-figure of Khafra carved over a thousand years earlier, and Haurun. Possibly from its position on the western desert looking towards the rising sun, reinterpreted by this time as the sun-god Harmachis (see HORUS section titled 'HARMACHIS') the sphinx suggested to the foreign artisans the god Haurun viewing the 'City of the East' which Canaanite legend has him founding. A temple to this god, the 'House of Haurun' as it was called, was constructed in front of the sphinx.

Haurun can be represented as a falcon as in the majestic granite and limestone statue (now in Cairo Museum) of the god protecting the pharaoh Ramesses II (Dynasty XIX) depicted as a child.

Haurun also figures in a magical spell against the dangers of wild animals such as lions or ferocious dogs; he provides the protection under his epithet 'the victorious herdsman'. There is an inherent contradiction (or dualism) in his character since his role as a healing god in Egypt must be balanced against his action as a god of doom in the Canaanite myth where Haurun is responsible for planting a 'tree of death'.

Heh

Anthropomorphic god, personification of infinity.

Heh is represented on temple walls, vases and jewellery with the force of an amuletic wish for untold millions of years of life.

Heh kneels, often on a basket which is the hieroglyph for universality, holding in each hand a palm-rib – the hieroglyph for 'year', and frequently carrying the sign of life or 'ankh' (see also OGDOAD).

Heka

God who embodies the concept of magical power and energy. In the Coffin Texts Heka is described as coming into being at the beginning of time at the will of the creator god ATUM to provide a supernatural strength which would pervade the universe and enable deities and mankind to function. In the Pyramid Texts Heka is a threatening force and in the spells where the king hunts and devours gods and men his own power is increased by their magic which he has swallowed. The Book of the Dead has spells which emphasise that the deceased will possess the universal magical power of Heka to counteract hazards in the Underworld. Also one spell is specifically directed against the crocodile trying to steal this magic. In later magical spells Heka is, along with RA, THOTH and SAKHMET, one of the protectors of OSIRIS, whose power is invoked to overcome crocodiles by blinding them. Heka is frequently depicted in anthropomorphic form in the Book of Gates standing in the boat of the sun-god during his nightly journey through the Netherworld. In the Second Hall, decorated in the Ptolemaic period, of the Mammisi in the Temple of Philae, Heka is the god who proclaims the enthronement of the son of ISIS – and symbolically the pharaoh himself – as ruler of Egypt, holding up the child in his arms.

Heket

Mammisi of Nectanebo, Dendera, Dyn. XXX.

Frog-goddess of birth.

Heket makes her debut in Egyptian inscriptions in the pyramids where, in a magical text destined to enable the king to ascend into the sky, she is one of numerous divinities that are said to equate with parts of the royal anatomy. Her connection with birth is first made explicit in a Middle Kingdom papyrus which contains tales of wonder set in the Pyramid Age. In the passage concerning the wife of the high priest of RA giving birth to the three kings who inaugurate Dynasty V, it is Heket in each instance who 'hastens' the last stages of labour.

Amulets and scarabs worn by women to protect them during childbirth often bear the image of the frog-goddess. Similarly, magical 'knives' of ivory, popular during the Middle Kingdom as devices to ward off threats to families, carry incisions representing Heket as a defender of the home. Possibly the title 'servant of Heket', carved on a musical clapper belonging to a lady Sit-Hathor, indicates that she was a midwife. The life-giving powers of Heket enabled her to be adopted as a benign deity fit to accompany OSIRIS, in whose temple at Abydos she receives wine from King Sety I (Dynasty XIX) and is labelled 'mistress of the Two Lands'.

There are remains of a temple to Heket at Qus in Upper Egypt where she is regarded as the wife of Haroeris (see HORUS section titled 'The struggle for the throne of Egypt'). Although it is not archaeologically extant, the best evidence of a cult centre to Heket is in an inscription in the tomb of Petosiris (fourth century BC) at Tuna el-Gebel in Middle Egypt. Petosiris, high priest of THOTH, relates how a procession in her honour was guided by the goddess Heket 'lady of Herwer' to the site of a sanctuary ruined by the annual inundation of the Nile. Petosiris takes this to mean that Heket wishes her temple there to be renovated and summons her scribe, giving him finance and orders for the construction of a new monument surrounded by a girdle-wall to prevent the flood-waters carrying it away.

Heret-Kau

 In the Old Kingdom there is a reference to a priest of this goddess whose name means 'she who is above the spirits' clearly emphasising her role as a dominating force in the Afterlife. She figures in temple-foundation rituals in the Delta alongside NEITH and ISIS.

Heryshaf

Ram-god prominent in Middle Egypt at Ihnasya el-Medina on the west bank of the Nile near Beni Suef.

His cult is mentioned as existing on this site as early as Dynasty I in the Old Kingdom annals inscribed on the Palermo Stone.

In reliefs and statuary Heryshaf is represented as having an anthropomorphic body in a pharaonic stance and wearing the royal kilt, while his head is that of a long-horned ram. His association with OSIRIS leads to his wearing the 'Atef' crown of that god, and his connection with RA results in the adoption of the sun disk surmounting his horns.

The name of Heryshaf means 'he who is upon his lake', referring to a topographical feature at his cult centre, probably the sacred lake in his temple, which in Egyptian religious concepts is an architectural attempt to recreate the primeval

waters. So Heryshaf is envisaged as emerging from the primal matter at the beginning of time. Regrettably, inscriptional evidence about Heryshaf is scant, so it is not possible to accept without reservations the attractive theory that 'he who is upon his lake' is the lotus plant arising out of the waters to open up and reveal the young sun-god.

The Greek author Plutarch renders Heryshaf as 'Arsaphes' and gives its meaning as 'manliness'. This is probably not to be taken as a general observation on the procreative inclinations of the ram, but more likely as deriving from an original (and typical) Egyptian play on words: between 'shaf' meaning 'his lake' and a word of similar consonantal sound, translating as 'respect' or 'manly dignity'.

In Greek terms Heryshaf became 'Herakles'. Accordingly the name of the site most sacred to the god, called Hnes in Ancient Egypt (modern Ihnasya el-Medina), is given in Greek texts as 'Herakleopolis' or 'town of Herakles'. Hnes was the capital city of Northern Egypt during the years separating the Pyramid Age from the Middle Kingdom (known as the First Intermediate Period). It is at this time that the relatively locally based god became enhanced with a universality accompanying his identification as the 'Ba' (soul) of Osiris and the 'Ba' of Ra.

Archaeologists have discovered that the earliest structures in his temple at Hnes date from the Middle Kingdom (Dynasty XII). There is a literary reference from this period to the temple in a narrative known as the 'Eloquent Peasant': in his fourth attempt to obtain redress for the unwarranted seizure of his donkeys and the goods they were carrying, the peasant comes across the official to whom he has been putting his complaints coming out of the temple of Heryshaf. During the New Kingdom the temple at Hnes was greatly

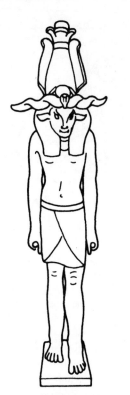

Gold figurine, *c.*700 BC, Boston Museum.

enlarged – especially under Ramesses II (Dynasty XIX) who was responsible for monolithic granite columns with palm-leaf capitals decorating the Hypostyle Hall. It is from that area that the exquisite gold miniature statuette of Heryshaf in the 'Atef' crown, now in the Boston Museum of Fine Arts, was discovered. This figurine gives the name of Peftuaubast, the ruler residing at Hnes, at the time of the invasion of Egypt by the Sudanese King Piye. Peftuaubast sided with Piye (Dynasty XXV) in his campaign of conquest, acknowledging him as his overlord and sending him tribute, doubtless some of it from Heryshaf's temple treasury.

The fullest description of the god is found on a stela originally set up at Hnes but discovered in the temple of ISIS at Pompeii and now in the Naples Museum. It is inscribed with the career of Somtutefnakht under the last native Egyptian pharaoh, through the second Persian Domination of Egypt beginning under Artaxerxes III in 343 BC to the conquest of Alexander the Great. Somtutefnakht, in his view guided by Heryshaf, collaborated with the Persians. The god also ensured that he remained unharmed during the turbulent period of the Greek invasion when, according to the inscription, there was colossal slaughter. Heryshaf then appears to Somtutefnakht in a dream advising him to return to his home town of Hnes and serve in the temple. Alone and through great peril on land and sea journeys, he reaches Hnes without even the loss of hair.

The god is described by the epithets:

'king of the Two Lands'
'ruler of the riverbanks'.

These titles ascribe the sovereignty of Egypt to Heryshaf. Solar symbolism is employed in the stela to invoke Heryshaf as a manifestation of Ra: the god's eyes are the sun disk and the moon. Heryshaf is ATUM who is here associated with the sacred 'naret' tree (sycamore?) of Hnes. As a primeval force Heryshaf is proclaimed creator of all life from the north wind which he breathes forth from his nostrils.

Hesat

Cow-goddess who gave birth to the king in the form of a golden calf. In general she is a milk goddess quenching the thirst of mankind with divine liquid described as the 'beer of Hesat'.

Hetepes-Sekhus   Underworld cobra-goddess who by virtue of her power as the

eye of RA annihilates the souls of OSIRIS's enemies. Her invincibility is enhanced by her entourage of crocodiles.

Horus

Falcon-god, 'lord of the sky' and symbol of divine kingship.

His name ('Har' in Egyptian) is probably to be interpreted as 'the high' or 'the far-off'. It appears in hieroglyphs in the royal protocol at the very beginning of dynastic civilisation *c*.3000 BC. The earliest occurrence of Horus, in complete hawk-form, is on monuments from the late Predynastic period, such as the palette showing a number of sacred creatures hacking at the walls of fortified towns. He continues to appear in the total falcon shape throughout Egyptian civilisation but his form, anthropomorphic to the shoulders with the hawk head becomes the most usual iconography.

Horus holding the heraldic plant of Lower Egypt. Statue of Senwosret I, Dyn. XII, Cairo Museum.

1 *Horus the child*

In the Pyramid Texts the god is once called 'Horus the child with his finger in his mouth'. This aspect of Horus refers to his birth and upbringing in secret by his mother ISIS. Born at Khemmis in the northeast Delta, the young god was hidden in the papyrus marshes, hence his epithet 'Har-hery-wadj' or 'Horus who is upon his papyrus plants'. This appears visually in a wall relief in the temple of Sety I (Dynasty XIX) at Abydos as a hawk on a column in the shape of papyrus reed. It is always possible – though not provable – that this imagery involving the god of kingship is behind the adoption of the shape of the papyrus as a column in royal architecture, first attested in the Step Pyramid complex of King Djoser (Dynasty III) at Saqqara. In the first century AD an instruction-document in Demotic (Papyrus Insinger)

uses, as an illustration that apparent misfortune can be reversed, the reference of Horus 'hidden behind the papyrus' becoming ruler of Egypt.

HARPOKRATES

From the Egyptian 'Har-pa-khered' literally 'Horus-the-child' the Greeks created the name of 'Harpokrates'. In this form Horus is as a rule iconographically depicted as a young vulnerable-looking child, sitting on the knees of ISIS, wearing the sidelock of youth and sometimes sucking his fingers. On a special category of objects occurring in the Late Dynastic Period, known as 'cippi', Harpokrates acts as an amuletic force warding off dangerous creatures: the naked child-god stands on the backs of crocodiles and holds in his hands snakes, scorpions, lions and antelopes. From a Demotic papyrus concerning the fortunes of Setne Khaemwase we have a reference to a temple of Isis and Harpokrates at Qift (Koptos). Although

Horus the child – 'Harpokrates' – on the lap of Isis. Bronze statuette, Bubastis, Dyn. XXVI, Kunsthistorisches Museum, Vienna.

pre-eminently the son of Isis, Harpokrates becomes representative of the concept of the divine child-god completing the union of the two chief deities in a temple. Consequently at Nag'el Madamud just north of Luxor a temple was built in honour of the god MONTU, his consort Raettawy (see under Montu) and their son Harpokrates.

HARSOMTUS

This version of Horus can be traced back to the Pyramid Texts as 'Har-mau' 'Horus the uniter'. The idea is the king as upholder of the unification of NORTH and SOUTH Egypt. Since in temple dogma the divine child of a god and goddess could be thought of as a manifestation of the pharaoh, Harsomtus comes to be used merely as 'filling' in a sacred triad. He is, e.g. the son of the elder Horus and HATHOR at Edfu temple. Similarly at the temple of Kom-Ombo the same couple

are the parents of Harsomtus under the name of 'Pa-neb-tawy' or the 'lord of the Two Lands'.

2 *Horus and the king*

In Ancient Egypt the evolution of divine kingship enabled the monarch to claim that his status as ruler was approved of by the chief gods and that moreover he himself was a deity and one of their number. Horus satisfied the first requirement by a successful legal action before the gods: the pharaoh therefore was in a supreme position, being seen as a manifestation of the 'living Horus' on the throne of Egypt.

According to the Turin Canon the late Predynastic rulers of Egypt were 'followers of Horus'. By the time of the unification of Upper and Lower Egypt in 3000 BC the ruler *was* Horus. On the palette in Cairo Museum, which shows King Narmer, the first ruler of a permanently united Egyptian state, the god Horus is shown holding a rope that passes through the nose of the defeated northern rival, symbolising the king's victory over the Delta. From this period onwards the King's name is introduced by the symbol of the Horus falcon, surmounting a rectangular shape which has a base part indicating a fortified wall. This was called the 'serekh' or 'proclaimer' of the king, whose name was written in the upper section of the rectangle.

3 *Horus the son of* ISIS: *Harsiese*

This form of Horus emphasises his legitimacy as the offspring of the union of Isis and OSIRIS. (Consult the entries under these deities for the events leading up to Horus's conception.) In the Pyramid Texts Harsiese performs the vital 'opening the mouth' ceremony on the dead king. This ritual, restoring faculties to the corpse for the Afterlife, would have been carried out at the time of burial by the successor-monarch (=Horus) upon his predecessor who has now become Osiris ruler of the Underworld. A clever – if a typical – pictorial statement of this rite being performed by one pharaoh upon another can be found on the wall of the sarcophagus chamber in the tomb of Tutankhamun (Dynasty XVIII). The new king in this case was an elderly statesman called Ay, unrelated to the young Tutankhamun and probably justifying his inheritance of the throne by depicting this ceremony with its imagery of filial devotion. In the role of dutiful son, Harsiese can be compared with two forms of Horus that imply the same idea of piety towards Osiris.

Horus 'iun-mutef'

The translation of the Egyptian means 'pillar of his mother' evocative of Horus's success in regaining the throne of his father – the raison d'être of ISIS's careful upbringing of her son. At funeral ceremonies the eldest son of the deceased – or mortuary priest – dressed in a panther skin, played the role of Horus Iun-mutef burning incense and scattering purified water before the coffin.

Harendotes

This is the Greek version of the Egyptian 'Har-nedj-itef' or 'Horus the saviour of his father'. This form of Horus refers to the vindication of his claim to succeed OSIRIS, rescuing his father's former earthly domain from the usurper SETH.

4 The struggle for the throne of Egypt

When he reaches maturity Horus becomes 'Harwer' or 'Haroeris' – the elder Horus now capable of seizing power. As early as the Old Kingdom it was envisaged that Horus wrested the kingship of Egypt from the god Seth: Horus takes his father's house from his father's brother Seth. Horus then triumphs over his paternal uncle. However, there is a problem in that our pharaonic sources indicate a conflation of two myths:

OSIRIS CYCLE	INDEPENDENT TRADITION
Brothers = Osiris and Seth	Brothers = Horus and Seth

The tradition of Horus and Seth as brothers feuding for the throne reflects the importance of these two cults. Normally Horus is in the ascendant, but there is indisputable evidence that the supporters of Seth were never suppressed. Royal propaganda refused to acknowledge that any conflict existed between the two gods: in Dynasty I King Anedjib uses the title 'Nebwy' or 'two lords' viewing Horus and Seth as a reconciled partnership. Later on, in Dynasty XII, Senwosret I has the sides of his throne carved with the figures of Horus and Seth facing each other across the symbol of 'unity' around which they tie the heraldic plants of North and South Egypt. However, for the purposes of stressing unequivocally the supremacy of Horus (by implication the king himself), the Osirian tradition absorbs some of the vicious fighting between the two brothers into its own account of the struggle for Egypt – with the necessity of Seth becoming the murderous brother of Osiris and hence the uncle of Horus.

From the Shabaqo Stone in the British Museum, a copy, carved in Dynasty XXV, of an original document from the Pyramid Age, there is a concise statement of the dispute between Horus and Seth. The god GEB is the judge and makes a preliminary decision to divide Egypt between the protagonists: Seth will be king of Upper Egypt and Horus will rule over Lower Egypt, the border being the 'Division of the Two Lands', i.e. the apex of the Nile Delta at Memphis where Osiris is said to have drowned. On reflection Geb revises this judgement awarding the whole 'inheritance' of Egypt to Horus. It is stressed that this result is amicably accepted by the disputants – the reed of Seth and papyrus of Horus being attached to the door of the god PTAH to symbolise that they were pacified and united.

Fortunately a fuller and more scandalous description of the trial survives in Papyrus Chester Beatty I written in the reign of Ramesses V (Dynasty XX). The following is a brief synopsis of passages germane to Horus's struggle both against Seth and for recognition as rightful heir to the throne.

The sun-god, in this tribunal, is not sympathetic to Horus's case to be ruler of Egypt, dismissing him as a youngster with halitosis and preferring the older claimant Seth (see also BANEBDJEDET).

Horus pleads that he is being defrauded of his lawful patrimony. There are now a series of episodes involving Horus and Seth, each trying to outwit the other and win over the court (see Isis for Seth's unintentional admission of guilt and his homosexual assault on Horus).

In one contest, in which the two gods as hippopotamuses intend to see if they can remain submerged under water for three months, ISIS refuses to take the opportunity of killing Seth with a harpoon. Horus, enraged, savagely attacks his mother and escapes into the desert. Seth finds him and cuts out his eyes. HATHOR, using gazelle's milk, restores Horus's eyes.

On another occasion Seth suggests a race in boats of stone. Horus secretly builds a vessel of pine covered with plaster to imitate stone. Seth's boat, 36 m of solid stone, sinks and he turns himself into a hippopotamus. Horus is prevented from slaying Seth by the other gods.

Eventually, after 80 years of conflict between the two gods, the tribunal awards Horus the throne of Egypt.

Symbolism of Horus's triumph over Seth (e.g. the pharaoh cutting the throat of an oryx or spearing a turtle) permeates many temple reliefs. It also lies behind the gilded wooden statuette of Tutankhamun standing on a papyrus boat, a lasso in one hand and a harpoon in the other: the king is in the act of spearing the hippopotamus Seth, superstitious reasons preventing his effigy from being included in the royal tomb.

5 *The eye of Horus*

The injury inflicted by SETH on the eyes of Horus mentioned earlier is alluded to in the Pyramid Texts where royal saliva is prescribed for its cure. The restored eyes of Horus become, in singular form, the symbol for a state of soundness or perfection – the 'udjat' eye. Its iconography consists of a human eye with the cosmetic line emanating from its corner, below which are the markings of a falcon's cheek. It became the protection sign par excellence. As an amulet the 'udjat' was placed in mummy wrappings or worn on a necklace. Apotropaically, in the Middle Kingdom, it was painted on the sides of rectangular coffins. However, it is only from the inscriptional evidence that we get some idea of its diversity and complexity of meaning. For example, the eye of Horus can stand for:

The strength of the monarch
Concept of kingship
Protection against Seth
Royal purification agent
Offerings at the festival of the waxing
    moon Wine.

There is even a reference to a cult of the 'udjat', since an official, Udjahorresne, living during Cambyses's invasion of

Horus the falcon and the 'Eye of Horus'. Tomb of Pashedu, Deir el-Medina, Dyn. XX.

Egypt in 525 BC, numbers among his titles 'priest of the Horus-eye'.

6 *Horus as sun-god*

As a cosmic deity Horus is imagined as a falcon whose wings are the sky and whose right eye is the sun and left eye the moon. From the reign of King Den (Dynasty I), on an engraved ivory comb, the hawk's wings as an independent entity convey the celestial imagery while a hawk in a boat suggests the journey of the sun-god himself. Textual evidence from the Pyramid Era refers to Horus as 'lord of the sky' or as a god 'of the east', i.e. region of sunrise. Three forms of Horus as a solar deity are particularly important.

HARAKHTI

This name means 'Horus of the horizon', referring to the god rising in the east at dawn to bathe in the 'field of rushes'. The Pyramid Texts mention this aspect of the god linked to the sovereign: the king is said to be born on the eastern sky as Harakhti. Also since the element 'akhti'

can be a dual form of the noun 'akhet', 'horizon', there is a play on words when the king is said to be given power over the 'two horizons' (i.e. east and west) as Harakhti. Naturally, the Egyptians had to accept that technically their pharaoh, as 'son of RA' the sun-god, could not achieve a total identification with this aspect of Horus, especially with the coalescence of this form of Horus with the Heliopolitan sun-god to become Ra-Harakhti. Thus Senwosret I (Dynasty XII) was appointed 'shepherd of this land' *by* Harakhti. But in laudatory or propagandist inscriptions the assimilation of the pharaoh to Harakhti is maintained, as for instance in the case of the Sudanese King Piye (Dynasty XXV) on his stela commemorating the conquest of Egypt.

HORUS OF BEHDET

The location of Behdet was in the marshy north-east Delta. It is not mentioned in the Pyramid Texts and the antiquity of the site as a cult centre of Horus (in relation to Edfu, e.g.) cannot yet be ascertained. The symbol of Horus of Behdet was the hawk-winged sun disk. It becomes a ubiquitous motif – e.g. in temple decoration of ceilings or gate lintels, or the upper frame of wall-reliefs and stelae.

HARMACHIS

This name from 'Har-em-akhet' or 'Horus in the horizon' aptly regionalises Horus as sun-god. Pharaonic inscriptions of the New Kingdom reinterpreted the sphinx at Giza, originally representing King Khafra guarding the approach to his pyramid, as Harmachis looking towards the eastern horizon (see also HAURUN).

7 *Localities with a Horus cult*

The two most important sanctuaries in terms of historical or archaeological evidence belong to Horus of Nekhen and Horus of Mesen.

HORUS OF NEKHEN

Probably assimilating an earlier falcon-deity 'Nekheny', Horus made this site (modern Kom el-Ahmar) his own by the Early Dynastic Period – an association lasting into the Graeco-Roman period when Nekhen became 'Hierakonpolis' or 'Hawk-city'. The exquisite gold falcon-head in Cairo Museum comes from a cult statue that stood in the Old Kingdom temple. Later in Dynasty XIII an official, Horemkauf, boasts how he was commissioned to bring a new cult image from the royal residence near Memphis all the way to Nekhen.

HORUS OF MESEN

This is the ancient name (connected with the idea of Horus as a harpooner) for modern Edfu. The magnificently preserved temple of Horus dates from the Ptolemaic period but Horus's sanctuary has stood here in one form or another since at least the beginning of the Pyramid Age. The reliefs show Horus

with his consort HATHOR and their child Harsomtus watching a myriad of rituals performed in their honour. One group of carvings represents a sacred drama, enacted by the priests, of Horus and the spearing of SETH in the form of a hippopotamus. This animal is annihilated – symbolically eaten in fact, as a cake in the shape of a hippopotamus – flying in the face of the tradition of the conflict where Seth is spared, because no detraction from Horus's supremacy can be permitted on this sacred site.

Other forms of Horus had sanctuaries on sites now almost totally bereft of archaeological remains, e.g. Horus Khenty-Irty.

HORUS KHENTY-IRTY

This falcon-god was worshipped in the south-west Delta at Ausim (Greek Letopolis) called Khem in Ancient Egypt, since at least Dynasty IV.

Finally, there were a number of names under which Horus was worshipped south of the first cataract of the Nile in Nubia.

HORUS OF BAKI

This is the ancient name for the fort of Quban, controlling vital gold supply routes.

HORUS OF BUHEN

Impressive fortress at the second cataract of the Nile – the south temple to Horus was built here during the reigns of Hatshepsut and Thutmose III (Dynasty XVIII).

HORUS OF MIAM

This is Aniba, the administrative centre of Lower Nubia which had a temple to Horus dating back to the Middle Kingdom. Like all regional forms of the hawk-god, Horus of Miam is not restricted to his name-site: there are depictions of him throughout Nubia – e.g. he stands opposite Seth raising his hands to the crown of Ramesses II in Nefertari's temple at Abu Simbel (Dynasty XIX).

Hours   Twelve Underworld-goddesses, daughters of the sun-god RA, represented in human form, each with a five-pointed star above her head. They figure among the deities on the walls of tombs in the Valley of the Kings which illustrate the religious compositions known as the Book of Gates and the Amduat.

These goddesses personify the reality of time over chaotic forces that would, if given the chance, render the universe of the sun-god non-existent. Accordingly Ra has given them the power of destiny so that they control the life-spans of beings that they live among, i.e. all living creatures subject to the progress of time. Possibly the ithyphallic form of OSIRIS in the Book of Caverns on one wall of the sarcophagus hall in the tomb of Ramesses VI (Dynasty XX), who is called 'he who conceals the Hours', symbolises a magical power desired by the monarch to halt the decay of time and live in ageless vigour.

Furthermore the Hours thwart the attempt of a hostile serpent called Hereret to produce anarchic powers from itself to challenge the order of the cosmos created by Ra – they swallow and annihilate these as they emerge out of the snake.

The imagery of some of the epithets attached to each of these goddesses emphasises their destruction of the enemies of the sun-god. For instance, the First Hour cuts open the heads of opponents, the Seventh drives away a threatening snake and the Tenth decapitates rebels.

Hu

    The god who personifies the authority of a word of command.

Hu came into being from a drop of blood from the phallus of the sun-god RA.

When, according to the theology of the Pyramid Age, the king becomes a lone star, his companion is Hu. The royal authority is maintained in the Afterlife by Hu acknowledging the king's supremacy and allowing the monarch to cross the waters of his canal.

It is tempting to correlate Hu with the power of the tongue of PTAH in the Memphite creation legend, commanding the universe into existence, at the instigation of Ptah's heart (see SIA).

I

Iah

${\text{Moon-god.}}$

In its earliest attestations the name Iah refers to the moon as satellite of the earth. Iah then becomes conceptualised as a lunar deity, iconographically anthropomorphic but whose manifestations, from the hieroglyphic evidence, can include the crescent of the new moon, the ibis and the falcon – comparable to the other moon deities, THOTH and KHONSU.

It is probable that contact with Middle Eastern states in Palestine, Syria and Babylonia was instrumental in the development of Iah as a deity. Certainly the zenith of Iah's popularity lay in the period following the Middle Kingdom when immigration from the Levant was high and princes from Palestine, known as the Hyksos rulers, dominated Egypt. These foreigners may well have looked for a lunar deity analogous to the Akkadian moon-god Sin who had an important temple at Harran in north Syria. Strangely, it is within the Theban royal family eventually responsible for the expulsion of these alien rulers that there is a definite inclination for names involving the moon-god Iah. The daughter of Seqenenra Taa (Dynasty XVII) is Iah-hotep ('Iah is content'). The founder of Dynasty XVIII was called Iahmose ('Iah is born') and the same element is in the name of his wife Iahmose-Nefertari. Most likely the Middle Eastern deity who gave the stimulus to the adoption of Iah is the influence behind the name Kamose, the brother of Iahmose, who began the final thrust against the Hyksos domination. Kamose ('the bull is born') might be the Egyptian equivalent of the epithet applied to Sin describing him as a 'young bull…with strong horns' (i.e. the tips of the crescent moon). This imagery would be totally compatible with the Egyptian concept of the pharaoh as an invincible bull (see APIS).

In the tomb of Thutmose III (Dynasty XVIII), the pharaoh whose campaigns took him to the banks of the Euphrates river, there is a scene where the king is accompanied by his mother and three queens, including Sit-Iah 'daughter of the moon-god'. Traces of his cult beyond this period are sporadic.

Ihy

${\text{Young god personifying the}}$ jubilation emanating from the sacred rattle.

The name of Ihy was interpreted by the Egyptians as 'sistrum-player' which was the raison d'être of this god. The sistrum was a cultic musical instrument used primarily (but not exclusively) in the worship of HATHOR, mother of Ihy. At Dendera temple Ihy is the child of the union of Hathor and HORUS and is depicted as a naked young boy wearing the sidelock of youth and with his finger to his mouth. He can hold the sacred rattle and necklace (menat).

In the temple complex the birth house or 'mammisi' was a sanctuary where the mystery of the conception and birth of the divine child Ihy was celebrated. His name is rarely found outside the confines of Dendera temple – e.g. occasionally in spells in the Coffin Texts or Book of the Dead where he is called 'lord of bread…in charge of beer', a possible reference to the celebrations at Dendera deliberately requiring a state of intoxication on the part of the acolyte in order to communicate with Hathor.

Imhotep

Historical high courtier under King Djoser (Dynasty III) who after deification becomes the embodiment of scribal wisdom and, as 'son of PTAH', of supreme architectural and creative skill.

Statue fragments attest that Imhotep was given the extreme privilege of his name being carved alongside that of Djoser Netjerykhet himself. He held the offices of chief executive (vizier) and master sculptor – the Egyptian priest Manetho, who wrote in Greek a history of Egypt in the third century BC, credits 'Imouthes' (i.e. Imhotep) with the invention of the technique of building with cut stone. It is likely he was the architect who planned Egypt's first large-scale stone monument: the Step Pyramid at Saqqara.

After his death Imhotep is remembered in Middle and New Kingdom scribal compositions as the author of a book of instruction – a well-known genre of Egyptian literature although the one credited to Imhotep has not survived. In the Late Period bronzes of Imhotep show him seated in scribal posture with a papyrus-roll open across his knees. This veneration for him leads to his deification – an extremely rare phenomenon in ancient Egypt (compare AMENHOTEP-SON-OF-HAPU, PETEESE and PIHOR, and PHARAOH sections titled 'Living king = deified through ritual' and 'Dead king = deified as royal ancestors').

In the Ptolemaic period Imhotep as a god is found in cult centres and temples throughout Egypt:

1 Objects dedicated in his name are found in north Saqqara.

2 At Thebes where he was worshipped in conjunction with Amenhotep-Son-of-Hapu he has a sanctuary on the Upper Terrace of the temple at Deir el-Bahari and is represented in the temple at Deir el-Medina.

3 At Philae there is a chapel of Imhotep immediately before the eastern pylon of the temple of ISIS.

An inscription, dated to the reign of the Roman emperor Tiberius, in the temple of Ptah at Karnak, gives some information on Imhotep's priesthood. It also emphasises Imhotep's ability as a healer, which had already produced identification in the Greek mind with Asklepios, their own god of medicine. His connection with Ptah – whose son he is considered to be by an Egyptian lady called Khreduankh – causes him to be seen as an agent capable of renewing his

Late Period bronze statuette, British Museum.

father's creative force in response to prayers. Taimhotep, a lady who died in the reign of Cleopatra VII (Ptolemaic period), left a poignant stela (now in the British Museum) on which is mentioned how she and her husband, high priest of Ptah, prayed to Imhotep for a son. In a vision or dream Imhotep requests the embellishment of his sanctuary in north Saqqara. The high priest commissions a monument for him involving 'sculptors of the house of gold'. Imhotep responds by causing Taimhotep to conceive a son who is born on his festival-day and named 'Imhotep-Pedibast'.

Ipy

𓉺𓏺𓏭 Benign hippopotamus-goddess first attested in the Pyramid Age where the monarch calls her his mother and requests her to suckle him with her divine milk. In another royal connection Ipy is carved as an amuletic force on the back of a statue of a Theban ruler of Dynasty XVII. Funerary papyri described Ipy as 'Lady of magical protection' and show her lighting a bowl of incense cones.

At Karnak to the west of the temple of KHONSU is the temple of a goddess called the Great Ipet who is none other than Ipy. In Theban theology this goddess rested on this spot when she was pregnant and gave birth to OSIRIS.

Ishtar

An astral goddess (although possibly androgynous in origin) worshipped in Mesopotamia as 'lady of battle' and as an embodiment of sexuality and fertility.

She is the Eastern Semitic counterpart of ASTARTE (who figures far more prominently in Egyptian theology) and the Akkadian equivalent of the Sumerian goddess Inanna. One of the most important Assyrian goddesses, her fame extends into the realm of the Hurrians and Hittites to the north. Her emblem, as on her gate in Babylon, is the eight-pointed star and her eminence is emphasised by her identification with the brightest planet Venus. Further, she is the daughter of the moon-god Sin.

Ishtar of Nineveh accompanies the Assyrian king into battle breaking the bows of his enemies, armed with her own quiver, bow and sword. Her animal, the lioness, symbolises her martial prowess.

It has been suggested that the voluptuous side of Ishtar – her pleasure in love, her 'beautiful figure' and 'sweet lips' as the texts tell us – is an inheritance from the Sumerian Inanna. Certainly, when lamenting the death of her consort Tammuz (Sumerian Dumuzi), Ishtar descends into the Underworld, all sexual activity ceased on earth. It would be tempting to make an analogy between Ishtar and ISIS or HATHOR but evidence from the Egyptian sources is lacking.

The role of Ishtar as a goddess of healing traverses frontiers in the Middle East. The best example comes from Egypt, preserved in one of the cuneiform letters from the diplomatic archive discovered at el-Amarna. Towards the end of his reign Amenhotep III (Dynasty XVIII) suffered a sickness or pain – if the mummy reburied under his name by priests living generations later is definitely that of this king, then the agony of his severe dental abscesses must have made him desperate for relief. To alleviate Amenhotep's illness his father-in-law Tushratta of Mitanni sent – on loan only – a statue of Ishtar of Nineveh to Egypt in the hope that the goddess's curing-power might operate through the divine effigy.

Isis

𓊨𓏏𓆇 Goddess of immense magical power, symbolic mother of the king.

Isis wearing throne symbol. Sarcophagus of Amenhotep II, Valley of the Kings, Dyn. XVIII.

The goddess's name is written in hieroglyphs with a sign that represents a throne, indicating the crucial role that she plays in the transmission of the kingship of Egypt.

Isis is shown as queenly in poise wearing on her head either the 'throne' symbol or a crown of cow-horns and the sun disk. An amulet known as the 'tyet', already regarded as sacred in the Pyramid Age, becomes her special symbol from the New Kingdom onwards. This consists of a girdle with a loop or knot on the front and seems to be connected with the sign of life (the 'ankh'), symbol of divine and royal power. In the Book of the Dead the tyet is described as being made of red jasper, suggesting its secondary interpretation as the blood of the goddess. In her role as a mother she could manifest herself as a sow – particularly the 'Great White Sow of Heliopolis'. She also had a form as the Isis-cow which gave birth to the sacred bull of Memphis (see APIS).

1 *Sister–wife of* OSIRIS

In the genealogy developed by the priests of Heliopolis, Isis was one of the children of GEB and NUT. As the 'sister whom Osiris loved on earth' she devotedly assists him in the government of Egypt. In the earliest references to the goddess in the Pyramid Texts she appears to foresee his murder by SETH, and is described as sitting despairing, weeping for her brother. After his death she – and her sister NEPHTHYS – mourn inconsolably in the shape of kites. She wearilessly seeks, and finds his body after her brother Seth had thrown it into the Nile; she reassembles Osiris's corpse after Seth had dismembered it and scattered the parts throughout Egypt (see Osiris for details of the myth). In the Great Hymn to Osiris on the stela of Amenemose (Dynasty XVIII) in the Louvre Museum, the goddess is envisaged as a kite protectively shading the god with her plumage, the breeze created by her wings providing breath for him. She then acts as a guard over the god. This is iconographically shown in some statues by the goddess standing in human form, stretching forward her arms from which grow wings to flank the figure of Osiris before her – a clear statement of how the Egyptians saw Isis as an example of supreme devotion to her husband. It is through her magic that Osiris makes her pregnant – the god now leaving Egypt for his role as Underworld king.

2 *Mother of* HORUS

It is in this aspect that the goddess was regarded as the vital link between deities and royalty, since the king was the living Horus on the throne of Egypt. In the Pyramid Texts it is stated that the ruler drinks divine milk from the breasts of his mother Isis. This is the imagery of the plethora of statuettes of Isis seated on a

Isis in cow-horn crown, holding ritual rattle and necklace. Temple of Sety I, Abydos, Dyn. XIX.

the assassination of his father. This close guarding of Horus from danger becomes a frequent point of reference in magical texts concerning cures for children's ailments resulting from hazards like scorpion bites, or accidental scalds. Isis called 'great of magic' is invoked to come to the child's assistance as if it were Horus himself. A spell against a burn, e.g. is recited over a concoction of human milk, gum and cat hairs, to be applied to the injured child: in it Isis, told that her son lies in the desert suffering from a burn with no water to cool him, gives the assurances that her saliva and urine (which she euphemistically calls 'the Nile flood between my thighs') possess the power to alleviate the pain.

3 Her tenacity and guile

When her son reached maturity Isis had to fight hard in the law-court of the gods for the award of his rightful inheritance of the Egyptian throne. In this respect she reveals her true nature as 'clever of tongue' and perseverance against obstacles put in her way by the most powerful gods. The Broad Hall of GEB is the scene for the litigation between Horus and SETH, the proceedings of which are preserved on a papyrus dating to Dynasty XX. An underlying motif in the account is the relationship between Isis and Seth, her brother. The blood-bond is, on one occasion, strong enough to soften the goddess's resolve on behalf of her son. When Isis has harpooned Seth, who is in the form of a hippopotamus, he appeals to her in the name of their consanguinity and she releases the barb from his flesh. However, this is only a momentary lapse. Two episodes will illustrate how Isis, by her guile and skill in magic, humiliates Seth in front of the gods presiding at the tribunal.

throne, suckling the young Horus who sits on her lap. The goddess was thought to have given birth to her son at Khemmis in the Delta, reinforcing the connection with the monarchy since the place-name in its ancient Egyptian form of 'Akh-bity' means 'papyrus thicket of the king of Lower Egypt'. Her role as a goddess protecting royal births is found in the Middle Kingdom story (in the Papyrus Westcar) foretelling a dynastic change: Isis receives into her arms each of the first three kings of the Dynasty V as Ruddedet gives them birth.

Isis intends to bring up Horus in secret so that he might eventually avenge

ISIS CAUSES SETH TO CONDEMN HIMSELF

Seth, annoyed at the sympathy Isis gains among some of the gods, refuses to continue with the lawsuit for the Egyptian throne while the goddess is present in the court. The tribunal adjourns to an island, with strict instructions being given to the ferryman not to bring Isis across the water. Isis disguises herself as an old woman wishing to take food to a boy looking after cattle on the island. Assuming the shape of a beautiful lady she entices Seth away from the court. She tells him how she is distressed because, following her husband's death, a stranger stole her son's inheritance of his father's cattle and evicted him. The righteous anger expressed by Seth is immediately turned against him by the goddess who declares her identity. He meets with little sympathy from the judging gods.

ISIS PROVES SETH GUILTY OF SEXUAL ASSAULT

During the dispute Seth makes a successful sexual attack on HORUS who takes some of the god's semen to his mother Isis as witness of the event. Isis determines to bring Seth into discredit with the gods. She obtains some of Horus's semen and spreads it over the lettuces growing in Seth's garden, which are then eaten by him. In front of the tribunal Horus asks for his semen to be summoned from the head of Seth who, to his chagrin, is left looking ridiculous. At the end of the litigation it is Isis who brings Seth in fetters into the court, where he concedes defeat.

In an episode involving the sun-god RA, Isis's craftiness has far-reaching implications for the ruling pharaoh although, it must be admitted, the surviving account exists only as an elaborate spell to cure a scorpion sting. The skeleton of the story is as follows:

> Isis 'more clever than a million gods' schemes to discover the secret name of Ra, knowledge of which conferred limitless power.
>
> Obtaining some saliva that Ra had dribbled from his mouth, she mixes it with earth and fashions it in the shape of a snake.
>
> Ra passes the snake and is bitten. He falls into a trembling agony, feverish with the poison.
>
> Isis offers to use her magic to alleviate the sun-god's pain in exchange for his secret name.
>
> Ra attempts to confuse the goddess by reciting a string of names, but Isis remains obdurate, refusing to cure the god until the true name is spoken to her. She even 'turns the screw' by causing the poison to burn into Ra more stringently.
>
> The sun-god divulges the secret to Isis who becomes 'the mistress of the gods who knows Ra by his own name'.

The most important element in the story is Ra's permission for Isis to pass the knowledge of his mysterious name onto her son Horus. Consequently the pharaoh, through the goddess's ruthless determination, as Horus, has a power no other god can rival.

4 *Her sanctuaries*

Isis as a universal goddess is worshipped in many temples of which a handful are:

Behbeit el-Hagar = ISEION This was a major cult centre of Isis in the north-east Delta on the Damietta branch of the Nile. Today Isis's temple's granite slabs and structures with fine reliefs of the goddess lie in ruins. Although it is an early sanctuary of the goddess – mentioned in the Pyramid Texts as providing the king with jars of water possessing the breath of 'Isis the Great' – archaeology has not yet discovered evidence of buildings prior to Dynasty XXX.

Temple of Isis 'mistress of the pyramid' at Giza In Dynasty XXI the chapel of one of the three satellite pyramids of queens, east of the Great Pyramid of Khufu.

Deir el-Shelwit Here, on the western bank of Thebes south of Medinet Habu, a small square temple was built under the Roman occupation of Egypt.

Temple of Sety I (Dynasty XIX) at Abydos There are three chapels and inner apartments, for Isis, OSIRIS and HORUS, in which there are the most exquisite and detailed representations of the goddess ever carved in pharaonic Egypt.

Temple of Augustus at Dendera A small sanctuary built to celebrate the birth of Isis, a day associated with falls of rain. The presence of Isis on terrain sacred to HATHOR, the goddess from whom she borrowed the cow-horn crown, is not surprising since both were bound up with the concept of kingship.

Temple of Isis on the island of Philae Now relocated on the neighbouring island of Agilqiya, this monument, with minor exceptions, belongs to the Graeco-Roman period. It has the distinction of outliving all other Egyptian temples as a place of worship and priestly rituals.

ISIS ABROAD

(For the goddess's connection with Byblos in Lebanon see OSIRIS.) In documents written in the Demotic script (the Petubastis story-cycle) there occurs a fragmentary saga, heavily influenced by classical Greek literature, involving an Egyptian, Pedikhons, and a Syrian, Queen Serpot, who rules a land of women-warriors. The climax is a single combat between them, before which Serpot invokes Isis as 'mistress of the land of women'.

There is a dichotomy between a few Roman writers and the archaeological proof, of the spread of the goddess's cult throughout the Mediterranean world and northern Europe. Isis is castigated by the satirist Juvenal AD (60–128) who mocks the exaggerated lengths to which her initiates go in celebrating the rituals. However, the popularity of Isis as the centre of a mystery cult was phenomenal. In this foreign development of Isis's cult the goddess surpassed Osiris in importance. Apuleius (born AD 125) has left a valuable description of the stages of initiation for a new acolyte (but is discreetly silent over the culminating rite). Her sanctuaries could be found on the Acropolis at Athens, on the island of Delos and at Pompeii. Christianity had an uphill struggle in eclipsing her worship.

Iusaas A goddess of Heliopolis whose name means 'she comes who is great'. Wearing a scarab beetle on her head she can easily be seen as a counterpart to the sun-god ATUM and like NEBETHETEPET plays a crucial role as the feminine principle in the creation of the world.

K

Khepri

Sun-god creator in the form of a scarab beetle.

The image of the scarab is almost synonymous with Ancient Egypt. The choice of an insect to convey one of the forms of the sun-god illustrates the keen eye of the Egyptian in observing nature and his imagination in trying to understand the universe. Khepri is the sun-god at dawn on the eastern horizon. His iconography is that of the scarab beetle (of which there are numerous varieties in Egypt) pushing the disk of the sun upwards from the Underworld to journey across the sky. In their own local environment the Egyptians would have noticed the scarabs busily rolling balls of dirt across the ground and translated this method of propulsion into an explanation of the sun's circuit. However, the analogy did not stop there. Observing that out of the ball emerged a scarab, apparently spontaneously, it was logical to see the insect as Khepri – 'he who is coming into being', i.e. self-created of his own accord

Khepri as hawk-winged scarab. Pectoral from the Tomb of Tutankhamun, Dyn. XVIII, Cairo Museum.

without undergoing the natural cycle of reproduction. The creator sun-god was therefore aptly manifest in the 'scarabaeus sacer' or dung beetle.

Inscriptional evidence for Khepri occurs in the pyramids of the Old Kingdom: a wish is expressed for the sun to come into being in its name of Khepri. The priesthood of the sun-god combined his different forms to assert that ATUM-Khepri arises on the primeval mound in the mansion of the BENU in Heliopolis. Referring to the myth of the sun-god's journey through the hours of night, Khepri is said to raise his beauty into the body of NUT the sky-goddess. From noticing the somewhat slimy consistency of the scarab beetle's dirt-ball, the earth is made from the spittle coming from Khepri.

From about the Middle Kingdom representations of Khepri, as the ovoid scarab, regularly occur in three-dimensional form carved as the amuletic backing of seals. These scarabs, by implication, connect the wearer with the sun-god. The underside could be incised, not just with the titles and name of an official, but also with good-luck designs, deities and the names of royalty used for their protective power. Kings would use the undersides of large scarabs to commemorate specific events – Amenhotep III (Dynasty XVIII) has left a number of these news bulletins which inter alia give information on his prowess at lion hunting and celebrate the arrival of a Syrian princess into his harem. The scarab could form the bezel of a ring or be part of a necklace or bracelet – the tomb of Tutankhamun has provided us with splendid examples of scarabs made of semi-precious stones like lapis lazuli set in gold. One of the young king's pectorals in particular stresses the dominance of Khepri the sun-god as well as being a masterpiece of the jeweller's craft: in the centre of the design is a scarab carved from chalcedony combined with the wings and talons of the solar hawk, representing Khepri who, as controller of celestial motion, is shown here pushing the boat of the moon-eye.

Paintings in funerary papyri show Khepri on a boat being lifted up by the god NUN, the primeval watery chaos. In some depictions Khepri coalesces with other conceptions of the sun-god to present the appearance of a ram-headed beetle. On a wall of the interior chamber in the tomb of Petosiris (fourth century BC) at Tuna el-Gebel, Khepri was carved quite naturalistically in low relief, painted lapis lazuli blue, wearing the 'atef' crown of OSIRIS. Less frequently Khepri could be shown as an anthropomorphic god to the shoulders with a full scarab beetle for a head. Bizarre as it might seem, the Egyptian artist has left some magnificent depictions of Khepri in this form – e.g. in the tomb of Nefertari (Dynasty XIX) in the Valley of the Queens.

Although relatively few examples are extant in museums or in Egypt, it seems likely that the major temples each possessed a colossal hard-stone statue of Khepri. Raised on a plinth, the scarab symbolised architecturally the concept that the temple was the site where the sun-god first emerged to begin the creation of the cosmos.

Kherty

A ram-god with a dual nature of hostility and protection. From Kherty the king has to be protected by no less a deity than RA. However, Kherty, as his name which means 'Lower One'

indicates, is an earth-god and so can act as the guardian of the royal tomb. The king's power over the winds is likened to the grasp of Kherty's hand.

In the Old Kingdom Kherty is eminent enough to figure as a partner of OSIRIS and his ram form leads naturally to a relationship with KHNUM. Kherty's major cult centre appears to have been at Letopolis, north-west of Memphis.

Khnum

  Ram-god, creator of life on the potter's wheel.

Khnum, called 'high of plumes, sharp of horns', had primarily an association with the Nile cataract. He controls the annual inundation of the river from the caverns of HAPY, the god personifying the flood itself. His importance at Elephantine can be traced back to the Early Dynastic Period although the archaeological evidence is predominantly from the New Kingdom and Graeco-Roman period. Rams sacred to Khnum have been discovered on Elephantine Island, mummified, adorned with gilded head-pieces and buried in stone sarcophagi. A stela was carved on a dominant rock on Seheil Island overlooking the first cataract which emphasises the antiquity of Khnum's cult at Elephantine. The inscription itself is a Ptolemaic copy (or forgery) of an original document dating to the reign of King Djoser (Dynasty III). There has been a seven-year famine which Djoser is anxious to halt. Khnum relents from preventing the Nile flood, on being assured of his temple's renovation and regular income of Nubian wealth, and Egypt prospers again.

In his supervision over the cataract region he is assisted by the goddesses SATIS and ANUKIS. He was also regarded in this aspect as lord of the cataract as the 'Ba' (soul) of the sun-god, hence his name becomes Khnum-RA. This strong connection with the river lies behind one of his titles 'lord of the crocodiles', intensified by the presence of the goddess NEITH, mother of the crocodile-god SOBEK, as the most important guest deity in his temple at Esna.

His other major role is probably derived from the procreative powers of the ram and the life-supporting river which make him eminently suitable as a creator-god. The iconography represents Khnum seated before a potter's wheel on which stands the being which he has moulded into existence. The god normally performs this task at the behest of another deity, e.g. in the theogamies on Theban temple walls (see AMUN) or in the story of the Two Brothers where Khnum is instructed to fashion a wife for Bata. It seems that Khnum breathes in the life force to the created being, as mentioned in the Westcar Papyrus where after the divine birth of the first three kings of the fifth-dynasty Khnum is said to put 'health' into each of their bodies.

It is the aspect of Khnum as 'potter' that is especially venerated in his main cult centre north of the first cataract at

Khnum moulding Ihy on potter's wheel. Mammisi of Nectanebo, Dendera, Dyn. XXX.

Esna. This temple which survives only in the form of one hypostyle hall surrounded by the modern conurbation is also sacred to Khnum in a manifestation strongly allied to the air-god SHU as war-champion of the sun-god. Important hymns provide a manifesto of the priests' belief in the supremacy of their god of the potter's wheel responsible for fashioning gods, mankind, cattle, birds and fish. The different speeches of the human race are also his gift. His consort at Esna (Neith having a totally independent role in this temple) is a minor lioness-goddess called Menhyt.

On other sites Khnum is found as the 'Ba' of GEB (at Herwer near modern el-Ashmunein in Middle Egypt) and the 'Ba' of OSIRIS at Shashotep (modern Shutb).

Khonsu

Moon-god especially prominent at Thebes.

The name Khonsu, 'wanderer', reflects the path of the moon across the sky. Most frequently shown human-headed, Khonsu as a sky-deity can have a hawk's head. The god's body is depicted in human form enveloped in a tightly fitting garment that does not permit his limbs to be differentiated. On his head is the crescent of the new moon in which the circle of the full moon rests. Around his neck is a loosely hanging necklace with the counterpoise on his back shoulders represented in profile. In his role of the divine child in a triad of deities he wears the 'lock of youth'. As a moon-god his sacred animal is the baboon, considered a lunar creature by the Egyptians.

The nature of Khonsu in the Pyramid Age is totally different from his character at Thebes in the New Kingdom. In the spell which aims to give the king power to hunt and eat certain deities, thereby absorbing their strength, Khonsu is a bloodthirsty god who helps to catch and slay these victims.

New Kingdom statue. Cairo Museum.

Khonsu as falcon-headed god. Papyrus of
Ramesses IV, Dyn. XX, British Museum.

At Thebes Khonsu is regarded as the
child of the union of AMUN and MUT,
appearing with them to complete the
'nuclear family' image in the temples on
the eastern and western banks of the Nile.
However, at Karnak he is given his own
precinct to the south of the first court of
the Great Temple of Amun. The pylon of
Khonsu's temple known as 'Benent' represented the starting point of the processional avenue south to Luxor temple. In
the New Year Festival at Thebes his statue
was transported on his sacred boat, with
a falcon's head at the prow and stern, to
join his parents for the celebration at the
temple of Luxor (see Amun section titled
'Amun em ipet resyt = Amun who is in
his southern sanctuary').

Khonsu has a number of forms at
Thebes found in inscriptions, for instance,
carved for Montuemhat the powerful
mayor of the city during the later part
of Dynasty XXV and the subsequent
traumatic Assyrian invasion. Montuemhat
boasts of the improvements carried out by
him at Karnak temple: he renovates the
sacred boats of:

Khonsu-pa-khered	Khonsu the child
The Three-Khonsu	Khonsu in Thebes, Nefer-hotep
	Khonsu Wen-Nekhu
	Khonsu Pa-ir-sekher ('he who governs' or possibly the 'provider')

Khonsu is also regarded as controlling destiny in his form Khonsu 'Heseb Ahau', 'Reckoner of the life-span'.

There are instances of Khonsu being involved with other deities outside of Thebes. At the Graeco-Roman temple of Kom-Ombo he is the child of the crocodile-god SOBEK and the goddess HATHOR. Also an obscure link exists with OSIRIS at Edfu temple where Khonsu is called the 'son of the leg', i.e. part of that god's body preserved there.

An interesting account of two cults of Khonsu at Thebes around the fourth century BC exists on a monument in the Louvre Museum, originally from Karnak (the Bentresh stela). The priests, authors of the stela – in order to give it more authority – perpetrate a pious forgery by ascribing the inscription to the reign of Ramesses II (Dynasty XIX) about 800 years earlier. The essentials of the document are as follows:

Ramesses on a tour of inspection in Syria falls in love with the daughter of the Prince of Bakhtan (= Bactria?).

The princess goes to Egypt as his Great Royal Wife Nefrura.

A request arrives from Bakhtan for help in curing Nefrura's younger sister, Bentresh.

The royal scribe Djeheutyemheb goes to Bakhtan and diagnoses that Bentresh is possessed by a hostile spirit. He informs the pharaoh.

In Egypt Ramesses consults Khonsu in Thebes Nefer-hotep.

Khonsu approaches the manifestation of himself specialising in healing and driving out demons, who is Khonsu pa-ir-sekher.

This Khonsu's statue is sent to Bakhtan, a journey of seventeen months.

To the amazement of the Bakhtan court, Khonsu cures Bentresh and the hostile spirit acknowledges his supremacy.

The Prince of Bakhtan deliberately detains the statue for three years and nine months until a dream of Khonsu as a golden falcon flying away causes a crisis of conscience.

Khonsu's statue returns to Thebes laden with treasure from the prince, which is handed over to Khonsu in Thebes Nefer-hotep – obviously the senior partner.

M

Maat

Goddess personifying all the elements of cosmic harmony as established by the creator-god at the beginning of time – including Truth, Justice and Moral Integrity.

Maat is shown as a lady wearing on her head an ostrich feather which can stand on its own instead of a full depiction of the goddess. The hieroglyphs of her name contain the symbol of a plinth representing the primeval mound upon which the creator-god emerged (see ATUM and KHEPRI).

The goddess's origins can be traced back at least as far as the Old Kingdom where she is already an integral part of the existence of RA and OSIRIS. Maat stands behind the sun-god or, in the Middle Kingdom, is described as being at the nostrils of Ra. It is not, however, until

Tomb of Sety I, Dyn. XIX, Florence Museum.

Dynasty XVIII that Maat is given the epithet 'daughter of Ra'. In the Pyramid Texts Osiris is called 'lord of Maat' and later frequently appears with her plinth symbol as the base of the Underworld throne on which he sits as judge of the dead. Similarly the deities of the ENNEAD in their role of tribunal judges are described as the 'council of Maat'.

Pharaohs see Maat as their authority to govern and stress how their reigns uphold the laws of the universe which she embodies. Amenhotep II (Dynasty XVIII) on his stela near the Sphinx at Giza claims that Maat was placed on his breast by AMUN himself. Numerous examples exist of the kings being called 'beloved of Maat', and they are depicted in temples proffering the effigy of the goddess in the palm of their hands before major deities. The ruler who forcibly emphasises his adherence to Maat on his monuments is Akhenaten (Dynasty XVIII) – the very pharaoh whom succeeding kings considered to have deviated immensely from her laws (see ATEN). Akhenaten 'lives by Maat' who can be seen next to him in a scene carved early in his reign in the tomb of his vizier Ramose at western Thebes.

The funerary papyri of the New Kingdom and later give many representations of Maat as the goddess crucial to the deceased reaching Paradise. In the Hall of the Two Truths (Maaty) the dead person's heart is placed in a pair of scales to balance against the image of the goddess Maat symbolising the truthful assertions of a blameless life given before the ASSESSOR GODS.

A hymn to Osiris praises that god for setting Maat throughout the 'Two Banks', i.e. Egypt. In this aspect Maat is justice

The Goddess Matt at the Weighing of the heart Papyrus of Anhai, Dyn. XX, British Museum.

administered by magistrates in the law courts. Possibly the title 'priest of Maat' relates to this part of an official's career as in the case of the 'royal secretary' Neseramun living under Osorkon II (Dynasty XXII). According to a classical source Egyptian law-officials wore an effigy of Maat when giving judgements – the British Museum possesses a small golden Maat on a gold chain that could be just such an ensign of authority.

A small ruined temple to Maat is in the southern sector of the precinct of MONTU at Karnak.

Mafdet

A panther-goddess whose ferocity prevails over snakes and scorpions.

The scratch of her claws is lethal to snakes, hence symbolically the barbs of the king's harpoon become Mafdet's claws for decapitating his enemies in the Underworld. When Mafdet is described as leaping at the necks of snakes, the imagery seems to suggest her form takes on that of a mongoose. In one epithet Mafdet wears braided locks, probably a reference to her displaying the jointed bodies of the scorpions which she has killed.

Mahaf

The ferryman who navigates the boat, provided by AKEN, along the winding waters of the Underworld. He also acts as a herald announcing the arrival of the king into the presence of the sun-god RA.

Mandulis   Sun-god of Lower Nubia.

Mandulis wears a crown of ram-horns surmounted by high plumes, sun disks and cobras. His name in Egyptian inscriptions is 'Merwel' but the Greek version, as found in the text known as the 'Vision of Mandulis' is used almost universally.

A chapel to Mandulis existed on the island of Philae off the eastern colonnade approaching the temple of ISIS, a goddess who seems to be regarded at least as his close companion. But it is in the temple of Kalabsha (now resited just above the High Dam at Aswan), architecturally impressive but sparsely decorated, that the best evidence of the cult of Mandulis can be found. Constructed on the site of an earlier New Kingdom sanctuary Kalabsha (ancient Talmis) took its present form during the reign of the Roman emperor Augustus. Mandulis, as represented on its walls, does not seem at all out of place among the other members of the Egyptian pantheon placed in his company. From the 'Vision of Mandulis' we find the unforced equation of this Nubian solar deity to Egyptian HORUS (compare section titled 'Horus as sun-god' under that god) and to Greek Apollo.

Mehen

Coiled serpent-god protecting the boat in which the sun-god RA travels through the Underworld. His coils envelope the kiosk on the deck of the boat. The earliest mention of the god occurs in a Coffin Text of the Middle Kingdom. Detailed representation of the 'coiled one' can be found in vignettes of funerary papyri and on the walls of tombs in the Valley of the Kings, especially Sety I (Dynasty XIX) and Ramesses VI (Dynasty XX).

Mehet-Weret

Cow-goddess of the sky.

Her name means 'great flood'. In the Pyramid Era Mehet-Weret represents the waterway in the heavens, sailed upon by both the sun-god and the king. She is also a manifestation of the primeval waters – consequently being sometimes considered as the 'mother of RA'. (Compare NEITH with whom Mehet-Weret identifies.) From vignettes in the New Kingdom funerary papyri the goddess is pictured as a cow lying on a reed mat with a sun disk between her horns.

Meretseger

Cobra-goddess dwelling on the mountain which overlooks the Valley of the Kings in western Thebes.

During the New Kingdom Meretseger had great authority over the whole Theban necropolis-area. She can appear as a coiled cobra or as a cobra with a female head and an arm projecting from the front of the snake's hood. An excellent carving of Meretseger is on the sarcophagus lid of Ramesses III (Dynasty XX) now in the Fitzwilliam Museum, Cambridge. Less frequently Meretseger is an equally poisonous, female-headed scorpion.

Her name translated is 'she who loves silence', aptly descriptive of a deity protecting secluded royal tombs.

The necropolis workers living at their village, known now as Deir el-Medina, or in huts in the Valley of the Kings have left stelae dedicated to Meretseger as a dangerous but merciful goddess. As a mark of respect they often use her dwelling place to describe her so she is addressed as the

Stela of Paneb, Dyn. XIX, British Museum.

'Peak of the West' ('Dehenet Imentet'). The inscriptions on these workmen's stelae reveal an admission of guilt normally absent from Egyptian monuments (compare PTAH section titled 'Ptah god of craftsmen'). Meretseger strikes down with blindness or venomous stings workers who commit crimes or make false oaths. (Working conditions may have contributed to the deterioration of eyesight and snakes and scorpions were always a hazard.) But Meretseger, who in her anger is a 'raging lion', will cure a person provided she is convinced of his repentance – as in the case of the draughtsman Neferabu (Dynasty XIX) who ends his stela with the words 'beware of the Peak of the West!'.

The demise of Meretseger is approximately coeval with the abandonment of Thebes as the royal burial-ground under Dynasty XXI.

Meskhenet

𓏞𓆄𓏏𓂝𓏤𓀀 Goddess presiding at childbirth.

In her form of a tile terminating in a female head (called in the Book of the Dead 'cubit-with-head') she represents one of the bricks upon which women in Ancient Egypt took a squatting position to give birth. Her presence near the scales in the Hall of the Two Truths, where the dead person's heart is examined and weighed to ascertain suitability for the Egyptian Paradise, is there to assist at a symbolic rebirth in the Afterlife. Her symbol of two loops at the top of a vertical stroke has been shown to be the bicornuate uterus of a heifer.

In addition to ensuring the safe delivery of a child from the womb, Meskhenet takes a decision on its destiny at the time of birth. In the Papyrus Westcar the goddess helps at the birth of the future first three kings of Dynasty V. On the arrival of Userkaf, Sahura and Neferirkara into the arms of ISIS, she approaches each child and assures it of kingship. Similarly she is the force of destiny that assigns to a scribe promotion among the administrators of Egypt.

A hymn in the temple of Esna refers to four 'Meskhenets' at the side of the creator-god KHNUM, whose purpose is to repel evil by their incantations.

Mihos   Lion-god, son of BASTET, called Miysis by the Greeks.

His local roots were at Leontopolis (modern Tell el-Muqdam) in nome 11 of Lower Egypt in the eastern Delta. Osorkon III (Dynasty XXII) erected a temple to him at Bubastis, the town sacred to the god's mother. Mihos's name is also found in amuletic papyri of the late New Kingdom.

Min

𓎟𓊵 Anthropomorphic god who is the supreme symbol of sexual procreativity.

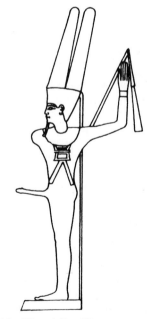

Temple of Karnak, Dyn. XII.

Also the protector-deity of the mining regions in the desert east of the Nile.

Min is shown standing with his legs closely linked and his arm raised from the crook of the elbow. The impression from two-dimensional representations of the god is that the arm is stretching out behind the body: this is the Egyptian artist avoiding any obscuring of the god's body, and statuary makes it quite clear that the god's arm is raised on his right side. The royal flagellum or whip rests semi-folded just above the god's upright fingertips on the raised arm – visually suggesting sexual penetration, although inscriptions (e.g. in Edfu temple) refer to the arm poised to destroy the god's enemies. Two high plumes rise from a low crown from which hangs a ribbon. The most distinctive feature of Min is his phallus projecting out at a right angle to his body, the symbol par excellence of the fertility god. On rare occasions Min can be depicted with a lion's head as in a chapel in the temple of KHONSU at Karnak.

The emblem of Min, comprising two horizontal tapering serrated cones emanating from a central disk, appears, prior to his anthropomorphic iconography, on predynastic monuments such as standards on boats painted on Naqada II pottery. Like the name of the god himself – Menu in Egyptian – no explanation for it has met with a consensus of agreement. Suggestions for the symbol range from a bolt of lightning or a circumcision instrument to a fossil belemnite. This emblem on a standard on a macehead from Hierakonpolis indicates that Min is counted among the allies of King Scorpion just prior to the lasting unification of Upper and Lower Egypt c.3000 BC.

Although there is a small element of doubt due to the monument dating from Dynasty V, the Palermo Stone, in mentioning the making of a statue of Min in Dynasty I, provides an image of the god as anthropomorphic and ithyphallic, indicating that this was his form from the beginning of Egypt's dynastic history. Sizeable fragments of three limestone colossal statues of Min, discovered at Qift and now in the Ashmolean Museum, could prove the point if they date to this archaic period. It is definitely a 'primitive' Min represented by these statues in the cylindrical body and the style of the wide beard. Incisings on the statues of elephants and sawfish are of a genre found on small ivories and cylinder seals of the late Predynastic Era and even support the archaeologically attested contact with civilisations flourishing in southern Iraq and Iran. But some scholars have doubted that the sculptures predate the Old Kingdom.

1 *Min and* HORUS

By the Middle Kingdom there was a deity Min-Horus combining attributes of the two gods. In the beginning it seems that the link between the gods stemmed from their associations with foreign lands – Horus as the god of the eastern Delta route into Palestine and Min as god of the eastern desert. In an inscription in the Wadi Hammamat the pharaoh Mentuhotep IV (Dynasty XI) regards his mining expedition as being under the protection of his 'father' Min. He sets the stela where Min resides, in a mountain which he calls 'the godly nest of Horus'. Also in the adventures of Sinuhe (set in early Dynasty XII) we meet with 'Min-Horus of the Hillcountries'. In the Graeco-Roman era the ensign of the two falcons indicating the district incorporating the god's temple at Koptos was interpreted as Min-Horus. The Greek writer Plutarch (AD 40–120) states that Horus is called Min, a name which he interprets as 'that which is seen' – an explanation possibly going back to an original Egyptian pun involving the name of Min and the verb to 'see' used in the past tense. The goddess ISIS is drawn into this amalgamation becoming the 'mother of Min'. In a charm against a fatal snake bite, Min is described as the 'son of the White Sow of Heliopolis' which is a periphrasis for Isis. At other times, however, Isis plays the role of Min's consort with Horus the child completing the divine family.

2 Sacred sites

While figuring as a universal deity in many temple reliefs all over Egypt, Min is thought to reside at two sites in particular.

QIFT (ANCIENT EGYPTIAN = 'GEBTU', GREEK = 'KOPTOS')

South of modern Qena and north of Luxor, this town lies at the western end of the Wadi Hammamat and was the starting-point for gold and stone mining expeditions into the eastern desert. Although sculptured reliefs of the Middle Kingdom date and New Kingdom temple foundation deposits have been discovered here, none of the extant temple ruins predate the Graeco-Roman period.

AKHMIM (ANCIENT EGYPTIAN = 'IPU' OR 'KHENT-MIN', GREEK = 'KHEMMIS' OR 'PANOPOLIS')

This site, north of Qena, has in its vicinity a rock-cut chapel decorated for the pharaoh Ay (Dynasty XVIII) and Queen Teye by the High Priest of Min, Nakht-Min (a name meaning 'Min is mighty'). The temple ruins to the west of the town are from the Graeco-Roman period. The Greek equation of Min with the god Pan led to the later name of the site as 'Panopolis'.

3 Min in the Pyramid Age

The god is likely to be the deity described in the Pyramid spells as 'he whose arm is raised in the east'. In a princess's mastaba tomb at Giza (Dynasty V) there is a reference to a feast celebrating the god – the 'procession of Min' – so his cult is obviously well established in terms of an organised priesthood. Relating to the god's temple at Qift are royal decrees from the end of the Old Kingdom exempting certain chapels (e.g. that built in the name of Queen Iput, mother of King Pepi I, Dynasty VI) from taxation.

4 Min in the Middle Kingdom

Some of the finest representations of the god in Egyptian art date to this era, such as the limestone relief in the Petrie Museum at University College London from Qift showing Senwosret I (Dynasty XII) performing part of his jubilee celebrations before Min. In the private Coffin Texts, the sexual prowess of the god is seen as a desirable quality to possess in the Afterlife, hence the deceased describes himself as the 'woman-hunting' Min. Some interesting epithets of Min occur in the hymn of Sobek-Iry (Dynasty XII) in the Louvre Museum. The god 'high of plumes' is the 'lord of awe' who humbles the proud. He possesses all the valued incense originating from equatorial Africa by his domination of Nubia – compare the Wadi Hammamat inscription of King Mentuhotep IV (Dynasty XI) which calls him 'ruler of the Iuntiu', i.e. Nubian bowmen.

5 The New Kingdom festivals of Min

The pharaoh, in the celebratory rituals surrounding his coronation, participated in a major procession and feast in honour of Min whose powers of fertility and regeneration could be seen as symbolising the vigorous renewal of sovereignty. At Thebes this festival has been carved on the second pylon of the Ramesseum, the mortuary temple of Ramesses II (Dynasty XIX) but a better preserved representation is found in the second court of the temple at Medinet Habu, built by Ramesses III (Dynasty XX):

A splendid pageant leaves the royal palace with Ramesses III carried on a palanquin. The king burns incense and pours sacred water before the statue of the god. In the procession that follows, the statue is carried on poles on the shoulders of priests practically hidden by a vast ceremonial cloth, Two priests also carry a cover to hide the god's statue from profane eyes when the procession reaches the point on its journey at which outsiders are allowed to view the pomp. The hieroglyphs contain hymns in honour of Min chanted by the chief lector priest. The queen and the 'White Bull', probably Min's sacred creature, take part in the ceremony at which statues of the ancestors of Ramesses III are carried by priests, emphasising the continuity of kingship and the coronation of the current pharaoh. Four sparrows are set free into the sky to carry news of the prospering sovereign and Min's festival to the points of the compass. Min's role as an ancient agricultural deity ensuring the fecundity of the crops is brought to the fore by the ritual of Ramesses cutting a sheath of emmer wheat. From a much later date in the Ptolemaic temple of Edfu the idea of Min as the bringer of prolific harvests lies behind the ritual of 'driving the calves' over the threshing-floor.

6 *Min's sacred lettuce*

Bouquets of flowers were offered to Min, as to other deities, with the idea of stimulating fruitfulness in the Nile Valley, e.g. the pharaoh Sety I (Dynasty XIX) offering flowers to a deity who is a combined form of Min and the ithyphallic form of AMUN, called Min-Amun-Kamutef. But one plant becomes the special emblem of Min, appearing on stands or chests near him, or carried by priests in his festivals, namely the long lettuce (lactuca sativa). This plant was supposed to assist the god – the 'great of love' as he is called in a text from Edfu temple – perform the sexual act untiringly. The symbolism stems perhaps not so much from the vaguely phallic shape of the lettuce as its milk-sap which could suggest the god's semen. Min is shown with the lettuce as early as Dynasty VI on the tax-immunity decrees from Qift. Over 2,000 years later the Roman Emperor Augustus is shown offering lettuces to the god in the temple of Kalabsha.

Mnevis

Sacred bull of the sun-god of Heliopolis.

Mnevis or 'Mer-wer' in Egyptian is an originally autonomous bull-god who becomes subordinated to the cult of RA-ATUM. The bull's hide is totally black and he wears the sun disk and Uraeus (see WADJET) between his horns. At Heliopolis the cow-goddess HESAT plays the role of the mother of Mnevis.

The sacred bull is the earthly representative of the sun-god, acting as a herald ('wehemu') for the divine communications to the priests of Heliopolis. Mnevis is also the intermediary for the interpretation of oracles, a phenomenon of Egyptian religion particularly in the later dynasties. The bull of the Heliopolitan solar theology is one of the few state-recognised survivors among the gods during the reign of Akhenaten (Dynasty XVIII). That pharaoh, as explicitly stated on his Boundary stelae, prepared a burial place, as yet undiscovered, for the sacred bull in the eastern cliffs behind his new capital at Akhetaten (see ATEN).

The temple of Heliopolis has all but disappeared but some burials of the Mnevis-bull under the Ramesside kings have been discovered to its north-east at Arab el-Tawil.

Although the names Mnevis-OSIRIS and Mnevis-WENEN-NOFER (see Osiris, section titled 'Osiris in the Middle and New Kingdoms') are attested, there is no close link between the bull of the solar cult of Heliopolis and the god of the Underworld. According to the Greek writer Plutarch, Mnevis was runner-up to APIS in being awarded official honours. While not stated, this must be on account of the importance of Memphis, residence of the Apis, as capital of Egypt.

Montu

Falcon-headed war-god of the Theban district.

Relief of Nebhepetra Montuhotep, Dyn. XI.

Montu enters the pantheon under the expansionist rulers of Thebes *c.*2000 BC. A number of the kings of Dynasty XI display the local allegiance to this militaristic deity by bearing the name Montuhotep ('Montu is content'). From now on Montu becomes the embodiment of the conquering vitality of the pharaoh. The quasi-historical narrative of the fugitive court official, Sinuhe, set in Dynasty XII describes how, after slaying the champion of a Syrian tribe, he raises his war cry and gives praise to Montu. At the beginning of Dynasty XVIII a ceremonial axe from the burial equipment of Queen Iahhotep represents Montu as a fierce, winged and crested griffin, an iconography clearly influenced by the same Syrian origin as that which inspired Minoan artists at Knossos. Over the griffin the pharaoh Iahmose 'beloved of Montu' slays a foreigner.

Montu's consorts are a Theban goddess Tjenenyet and the solar goddess Raettawy. In the later period Montu is associated with a sacred bull called Buchis whose distinguishing features are a white hide and black face. On the edge of the desert at Armant is the burial place of the bulls (known as the Bucheum) and of the cows who were the 'mothers of Buchis'. On present archaeological evidence sacred bulls were buried from the reign of Nectanebo II (Dynasty XXX) to the time of the Roman emperor Diocletian.

The cult centres of Montu in the Theban nome, from north to south, are at:

1 Medamud (ancient Medu) – north-east of modern Luxor – where a sanctuary founded by Senwosret III (Dynasty XII) was expanded during the New Kingdom and Graeco-Roman period.
2 Karnak, where a precinct for Montu 'lord of Thebes' lies north of the main temple of AMUN.

3 Armant (Hermonthis), originally the major sanctuary from the early Middle Kingdom to the Graeco-Roman era. Luckily the ruins were drawn by early nineteenth-century visitors to Egypt before the temple was used as a quarry for stone for a sugar factory.

4 Tod, where during the Middle Kingdom the temple of Montu 'lord of Djerit' received from Amenemhat II (Dynasty XII) four 'treasure chests' of diplomatic gifts from Syria, the Aegean and Mesopotamia, now displayed in the museums of Cairo and Paris. The scant ruins are of Graeco-Roman date.

Mut

Pre-eminent goddess of Thebes.

Mut's name is the same root as the Egyptian word for 'mother' and this reveals part of her character in that, like HATHOR or ISIS, she is one of the pharaoh's symbolic mothers.

Her iconography is predominantly anthropomorphic: a slim lady in a linen dress, often brightly coloured blue or red in a pattern suggesting feathers, wearing a head-dress in the shape of a vulture surmounted by the combined crowns of Upper and Lower Egypt. She holds the lily sceptre of the south.

Mut can also appear as a lioness-headed goddess. The lion is the main manifestation of Mut, more important than the vulture symbolised on her crown or in the hieroglyph that writes her name. Developing from the lion imagery is the association of Mut with the cat, i.e. a vaguely leonine creature that can be approached and stroked. Her name can be written with the sacred cat and naturally she coalesces with the northern cat-goddess to become Mut-BASTET. In religious texts Mut is

Papyrus of Ramesses IV, Dyn. XX, British Museum.

described as being present in Heliopolis with RA to split the 'ished' tree. Dedications to the goddess in the form of cat statuettes far outweigh those of Mut as the vulture.

At Thebes she supplants AMAUNET, the original consort of AMUN, to become the god's chief wife. She appears on all the major temple walls enthroned beside Amun or as 'mistress of the nine bows' (= symbolic enemies of Egypt), standing by him as he proffers a pharaoh the scimitar of war. She becomes adopted as the mother of KHONSU to complete the Theban sacred triad.

Her temple precinct was connected to Amun's sanctuary by a processional road through the series of pylons leading off to the south. The goddess's sanctuary was called 'Isheru', the hieroglyphs for which contain, not fortuitously, the symbol of a recumbent lion. In addition to the main temple of the goddess where she was worshipped with Amun-Kamutef, the sacred lake and subsidiary temples from the Dynasty XVIII survive but the whole precinct is greatly ruined. It was in this enclosure that Amenhotep III set up the numerous statues of Mut's northern counterpart, the lioness-goddess SAKHMET.

N

Nebethetepet

⟨hieroglyphs⟩ A goddess of Heliopolis whose name 'mistress of the offering' conceals a more intellectual concept. Like IUSAAS she is a feminine counterpart to the male creative principle embodied in the sun-god ATUM. She is therefore transformed from merely a manifestation of HATHOR at Heliopolis into an integral element of the creator-god, namely the hand with which he grips his phallus prior to bringing the Egyptian cosmos into being.

Nefertum

⟨hieroglyphs⟩ God of the primeval lotus blossom.

The name of Nefertum has the notion of 'perfection'. He is the blue lotus out of which, according to one myth, the sun rises. In a description in the Pyramid Texts Nefertum is the lotus blossom in front of the nose of RA – the textual equivalent of courtiers holding the plant in their hand and breathing in the scent of the lotus. In art Nefertum is normally anthropomorphic wearing a head-dress in the shape of the lotus plant, embellished with two plumes and two necklace-counterpoises (Hathoric symbols of fertility).

Sometimes the god is portrayed lionheaded by association with leonine mother goddesses: at Memphis Nefertum is the son of the lioness-goddess SAKHMET and, although it is never explicitly stated, he becomes by implication the child of the union of the goddess and PTAH. At Buto in the Delta Nefertum is the original son of WADJET, a cobra-goddess who can

Tomb of Horemheb, Dyn. XVIII.

take leonine form. Similarly the feline goddess BASTET has a claim to being the god's mother. As a child, he can be depicted seated on a lotus blossom, reminiscent of the young sun-god.

Nehebu-Kau

⟨hieroglyphs⟩ A snake-god, 'He who harnesses the spirits', whose invincibility is a source of protection both in Egypt and in the Underworld.

In the Pyramid Texts Nehebu-Kau is called 'son of Selkis (see SERKET)', the scorpion-goddess, emphasising his role in later spells of restoring the health of victims of venomous bites. Protective of royalty, Nehebu-Kau receives the monarch in the Afterlife and provides a meal. A Middle Kingdom spell identifies the deceased with this snake-god who is not subject to any magic, nor vulnerable to fire and water. One source of his power lies in the magical force of the number 'seven' in the 'seven' cobras which he swallowed. In a spell concerning the welfare of his heart in the Afterlife, the deceased requests other deities to give him a good recommendation to Nehebu-Kau. There is a hint in the Old Kingdom that Nehebu-Kau's power needs to be controlled by the sun-god ATUM pressing a fingernail on the snake's spine.

Another tradition makes Nehebu-Kau the son of the earth-god GEB and the harvest-goddess RENENUTET. Consequently his chthonic and fecund power provides other deities with their vital strength.

Neith

Creator-goddess of Sais.

The goddess's name has been derived from the word meaning 'that which is' which, while not totally convincing, suits her procreative aspect and seems preferable to the etymology which would give it the sense 'the terrifying'. The goddess does have an undeniably bellicose side to her nature but it has been greatly overstated.

Her most ancient symbol is the shield with crossed arrows, which occurs in the Early Dynastic Period, e.g. engraved and inlaid in blue paste on a gold amulet in the shape of a cockroach from a first-dynasty tomb at Naga ed-Deir. This warlike emblem is reflected in her titles 'mistress of the bow ... ruler of arrows'. The hieroglyph writing her name comprises two bows bound in a package. The warrior imagery behind these symbols led to the Greek identification of Neith with Athene.

Iconographically the goddess is represented as a lady wearing the red crown of Lower Egypt. The earliest occurrence of Neith in the northern crown comes from the sun temple of King Userkaf (Dynasty V) at Abu Ghurob. Historically it was the Delta which in 3000 BC succumbed to the onslaught of the ruler of the south, becoming incorporated with Upper Egypt

Neith, on right, opposite Serket, at theogamy of Amun and Queen Mutemwiya. Temple of Amenhotep III, Luxor, Dyn. XVIII.

into one unified state. The northern goddess Neith, whose home town was Sais (modern Sa el-Hagar) in the western Delta, was one of the most prominent deities of the conquered kingdom. It seems a plausible suggestion therefore that an early ruler of Dynasty I, Hor-Aha, founded a temple to Neith at Sais, possessing the political foresight to placate the defeated northerners by a gesture of goodwill towards their goddess. In addition the red crown of Sais and the town's palace-emblem of the 'bee' both became symbols of immense importance to the monarchy of dynastic Egypt. By the Old Kingdom at the latest Neith was an integral element of the state pantheon with a sanctuary at Memphis. There, by analogy with the host-deity PTAH 'south of his wall', she was termed as being 'north of her wall'.

In the Roman period inscriptions were carved on the columns of the temple of Esna in Upper Egypt attempting to give

Neith, a goddess of impeccable northern credentials, southern origins. It is important, however, because it stresses the dominant feature of Neith which is her role as creator. According to the Esna cosmology the goddess emerged from the primeval waters to create the world. She then follows the flow of the Nile northward to found Sais in company with the subsequently venerated lates-fish. There are much earlier references to Neith's association with the primordial floodwaters and to her as the demiurge: Amenhotep II (Dynasty XVIII) in one inscription is the pharaoh 'whose being Neith moulded'; the papyrus (Dynasty XX), giving the account of the struggle between HORUS and SETH, mentions Neith 'who illuminated the first face' and in the sixth century BC the goddess is said to have invented birth.

This abovementioned papyrus relates a brief passage that brings Neith into the struggle over the throne of Egypt as a wise counsellor:

> *Banebdjedet* urges *Ra* to seek the advice of Neith the Great to solve the eighty-year dispute. Neith's advice, which is the course eventually but not immediately adopted, is to award the throne to Horus (also to compensate Seth by giving him the goddesses *Astarte* and *Anat* as his wives). Aggressively Neith threatens in her letter to the court that if Horus does not win she will grow angry and the sky will crash to the earth.

By the Pyramid Era Neith was regarded as the consort of Seth and the mother of SOBEK, in this role aptly described as 'nurse of crocodiles'. This concept of Neith as divine mother extends to other deities, such as ISIS and even to the sun-god Ra himself. In this aspect she necessarily transforms into a sky-goddess with the title of the Great Cow. In complete contradiction to her maternal

relationship to Ra, late inscriptions in the Esna temple call the goddess mother of the serpent APOPHIS, arch-enemy of the sun-god, ascribing his birth to the saliva spat out by Neith into the primeval water.

Nekhbet

 Vulture-goddess of Nekheb (el-Kab), upholding the monarch's sway in Upper Egypt.

Iconographically the goddess is often shown with wings spread, grasping the symbols of 'eternity' in her claws. She also appears as a vulture at rest in statuary or as an element in one of the king's titles (see PHARAOH). With one wing outstretched before her she is a protective symbol carved above royal or ritual scenes.

Nekhbet was favoured by the rulers of South Egypt whose capital was nearby on the opposite bank of the Nile to el-Kab at Nekhen (Hierakonpolis, modern Kom el-Ahmar). This adoption led to her being recognised as one of the 'two Mighty Ones' – the tutelary goddesses of the kingdoms united into one state c.3000 BC.

Important epithets for the understanding of the nature of Nekhbet ('she of Nekheb') can be gleaned from the Pyramid Texts. The king's mother is named as the 'Great White Cow who dwells in Nekheb' and possesses hanging breasts. Here the allusion is to Nekhbet as a mother-goddess for which the cow-imagery is traditional in Egyptian thought (compare HATHOR and HESAT). In

Pectoral from Tomb of Tutankhamun, Dyn. XVIII, Cairo Museum.

royal birth-scenes Nekhbet takes the role of protective nurse to the monarch (e.g. in the mortuary temple of Sahura at Abusir). This led to a later identification with the Greek goddess of childbirth Eileithyia.

Also in the Pyramid Texts she is called 'White Crown', symbolic headdress of the king as ruler of Upper Egypt, and 'mistress of the Per-wer', i.e. the shrine par excellence of the southern kingdom. In this respect she is the counterpart to WADJET of the north whom she occasionally accompanies on the front of the royal headdress. She can even take the serpent-form of the northern goddess – normally to form an heraldic device around the sun disk or royal name.

Her cult-sanctuary at el-Kab is impressive in size but devastated. The presence of a Middle Kingdom shrine is attested as are constructions from Dynasty XVIII but the present ruins date to the last native rulers of Egypt (Dynasties XXIX–XXX).

Neper

 God of grain.

In a procession of deities carved in the reign of Sahura (Dynasty V) Neper's body is dotted to represent grains of corn. The hieroglyphs that write his name similarly include the symbols of grain.

He represents the prosperity of the barley and emmer wheat crops which the Egyptians cultivated. The pharaoh Amenemhat I (Dynasty XII) is described as responsible for the ripening of the grain and called 'beloved of Neper'. Being dependent, however, on the silt brought by the Nile flood he is subordinated to HAPY who is proclaimed 'lord of Neper'.

His association with agriculture is as early as, if not predating, that aspect of OSIRIS. He also resembles that god inasmuch as the Coffin Texts characterise Neper as a god 'living after he has died'. Accordingly the latter has no problem assimilating Neper into his own nature (see also RENENUTET).

Nephthys

Funerary goddess with a subordinate role in the OSIRIS myth.

Her own personality is lost behind the bland meaning of her name 'neb-hut' – 'lady of the mansion', the hieroglyphs for which she wears as a symbol on her head. Nephthys is the daughter of GEB and NUT, and nominally partners SETH to balance the couple ISIS and Osiris. According to a late tradition Nephthys had a liaison with Osiris, the result of the union being the jackal-god ANUBIS.

She occurs in the Old Kingdom alongside Isis as a protectress of the monarch: she escorts him into the darkness of the Underworld and weeps violently for him as her brother Osiris. Vague identifications occur indicating that the goddess's original role might well have been of greater prominence than the shadowy character of the Osirian legend. Nephthys

Tomb of Nefertari, Dyn. XIX.

suckles the king who is described as her menstrual blood. Her funerary association is evident when the king is urged to escape from the tresses of Nephthys which symbolise the mummy wrappings, necessary but feared as an impediment. The goddess can take the form of a kite guarding the funerary bed of Osiris – an inscription from the reign of Thutmose III (Dynasty XVIII) calls her 'Nephthys of the bed of life'. She is in the company of the tutelary goddesses into whose care the mummified organs in their respective jars are placed (see SONS OF HORUS).

Nome gods Pharaonic Egypt was divided into forty-two administrative districts or nomes. Each nome had principal deities but on temple walls all the nomes are personified as androgynous figures bearing the ensigns of their districts on their heads.

Ensign	No.	Location	Title	Important Deities
The Nome gods of Lower (North) Egypt				
	1	Memphis area	White Wall	PTAH, SOKAR, APIS
	2	South-west Delta apex	Foreleg	HORUS of Letopolis, KHERTY
	3	North-west Delta flanking Libyan Desert	West	HATHOR
	4	South-west Delta	Southern Shield	NEITH
	5	Sais area to coast	Northern Shield	Neith
	6	Mid-Delta to coast	Mountain Bull	RA

(continued)

Continued

Ensign	No.	Location	Title	Important Deities
	7	North-west Delta along Rosetta branch of Nile	Western Harpoon	HA
	8	East Delta along Wadi Tummilat to Bitter Lakes	Eastern Harpoon	ATUM of Tell el-Maskhuta
	9	Mid-Delta to Busiris	Andjety	OSIRIS of Djedu ANDJETY
	10	South-east Delta around Athribis	Black Ox	Horus
	11	Mid-east Delta	Ox-count	SHU, TEFNUT and MIHOS of Leontopolis
	12	North-east Delta from Sebennytos to coast	Calf and Cow	ONURIS
	13	South-east Delta apex	Prospering Sceptre	Atum, IUSAAS and MNEVIS of Heliopolis
	14	East Frontier coastal Delta to Pelusium beyond modern Port Said	Foremost of the East	SETH
	15	North-east Delta along Damietta branch of Nile	Ibis	THOTH of northern Hermopolis

Continued

Ensign	No.	Location	Title	Important Deities
	16	North-east Delta from Mendes to coast	Fish	BANEBDJEDET HATMEHYT
	17	North-east Delta coast to West of Damietta branch of Nile	Behdet	Horus of Behdet
	18	North-east Delta around Bubastis	Prince of the South	BASTET
	19	North-east Delta incorporating Tanis	Prince of the North	WADJET of Nabesha
	20	North-east Delta above Wadi Tummilat	Plumed Falcon of Sopedu	SOPEDU

The Nome gods of Upper (South) Egypt

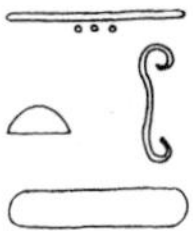	1	First cataract of the Nile to Gebel el-Silsila	Ta-Sety	ISIS at Philae KHNUM, SATIS and ANUKIS of Elephantine, Haroeris (see Horus, section titled 'The struggle for the throne of Egypt') and SOBEK of Kom-Ombo
	2	Edfu area	Throne of Horus	Horus of Mesen
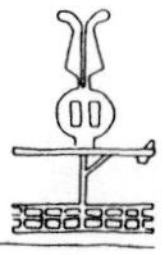	3	Hierakonoplis to north of Esna	Shrine	Horus of Nekhen NEKHBET of El-Kab Khnum, Menhyt (see Khnum), Neith of Esna

(*continued*)

Continued

Ensign	No.	Location	Title	Important Deities
	4	Armant and the Theban area	Sceptre	MONTU, AMUN, MUT, KHONSU, Sobek of Sumenu
	5	Area around Koptos	Two Falcons	MIN of Koptos, Seth of Nubet
	6	Most of the east to west bend of the Nile	Crocodile	Hathor
	7	The Nile's return to its south-north direction around Nag Hammadi	Sistrum	BAT
	8	Area around Abydos	Great Land	Khentamentiu (see Osiris), Osiris, Onuris
	9	Area around Akhmim	Min	Min
	10	North of Qaw el-Kebir	Cobra	Seth of Tjebu, Mihos
	11	Smallest Nome in Egypt on west Bank of Nile around Deir Rifa	Seth	Seth
	12	East Bank of Nile around Deir el-Gebrawi opposite Asyut	Viper Mount	ANTI
	13	West Bank of Nile around Asyut	Upper Sycamore and Viper	WEPWAWET, ANUBIS

Continued

Ensign	No.	Location	Title	Important Deities
	14	Vicinity of Meir and el-Qusiya (Cusae)	Lower Sycamore and Viper	A god taming two serpentine-necked quadrupeds, Hathor
	15	Area around el-Ashmunein and Antinoopolis, incorporating el-Amarna	Hare	Thoth of Hermopolis OGDOAD, ATEN
	16	From Beni Hasan to north of el-Minya	Oryx	PAKHET
	17	Vicinity of Samalut	Jackal	Anubis
	18	East Bank of Nile including el-Hiba to opposite el-Lahun	Anti	Anti
	19	West Bank of Nile from el-Bahnasa (Oxyrhynchus) to Biba	Two Sceptres	Seth, Mormyrus fish
	20	West Bank of Nile around Beni Suef	Southern Sycamore	HERYSHAF
	21	West Bank of Nile around el-Wasta and Meidum	Northern Sycamore	Khnum, God-king Sneferu (Dynasty IV)
	22	Northernmost Nome of Upper Egypt stretching along east Desert from Atfih towards Memphis	Knife	Hathor

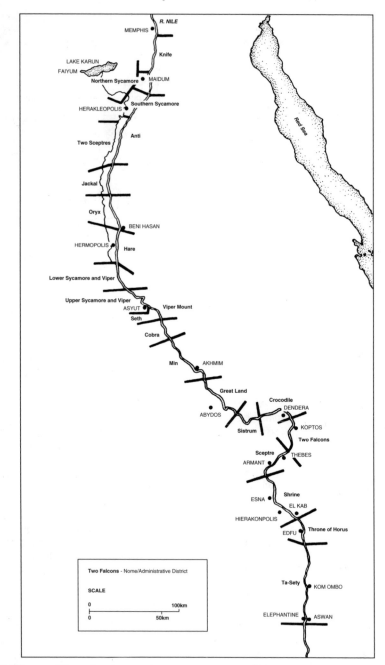

The Nomes of Upper Egypt.

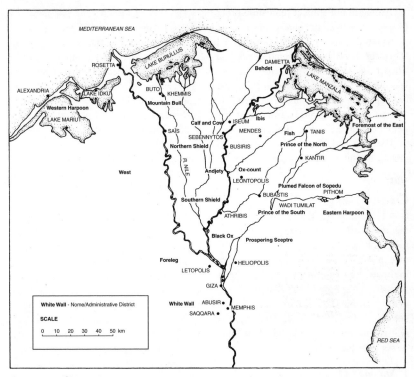

The Nomes of Lower Egypt.

Nun

⭕⭕⭕ God personifying the primeval waters out of which emerged the creator-god.

Nun is called 'father of the gods' but this emphasises only his unrivalled antiquity as an element of the Egyptian cosmos – in terms of importance he is superseded by the creator sun-god (see ATUM). Nun has a continual existence unaffected by mythology or events and plays no part in religious rituals, possessing no temples or priesthood. When represented on tomb walls or in religious papyri, Nun's arms thrust the sun at the twelfth hour of the night into the horizon to begin its journey in the day-boat (see KHEPRI and RA).

The sacred lakes in temple enclosures (e.g. at Karnak or Dendera) symbolised the primordial waters, enhancing their practical function for priestly ablutions. At Heliopolis when the Sudanese ruler Piye (Dynasty XXV) visited the temple he claimed that like the sun-god Ra he washed his face in the 'river of Nun'.

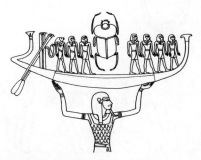

Nun raising solar boat. Papyrus of Anhai, Dyn. XX, British Museum.

Although not subject to cosmic order (MAAT), the watery chaos of Nun is considered beneficial. Amenhotep III (Dynasty XVIII) constructed a pool at Thebes in which the god Nun (i.e. the lake-water) delighted. Sometimes the god can represent the Nile, as in the hymn to KHNUM where it is said that mankind and gods feast on the fishes of Nun.

For Nun and Naunet, his consort, as creator divinities see OGDOAD.

Nut

⊙⌒

▭   The sky-goddess. Nut is one of the personifications of the cosmic elements evolved by the priests of Heliopolis to explain the physical universe. She is the daughter of SHU the air-god and TEFNUT. The Egyptians visualised her mainly as human in form but she can appear as the Sky Cow. In an early text Nut is imagined as a bee wielding great power over the gods.

1 *Nut and* GEB

The sky-goddess united with her brother the earth-god and as a result gave birth to the gods and goddesses really belonging to the Osirian cycle of myth, incorporated into the Heliopolitan pantheon in recognition of the growing popularity of that cult. These children of Nut are OSIRIS, ISIS, SETH and NEPHTHYS. In Egyptian iconography the sexual union between Nut and Geb is occasionally symbolised by the phallus of the prone earth-god reaching towards the goddess's body. However, Nut is more frequently depicted arching her body over the god, separated from him by the air-god Shu – either standing between the couple supporting the body of the goddess on his upraised hands, or sailing between them in a boat. Although in Egyptian art it appears as if Nut is stretching her body with her arms and legs tightly together, the actual concept of the sky-goddess is that her fingers and her toes touch the four cardinal points. This visualisation of Nut and Geb as apart is the probable source of the Greek interpretation of the myth of the difficult birth of the children of the sky-goddess, as related by Plutarch (AD 40–120). Fearing an usurpation of his own power the sun-god ('Helios') utters a curse on the pregnant sky-goddess ('Rhea') to prevent her giving birth on any day of the then 360-day year. Only by the moon-god's ('Hermes') winning sufficient light for five extra days (the epagomenal days of the Egyptian calender considered as gods' birthdays) was Nut able to go into labour and produce her children (with the addition in this version of the god HORUS, called 'Apollo').

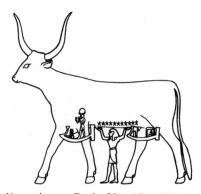

Nut as sky-cow. Tomb of Sety I, Dyn. XIX.

Greenfield Papyrus, Dyn. XXI, British Museum.

Probably from the Egyptian idea that Nut swallowed the solar god and his entourage to give birth to them again at dawn, the notion arose that the earth-god Geb became angry with the sky-goddess for eating her 'children'. In the cenotaph of Sety I at Abydos Nut's swallowing of celestial deities is likened to a sow devouring her piglets.

2 *Nut and the sun-god*

Naturally there is a close relationship between the sky-goddess and the sun, the most important feature of the sky. For example, Nut is the 'lady of Heliopolis' (centre of sun worship) dwelling there in the 'lower mansion'. Although the priests interpreted the goddess as the creator sun-god's grandchild it is clear that the underlying concept of Nut is that of the 'great who gives birth to the gods'.

She keeps the forces of chaos from breaking through the sky and engulfing the world – her body is in fact the firmament dividing the cosmos, created by the sun-god and governed according to his vision of order (personified as MAAT), from the amorphous, primeval matter merging with which would be tantamount to non-existence. The thunder which must have seemed ominous as it echoed around the sky was euphemistically explained away as the laughter of Nut.

The Egyptians painted the royal tombs at Thebes with two discrepant myths about the disappearance of the sun at night. The tomb walls in the Valley of the Kings show the sun's journey through the Underworld. The ceilings, imitating the sky, reflect the belief that the sun-god was swallowed by Nut. A detailed representation can be found on the ceiling of the sarcophagus chamber of Ramesses VI (Dynasty XX). Nut is painted twice on a colossal scale, depicting the day and the night sky. The sun-god sails in his barge along the elongated body of Nut until evening, when the disk of the sun approaches the mouth of the sky-goddess to be swallowed. The sun travels with the stars through the hours of night safely inside the goddess's body. At dawn, the red glow of which was called the 'daughter of Nut', the disk of the sun-god is seen emerging from the vulva of the sky-goddess. How Nut maintains the equilibrium of the sun's course is not investigated by the Egyptians but attributed to inexplicable factors summed up by her epithet 'shetayit' or 'mysterious one'.

3 *Nut as a funerary deity*

In the Pyramid Texts the goddess is said to enfold the king in her 'soul' or to

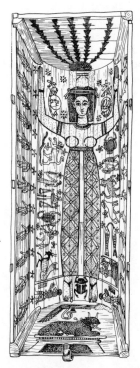

Coffin of Soter, second century AD, British Museum.

uncover her arms for the monarch. These are euphemisms for the pharaoh being placed in his coffin and buried. Death as termination of life is denied and the king is with Nut living in the sky. Elsewhere in the texts this sentiment is more fully expressed: the king goes to Nut in her name of 'sarcophagus' embraces her in her name of 'coffin' and rests in her name of 'tomb'. Royal stone sarcophagi some-times show Nut carved in high relief with stars, in whose number is the soul of the king, at her head (e.g. the interior of the anthropoid lid on the sarcophagus used for the burial of King Psusennes (Dynasty XXI) at Tanis). This notion extends to the courtiers, as we can see from the image of Nut decorating the interior of mummy – cases symbolising the deceased protected by and linked with the sky-goddess. Apposite to this aspect of Nut is a poignant passage in the Middle Kingdom narrative of the fortunes of Sinuhe, a palace official who spent his life in self-imposed exile in the states of the Levant: the pharaoh invites him by letter to return to Egypt for his old age and so that he can receive proper burial rites – including lying in his coffin in a mummy-case of gold and lapis lazuli, with Nut the 'mistress of all' above him for eternity. Nut as a deco-ration on coffins survives into the Roman period. The coffin of the archon Soter (second century AD) from Thebes has a painting of Nut in a red linen dress on which is a pattern representing the stars: the only innovations to traditional iconog-raphy are in Nut's Hellenistic hairstyle, jewellery and dress, and in the addition of the signs of the classical zodiac down either side of the goddess's body.

In vignettes in the Book of the Dead and Theban tomb paintings, the sky-goddess is shown in the Underworld as a lady rising from the trunk of the sycamore tree. In this aspect she is the magical force behind the spell enabling the deceased to breathe air and never be without water in the Afterlife. Nut pours water and proffers loaves indicating that there will always be an abundance of life-sustaining produce in the Underworld.

O

Ogdoad   Eight deities representing the primeval chaos before the emergence of the sun-god.

The four gods are in the form of frog-headed beings and the four goddesses are snake-headed. When the sun-god is depicted coming into existence these divinities can appear as baboons greeting the rising sun. The Ogdoad are:

God	Goddess	Nature
NUN	Naunet	Primordial abyss
HEH	Hauhet	Infinity
Kek	Kauket	Darkness
AMUN	AMAUNET	Hidden power

The concept of these deities in pairs reveals the Egyptian view of the creative principle as parthenogenetic. The Ogdoad are envisualised as entities of the cosmic matter in primeval time sufficiently forceful to produce out of themselves the mound upon which lay the egg containing the young sun-god. The catalyst for this event is the permeating creative power of the serpent Kem-Atef (see Amun in section titled 'Amun as creator').

Their main cult centre, where the sun-god came into being on the 'island of flames', was 'Khemnu' or 'Eight town' – still surviving in the modern name of this site in Middle Egypt as el-Ashmunein. The supremacy of the god THOTH at Khemnu led to the place being called Thoth-town – in Greek, Hermopolis. The Ogdoad also had a sanctuary in the Small Temple (dating from Dynasty XVIII – Roman period) at Medinet Habu in western Thebes.

Onuris

    Warrior- and hunter-god originating at This near Abydos.

Onuris is depicted as a bearded, spear-carrying man wearing a crown of four high plumes. In Egyptian his name is Anhur and means 'the one who leads back the distant one' – referring to the myth where the god journeyed to the south to bring back into Egypt the lioness who became his consort, Mekhit. In some statues of the god the spear is replaced by a rope suggesting the capture of the lioness-goddess.

Onuris as a warrior-god with a crown of plumes easily assimilates to MONTU and SOPEDU and also has a strong rapport with HORUS whose claims he vociferously advocates in the tribunal judging the rights to the Egyptian throne. His iconography as 'lord of the lance' therefore suggests a further link with Horus by symbolising the spearing of the god SETH. This extends to interpreting Onuris as the hunter and slayer of all enemies of Egypt and the sun-god RA.

The most frequent identification is made between Onuris and the god SHU, with the epithet of 'son of Ra'. This amalgamation is enhanced by the fact that the lioness Mekhit can symbolise the vengeful Eye of the sun-god in the tradition of other daughters of Ra such as SAKHMET and especially TEFNUT. It is the latter goddess who, according to Heliopolitan mythology, was brought back to Egypt by her brother–husband Shu from Nubia where she was a raging desert lioness.

Onuris with his lioness-consort Mekhit. Late Period bronze dyad, Musée des Beaux-Arts, Budapest.

Onuris's main cult centre in the later period of Egyptian civilisation was in the Delta at Samannud (ancient Sebennytos) where a temple to Onuris-Shu dated from the reign of Nectanebo II (Dynasty XXX).

In the Ptolemaic period Onuris is seen by Greeks as the Egyptian equivalent of their war-god Ares. This martial deity continues into the Roman era where, for example, the emperor Tiberius can be seen carved on one of the column-shafts before the hypostyle hall of the temple of Kom-Ombo wearing the plumed crown of Onuris.

Orion

The constellation of Orion, called Sah in ancient Egypt, has close affinities with OSIRIS and the king.

Orion is imagined as being swallowed at dawn by the Underworld but having the power to emerge again into the sky. In the Afterlife the king reaches the firmament as Orion who bestows on him the authority of a 'great force'.

In the identification of Osiris with Orion the underlying motif appears to be the link that the constellation has with the star Sirius (SOTHIS): the renewal of life via the Nile flood, announced by the heliacal rising of the Dog-star, emphasises the connection between Osiris and vegetation. Another concomitant factor between the two gods is that Orion has freedom of movement striding across the sky in the same way that Osiris, according to the Coffin Texts, will not be hindered in his rule over Upper Egypt.

In the New Kingdom funerary texts Orion reaches his land by rowing towards the stars, an image which is depicted on the ceilings of some tombs and temples (e.g. Esna) by a god in the pharaonic White Crown standing on a papyriform boat sailing across the sky.

Osiris

God whose domain is Duat – the Egyptian Underworld.

He is depicted in human form, as in his earliest appearance yet attested on a block from the reign of King Djedkara Izezi (Dynasty V) which shows the head and part of the upper torso of a god, above whom are the hieroglyphic symbols of Osiris's name. In fuller iconography his body is portrayed as wrapped in mummy

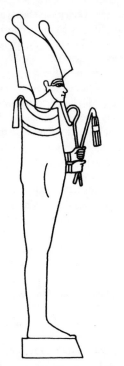

Osiris 'Foremost of the Westerners'. Tomb of Sety I, Dyn. XIX.

corn-god bearing a Berber name which means the 'old one'. His name has been split up by others to mean 'he who occupies the throne' or 'he who copulates with ISIS'. It has even been suggested that behind Osiris there lurks an original mother-goddess whose name might be interpreted as 'she who belongs to the womb'. However, the most likely explanation seems to be the simplest: Osiris's name is connected with the word 'woser' which would give the sense of the 'Mighty One'.

1 Osiris in the Pyramid Age

HIS ANCESTRY

A genealogy for Osiris exists in the texts carved on the walls of the pyramids from the end of Dynasty V onwards. This pedigree is clearly an attempt by the priests of the sun-god at Heliopolis to incorporate Osiris into their theology, cleverly subordinating him by two generations to their own principal deity:

	ATUM			
SHU		TEFNUT		
GEB		NUT		
Osiris	Isis	SETH	NEPHTHYS	THOTH

Osiris is described as the first born of the children of Geb and Nut, his birthplace being given as Rosetau, located in the western Desert necropolis near Memphis, but really signifying the entrance into the Underworld.

HIS EPITHETS

The titles used to describe Osiris are of great value in trying to elucidate his nature although for the most part they seem to be drawn to Osiris from other deities. This is an indication of Osiris's success story as a universal god, capable

bandages from which his arms emerge to hold the sceptres of kingship – the crook and the flail. His distinctive crown known as the 'Atef' comprises a ram's horns at its base, and a tall conical centrepiece sporting a plume on each side.

The writing of his name has attracted much attention from scholars hoping to discover an etymology behind it which could lead to conclusive proof concerning Osiris's origins. Few theories have met with even a quorum of acceptance and most remain unconvincing. From the symbols of the eye and the throne, Osiris has been given 'roots' both east and west of the Nile, e.g. in Mesopotamia as the god Marduk, and in Libya as an alleged of absorbing different divinities into his own personality:

Foremost of the westerners (in Egyptian, Khentamentiu)   This stresses the role of Osiris as a protective funerary god. To the west of the Nile is where the majority of cemeteries are situated, the region where the sun set and descended into Duat. Originally this title applied to an ancient jackal-god worshipped at Abydos.

He who dwells in Andjet   This title refers to Osiris's centre of Busiris in the Delta. Possibly the local god of this site, ANDJETY, was the source of the regalia in the iconography of Osiris.

He who dwells in Heliopolis   By this description Osiris is related to the resident deities of the ancient centre of sun worship.

He who dwells in Orion with a season in the sky and a season on earth   This formula connects Osiris with an important constellation of stars and signifies an astral element in him which contrasts with the predominant chthonic aspect. The imagery is probably attracted from one of the manifestations of the king in the Afterlife where he becomes a *Star-god*.

He who dwells in the house of SERKET This brings Osiris into close proximity with the scorpion-goddess who has an important role in the mortuary cult as protectress of human remains.

He who is in the God's tent   Here the booth where the embalmers turned the corpse into a mummified body is placed under Osiris's protection. It seems probable that this role is borrowed from ANUBIS. The descriptions that accompany this title however are particularly suitable for Osiris:

'He who is in the fumigation', i.e. the incense-burning that accompanied the embalming ritual. This idea of an aromatic atmosphere counteracts the fear which the Egyptians had of the god of the Underworld being associated with the stench and corruption of death. In fact in one passage in the Pyramid Texts it is explicitly stated that in the next life the king will not tread on the 'putrefaction of Osiris'.

'He who has been put in the box', namely the sarcophagus. This has been taken as a reference to the way in which Osiris was murdered by Seth in the legend given by the Greek writer Plutarch (AD 40–120). It seems highly unlikely that this is the case and the epithet is best regarded as extending Osiris's protection to the container of the corpse.

'Put in the shrine', i.e. the funerary shrines in the shape of ancient sanctuaries which were placed over the sarcophagus as in the case of the four gilded shrines of Tutankhamun.

'Put in the cloth', a reference to the linen bandages which wrap up the embalmed body for greater security.

The emphasis from the above titles is on Osiris's association with funerary procedures and burial, applicable only to the king to begin with but gradually extending to the population in general.

OSIRIS AND THE KING

In the Old Kingdom there is a nexus of paramount importance between the monarchy and Osiris. Once the ruler of Egypt has died he becomes Osiris, King of Duat. The divinity of the pharaoh embodied in the form of HORUS on the throne of Egypt takes on a new manifestation as monarch in the Underworld. Consequently, in the texts decorating the burial chamber of the last pyramid built in Dynasty V and those constructed in Dynasty VI, the dead king is sometimes referred to under the god's name, e.g. Osiris Unas or Osiris Pepi. The belief that the king has undergone a transformation of state and has not on death reached a termination of existence is further emphasised by graphic phraseology, such as asserting that he has departed 'alive' to sit on the throne of Osiris to give orders to the 'living'.

In contrast to this correspondence between the king and Osiris, sentiments can be found that reveal an apprehension or dread of the ruler of the Underworld. This reflects the underlying desire of the monarch to be with the sun-god in the sky as a visible phenomenon rather than to dwell in the unknown and forbidding regions of Duat. Therefore one text informs us that RA will not hand over the king to Osiris while another orders the Underworld-god to leave the royal tomb free of his 'evil'. Even later when the tutelary role of Osiris extends beyond the sphere of royalty in the Middle Kingdom, there exist in the Coffin Texts descriptions of Osiris that conjure up a picture of a threatening demon. He glories in slaughter, utters malignant spells against a dead person and runs a 'mafia' consisting of executioners called 'Osiris's butcherers painful of fingers' or 'Osiris's fishermen'. However, this darker aspect of Osiris is never allowed to outweigh his role as the personification of dead kingship.

THE FATE OF OSIRIS

The inscriptions of the Pyramid Age provide an extremely 'spartan' account of the legend of Osiris's rule over Predynastic Egypt being brought to an end by his assassination at the hands of his brother Seth. This earthly life attributed to the god seems an interpolation into the Osiris cycle of myth, possibly to make his paternal relationship to the Egyptian king (who of course is the manifestation of Osiris's son and

instrument of vengeance, the god Horus) more comprehensible. Certainly Osiris's rule over Egypt is a shadowy concept in comparison to his full-blooded government in the Underworld. We are told that the 'Great One', i.e. Osiris, fell on his side (meaning that he collapsed dead through some outside agency) on the river bank of Nedyet, identifiable as his cult centre Abydos. From the Middle Kingdom Coffin Texts it is explicitly stated that it was Seth who attacked Osiris in the land of Gahesty and killed him on the bank of Nedyet. At no time in ancient Egypt is Osiris's murder at the hands of Seth pictorially represented. The god seems to be resisting the state of death for following an epithet, 'he who is in Nedyet', are phrases asserting his detestation of sleep (= dying coma) and his hatred of inertness (= 'rigor mortis'). There is also an allusion to the death of the god by drowning near Memphis. But this connection of Osiris with water is only developed in the later period when it seems to be regarded as a blessed fate to drown in the Nile (see PETEESE and PIHOR). The devotion of his elder sister, the goddess Isis, which was to become a highly developed motif in later accounts, is already present in this early documentation of the myth. After a search she finds Osiris on the river bank and 'gathers up his flesh' which seeing that no mention is made of any dismemberment of Osiris's body, found in the later tradition, probably means that she used her magical powers to arrest his decomposition. Onto the scene now come the gods Thoth and Horus, who are to be found flanking the pharaoh in a number of royal rituals and are therefore admirably suited to assist the potential monarch of Duat. They raise Osiris up onto his side – a vivification reminiscent of the two gods pouring symbols of life over a pharaoh depicted on numerous temple walls. The embalmment ritual is then carried out at Abydos. To all intents and purposes Osiris now disappears from the struggle for the throne of Egypt – if ever he were originally involved in this legend – and becomes the Underworld ruler, leaving his sister Isis and the gods Horus and Seth as the main protagonists.

2   *Osiris in the Middle and New Kingdoms*

Although they were originally addressed to Anubis, in Dynasty IV, Osiris gradually finds a place in the funerary formulae found in courtiers' tombs intended to ensure that food offerings, linen and alabaster jars of perfume will never be lacking for the deceased. This is done, however, only through the intervention of the king. So Osiris had become a major protective deity of private burials by Dynasty V; it is not until long funerary texts become 'de rigueur' on the coffins of officials in Dynasties XI–XII and elaborate papyri full of vignettes and spells accompany the courtier's body into the tomb from Dynasty XVIII onwards that the relationship between non-royal personages and Osiris is documented in detail, and the different aspects of the god's character are richly portrayed.

THE PLETHORA OF HIS EPITHETS

A conscious attempt to reflect the universality of Osiris lies behind the massive increase during this period in geographically descriptive and characterising titles. For example, from the Middle Kingdom texts Osiris is the 'Great Inert' or mummified corpse brought together by Isis and Nephthys – presumably from the dismembered and scattered limbs following his murder. In his primary 'raison d'être' he is 'king of those who are not', namely the dead envisaged as 'living' in Duat. In the New Kingdom we meet more and more with Osiris as 'Lord of the Living' (in this case clearly emphasising the Egyptian denial of death since it refers to those in the Underworld), 'Lord of the Universe' and 'Ruler of Eternity'.

Possibly the best illustration for the diversification of Osiris can be found in Spell 142 of the Book of the Dead which is concerned with listing all the numerous names of the god that the deceased might require journeying through the Underworld. Here is a short selection describing Osiris as:

Presiding over Rosetau, i.e. the necropolis as entrance to the Underworld
Dwelling in the Lake of Buto
Dwelling in Memphis
The Ape
Lord of the Two Plumes
The Terrible.

Other titles mention Osiris Hemag connected with the palace at Sais and Osiris SEPA connected with Heliopolis. By now the former royal prerogative of identification with Osiris ruler of Duat has extended to officials so that their anticipation of unassailable status in the Afterlife is expressed by the prefix 'Osiris' before their own names.

OSIRIS WENEN-NOFER

There is every likelihood that the name Wenen-nofer was borrowed from another divinity as a euphemism disguising the decay of death. It can be translated as 'he who is everlastingly in a fine condition', or it could also be taken to mean the 'beneficent being'. This epithet can stand on its own and from it derives the Greek equivalent of Onnophris.

OSIRIS AND RA

It was the fear of the possible gloom pervading the Underworld that led the

Egyptians to interpret Osiris as a counterpart of the sun-god below the earth. Consequently, Duat would always have a share of the solar light; Osiris and Ra embrace one another to become the 'Twin Souls'. In an effort to link the sun-deity to the Osirian legend, Ra supervises Osiris's funeral ceremonies. But there is a rivalry between the two gods, reflected in a short 'public' dialogue. Osiris stresses his own importance as an agricultural deity in producing emmer wheat and barley which keep alive both gods and men. Ra's only and rather petulant reply is that the crops exist regardless of Osiris. Osiris gives the final self-righteous rejoinder: Ra's government allows the unjust to thrive but in the domain of Osiris there are fearless messengers ('weputiu') to bring the hearts of the wicked to the Hall of Judgement for punishment. These agents respect no status so that both gods and humans are under Osiris's rule.

OSIRIS AS A GOD OF GRAIN

The role of the god in agriculture is not a primal one but comes naturally through the association of the motif of the murdered Osiris emerging as the dominant divine force in the Underworld, and the cycle of seedtime and harvest. The earliest unambiguous reference to Osiris and corn occurs in the Dramatic Ramesseum Papyrus (Dynasty XII), a commentary on, or directory of, ritual. Osiris is the barley which is 'beaten' (i.e. threshed) by the god Seth in the form of the ass. This is described as 'hacking the god to pieces'. From other Middle Kingdom texts the identification of Osiris with barley extends to analogising him with the grain-god NEPER. There is a ceremony found in the Ptolemaic period called 'driving the calves' for which antecedents can be found in Dynasty V

and the New Kingdom. The essence of this ritual originally seems to encourage divine intervention to bring bumper harvests by the hoofs of calves threshing grain on a floor sacred to the god. However, it was also interpreted as an apotropaic rite where the calves, by trampling over the threshing-floor, now symbolising the grave of Osiris, hid the spot from the god's enemies.

The most explicit evidence of Osiris as a grain-god is archaeological. In the New Kingdom wooden frames were placed in the burial chambers of some royal and private tombs which supported an 'Osiris-bed'. This was a model of the god filled with silt in which barley had been planted. The sproutinsig of the crop – 8 in. high in an example from the tomb of Yuya and Tuyu (the parents of Queen Tiye, Dynasty XVIII) in the Valley of the Kings – implied the resurrection of the deceased in the Underworld. The same symbolism is found in one of the late New Kingdom Mythological Papyri: Osiris 'he who is in the grain of the gods' lies ithyphallic on desert sand, indicating his coming to life in the barren terrain which surrounds his tomb. The motif of the continual cycle of crops and vegetation accounts for the colour of the pigments used to represent the flesh of Osiris. His face and hands can be painted black to evoke the Nile silt from which the barley and emmer emerge; his flesh can appear green, the colour of living vegetation and of the fields before the summer ripening of the crop.

OSIRIS AND THE IMPREGNATION OF ISIS

In the pharaonic period the span of years spent by Osiris in Egypt is a prelude to the universal acclamation of his son and heir Horus as the rightful possessor of the throne. The effectual transmission of the kingship from the murdered father via

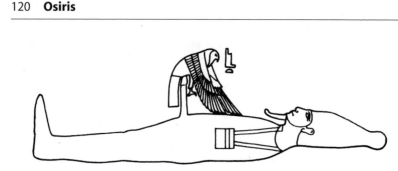

Osiris impregnating Isis as a kite. Temple of Sety I, Abydos, Dyn. XIX.

the usurper-brother to the son is due to the magic and guile of Isis, sister–wife of Osiris. Through her skills the dead god is sufficiently vivified to have sexual intercourse with her, leading to the conception of his avenging son Horus. The vital moments of this congress are carved on the walls of the chapel of SOKAR in the temple of Sety I at Abydos. In one relief Osiris prone on a couch manually stimulates his phallus into an erection. On the opposite wall Osiris's phallus (now maliciously hacked out of the relief) penetrates Isis who hovers over it in the form of a kite. The goddess in human form stands at one end of the couch and hawk-headed Horus the future son of this union at the other, completing the divine triad and leaving by this anticipatory carving no doubt as to the success of Osiris's last deed on earth. From Karnak there is an inscription calling Osiris 'he who resides in the house of conception' alluding to the impregnation of Isis and the consequent birth of Horus.

OSIRIS AND THE 'DJED' COLUMN

Before the earliest attestation of Osiris's cult the symbol that was to become so representative of the god already existed. It is called the 'Djed' column, a word meaning 'stability' or 'continuity of power'. It is found e.g. surmounting the design of a granary in one of the decorations formed from blue glazed composition tiles in the subterranean galleries of the Step Pyramid of King Djoser (Dynasty III) at Saqqara. Its shape of a pillar with flattened terminals and four horizontal bars across its upper length has given rise to numerous suggestions as to what it is. Could it be an altar from a Predynastic sanctuary? Or perhaps four altars in a row but depicted as if superimposed, which would be quite in keeping with spatial rendering in Egyptian art? What about it being a bundle of reeds or an artist's easel such as the vizier Mereruka is shown using on the inner entrance wall of his tomb near the pyramid of Teti (Dynasty VI), his king? Is it perhaps an attempt to visualise a concept like the four regions of the Egyptian world – Libya, Nubia, Middle East and Mediterranean? It is better to admit that at present its origins escape us and accept the later interpretations of the symbol that the Egyptians themselves evolved when it became inseparable from the cult of Osiris. Thus in the Book of the Dead a 'Djed' column of gold is called the vertebrae or backbone of Osiris. There are papyri and temple reliefs showing the 'Djed' surmounted by the Atef crown of Osiris and given human arms which hold the crook and flail. The ceremony of 'erecting the "Djed" column' is mentioned as part of the enthronement ritual of Senwosret I in Dynasty XII. The 'Djed' is involved in an important ritual of the

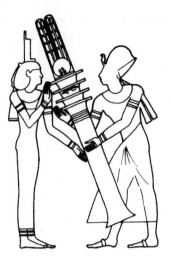

Isis and the Pharaoh raise the Djed-pillar. Temple of Sety I, Abydos, Dyn. XIX.

Museum belonging to a high-flying treasury official, Ikhernofret, who lived in the Middle Kingdom during the reign of Senwosret III (Dynasty XII), gives a tantalising glimpse of the 'mysteries' of the god. Ikhernofret was commissioned by the king to use Nubian gold to decorate the cult statue of Osiris at Abydos. He also constructed a new shrine for the god's statue carved out of cedarwood and inlaid with gold, silver, bronze and lapis lazuli. For the ceremonial drama the shrine and statue were conveyed on symbolic boats carried on the shoulders of the priests. Ikhernofret supervised the construction of the god's special boat known as the 'neshmet'. The ritual of the festival is now all too succinctly summarised.

royal jubilee celebrations. In this festival, which in essence is a ceremony of rejuvenation for the pharaoh, a gilded wooden 'Djed' column is raised from a prone to upright position by the king. It receives a ritual performed in a similar way to that for a divine cult-image, being presented with offerings and linen garments. An official called Kheruef has depicted in his tomb at Thebes the ceremony of erecting the 'Djed' carried out by King Amenhotep III and Queen Tiye in Dynasty XVIII. The location is Memphis or Busiris (see Sanctuaries of Osiris). By incorporating the 'Djed' into the monarch's jubilee the strength and stability of the kingship of Egypt becomes analogous to the unshakeable jurisdiction of Osiris in Duat.

FESTIVAL OF OSIRIS

Pharaonic sources are discreet to the point of irritation in unveiling the legend of Osiris as it was enacted in an annual festival drama at Abydos. A stela in Berlin

Procession of WEPWAWET This ancient canine deity acts as the herald of the god Osiris, leading the ceremonial journey. At this point Ikhernofret fends off an attack on the 'neshmet' made by priests symbolising the god's enemies.

Great procession Ikhernofret conducts this focal point of the drama where the shrine of Osiris is carried on another boat in a funeral procession from his temple south-west to his symbolic tomb in a region called 'Peqer'. On this journey a major struggle against the god's foes is enacted in which Ikhernofret protects Osiris (called here Wenen-nofer). The shore of Nedyet is given as the name of this place where Osiris's opponents are destroyed – the very place where the god was slain by Seth.

Return to the temple Ikhernofret organises the shrine and the ceremonial boats to be taken onto the 'great barque' and conveyed along the Nile back to the Abydos temple into which the god is carried on his 'neshmet' for the final purification ceremonies.

The ruler of the Underworld naturally ensures that the souls of the wicked and undesirable do not survive to live in his realm. In the law court Osiris sits on his throne holding his sceptres and supervises the judgement of the new applicants for Paradise. Osiris in a judicial connection, or at least as upholder of honesty and upright behaviour, is attested as early as the Pyramid Era where he is called 'lord of MAAT', i.e. the goddess of cosmic order who later represents the 'truth' against which all answers must be weighed in the aggressive interrogation of the dead person's soul. This association with the goddess persists into the Late Period, for at Karnak Temple inscriptions from an edifice built by the Divine Adoratrice of Amun, Ankhnesneferibra (Dynasty XXVI), in honour of Osiris Pameres describes the god as 'united with Maat'. In the iconography of Osiris, the god is frequently depicted standing on a plinth tapering to a point which is the hieroglyph for 'truth'. In royal tombs a mummiform figure, on whom rests a pole-beam balance, stands before Osiris. Nearby is a boat in which a monkey brandishes a stick above a pig – a reference to the humiliation of Seth, brother–enemy of Osiris. His nine agents will cut to pieces the souls of criminals. In private funerary papyri the examination of souls and condemnation of those unfit for an Afterlife in Duat is carried out on Osiris's behalf by the ASSESSOR GODS. Successful candidates are then led into the presence of enthroned Osiris by his son Horus.

3 *Sanctuaries of Osiris*

Since the god is universal his cult places are not confined to any one district of Egypt but are found throughout the Nile Valley. The hymn to Osiris inscribed on the Louvre Museum stela of Amenemose,

a New Kingdom cattle overseer, enumerates a number of sites where the god is worshipped:

The Delta sites of Letopolis and Heliopolis
Memphis the capital city
Herakleopolis, where the local priests boasted that the tomb of Osiris was situated, over which grew a sacred tree Hermopolis.

However, one site in Lower Egypt and one in the south possessed the sanctuaries most sacred to Osiris.

DJEDU

The hieroglyphs spelling out the name of this town in the mid-Delta employ two 'Djed' columns. It is often referred to by its Greek name Busiris (first coined in the fifth century BC by Herodotus) which derives from the Egyptian 'house of Osiris' meaning the god's temple. The antiquity of the sanctuary to Osiris is proved by its mention in invocation formulae found in Old Kingdom courtiers' tombs.

IBDJU

This most important and oldest sanctuary of the god, situated in Upper Egypt not too far from modern Balliana, was rendered into Greek as Abydos, the name by which the site is generally known today. Part of the impressive mudbrick enclosure of the Old Kingdom temple of Osiris is still extant. The tomb of Osiris was claimed to be near the desert escarpment – a reinterpretation by the Ancient Egyptians of a monument constructed in the First Dynasty for King Djer. However, the fullest evidence of the hallowed regard for the Osiris cult at Abydos comes from the magnificent temple reliefs carved during the reign of Sety I of Dynasty XIX. Every stage of the daily ritual is portrayed as being performed by the king – unbolting the god's shrine, dressing and adorning the statue inside and providing incense and nourishment. Behind this temple a monument known as the Osireion contained a symbolic tomb of the god and a representation in architecture of the primeval mound. Abydos had a distinctive emblem, implying Osiris, of a pole supporting a 'beehive' shape from which emanate two tall plumes. This symbol became interpreted as a reliquary containing the god's head – an attempt to explain each of the cult centres of Osiris as a place where a part of his corpse was buried.

OSIRIS AT KARNAK

With the exception of the temple of PTAH all the area north of the temple of Amun up to the boundary wall of the precinct was sacred to Osiris. He is particularly in evidence in the chapels built by the Divine Adoratrices of Amun, e.g. under Amenirdis and Shepenwapet in Dynasty XXV Osiris is mentioned in conjunction with the sacred persea tree and in the next dynasty under Ankhnesneferibra a chapel was dedicated to Osiris Wenen-nofer 'lord of offerings'.

On a monument of Ptolemy XII which also bears the cartouche of Tiberius Osiris is called 'he of Koptos who presides over the mansion of gold', placing the god in the role of protector of the gold mined in the eastern Desert and brought to the Theban treasuries.

OSIRIS AT BIGA

The island of Biga, known as Senmet in Egyptian, south of Aswan and immediately west of the temple of Isis on Philae, was at some date regarded as possessing the tomb of Osiris (statues and inscriptions indicate worship here from at least Dynasty XVIII). Osiris's body was brought here to the 'high hill…twice hidden, twice secret' on the back of a crocodile. The god's ritual was

linked to the festival of the goddess on the neighbouring island whose statue was brought to the Abaton (the holiest sanctuary equatable with the Egyptian term 'pure mound') on Biga to be with Osiris. This sacred spot, however, cannot now be located and there are very few remains of even the latest archaeologically attested sanctuary on the island built under Ptolemy XII.

4 *The Osiris legend according to Plutarch*

The Greek writer Plutarch (AD 40–120) has left an account of the god's myth in a work 'Peri Isidos kai Osiridos' – i.e. 'About Isis and Osiris'. In it there are perceptive comments on the god, heavily intermingled with Greek speculations.

OSIRIS'S DEATH

Osiris and Isis ruled over an Egypt which he personally had transformed from barbarism into a civilised state of growing crops, observing laws and honouring the gods. This was done by the power of his songs, not weapons, leading to an identification in the Greek mind with their god Dionysus. His brother Seth (called Typhon by Plutarch) enlisted the help of seventy-two conspirators and a Nubian queen to overthrow Osiris. An exquisite chest was made exactly to Osiris's measurements and light-heartedly offered at a banquet as a gift to whomever fitted inside it. Once Osiris took his turn the plotters slammed the lid down, covered the chest with molten lead and threw it into the Tanitic mouth of the Nile to be carried out into the Mediterranean Sea.

OSIRIS AND BYBLOS

The chest was eventually washed up on the shores of the Lebanon at Byblos and enfolded in the trunk of a heath-tree. The king of Byblos cut the tree for use as a column in a temple. Isis rescued the chest containing the body of her husband, leaving the wood of the heath-tree to be venerated in her temple at Byblos. There is no trace of the Byblos episode in the pharaonic myth but Plutarch has been held by some to reflect a lost tradition of the origins of Osiris lying in the Lebanon. This suggestion is not at all likely and the probable source for the Byblos setting is remembrance of the extensive trade in timber (especially cedars) that Egypt had with the Lebanon, certainly on preferential terms, from the Pyramid Age to the New Kingdom.

THE DISMEMBERMENT OF OSIRIS

Plutarch's source for the separate burial of parts of the god's body is a late feature of the myth in Egypt, not found prior to the New Kingdom. Isis brings the chest to the Delta, then neglects it while she goes to Buto to her child Horus, already born in this version of the legend. Seth, hunting by moonlight, discovers the chest. He cuts Osiris's body into fourteen parts and scatters them throughout the Nile Valley. Isis pursues each severed part, holding a burial ceremony wherever she comes across one. According to Plutarch this explains the location of Osiris's tomb being claimed by many temples. Ptolemaic temples such as Dendera and Edfu provide texts mentioning fourteen, sixteen and forty-two parts – the latter enabling a part of the god's body to rest in every nome or administrative district of Egypt. Sites claiming pieces of Osiris include:

Sebennytos	upper and lower leg
Herakleopolis	thigh, head, two sides and two legs
Athribis	heart
Abydos	head
Edfu	leg
Biga Island	left leg

A problem arose for Isis in that Osiris's phallus, thrown into the Nile by Seth, had been eaten piecemeal by the lepidotus, phragus and oxyrhyncus fish. The goddess manufactured an artificial organ for the god around which the Egyptians established a cult and festival. In the pharaonic tradition, however, the phallus is preserved intact and buried at Memphis.

P

Pakhet

A lioness-goddess worshipped particularly at the entrance of a wadi in the eastern desert near Beni Hasan.

Her name is very evocative of her nature, meaning 'she who snatches' or the 'tearer'. In the Coffin Texts Pakhet the Great is described as a night-huntress with sharp claws.

It is easy to see Greek settlers seeing in Pakhet characteristics of Artemis, goddess of the chase. Speos Artemidos (cave of Artemis) became the common designation of Pakhet's rock-chapel near Beni Hasan, carved out of the limestone in Dynasty XVIII under Hatshepsut and Thutmose III.

Panebtawy

A youthful god who is the divine child of Haroeris (see HORUS section on 'The struggle for the throne of Egypt'), and TASENETNOFRET in the western sanctuary of Kom-Ombo temple. As 'the lord of the Two Lands' he represents the idea of the pharaoh as son of the god Haroeris, hence the legitimate ruler of Egypt.

Pelican

The Pelican (Henet in Egyptian), found in livestock scenes on the walls of courtiers' tombs, figures in royal funerary texts from the Pyramid Age as a protective symbol against snakes. The description of the Pelican falling into the Nile seems connected with the idea of scooping up in its prominent beak hostile elements under the guise of fish – a concept comparable to the dragnets and bird nets used for trapping sinners in the Underworld.

That the Pelican is a divinity must be assumed from the reference to it in the Pyramid Texts as the 'mother of the king', a role which in religious documents can only be ascribed to a goddess. In non-royal funerary papyri the Pelican has the power of prophesying a safe passage for a dead person in the Underworld. The open beak of the Pelican is also associated with the ability of the deceased to leave the burial chamber and go out into the rays of the sun, possibly an analogy made between the long cavernous beak of the pelican and the tomb shaft.

Peteese and Pihor

Two deified brothers, sons of Kuper, who seem to have lived in the vicinity of Dendur in Lower Nubia about Dynasty XXVI. The reason for their elevation to minor gods is not stated, but quite possibly they met their death in the Nile, a fate having connotations with OSIRIS. Establishing 'laissez-faire' guide lines for Roman policy towards Egyptian religion, Augustus built a modest temple in honour of the brothers on the west bank at Dendur. In some instances the reliefs show Peteese and Pihor as 'upstart' deities making offerings to their superior, the goddess ISIS. (Dendur temple, dismantled to avoid being permanently covered by the lake created by the completion of the High Dam at Aswan in 1971, is now part of the Metropolitan Museum of Art, New York.)

Pharaoh

Kingship in ancient Egypt is set apart from coeval Near Eastern monarchies by virtue of its holder being regarded as the 'perfect god'. The major features of the cult of the divine ruler, called in the Pyramid Age 'essence of all the gods', can be summarised as follows.

The pharaoh Ramesses III Dyn. XX, Great Harris Papyrus, British Museum.

Pharaoh as Horus spearing Seth. Statuette from the Tomb of Tutankhamun, Dyn. XVIII, Cairo Museum.

1 *King* = HORUS

The earliest title carried by the pharaoh is that equating him with the hawk-god legitimately awarded the throne of Egypt by a tribunal of deities – hence the Horus Narmer (Dynasty I). Another element in the royal titulary calls the pharaoh 'Horus of gold', the metal ('flesh of RA') enhancing his divinity as well as the title-device itself being capable of a secondary interpretation as the triumph of Horus over SETH.

2 *King* = *son of* RA

The link between the monarch and the most important of all Egyptian deities is vital. A papyrus relates how the wife of a high priest of Ra made pregnant by the sun-god gives birth to three future pharaohs. These are the kings of early Dynasty V – the period that first witnesses the great influence of the sun-cult – and from now on the pre-coronation name of the king in the royal protocol is introduced by the title 'Son of Ra'. (For the emphasis of a divine parent for the king, see AMUN section titled 'The Theban theogamy'.)

3 *King* = *ward of* NEKHBET
and WADJET

Although the kingdom of united Egypt came into being (*c.*3000 BC), there is always the underlying concept that the state is really 'Two Lands'. The pharaoh is protected therefore by those goddesses of North and South Egypt that had been taken as national emblems by the Predynastic rulers, i.e. before the unification. Thus, one of the royal titles means 'the Two Mistresses' stressing that the pharaoh is defended by the vulture-goddess of Upper Egypt and cobra-goddess of the Delta. Another title of one of his five 'great names' taken on accession to the throne emphasises the king's attachment to each of the original separate kingdoms by describing his divinity as including their sacred emblems: 'belonging to the sedge-plant (= south) and the bee (= north)'. It should be mentioned that a different interpretation of these emblems gives the translation 'Dual King' relating to worldly and divine aspects of the pharaoh's role. Also in the regalia the Lower Egyptian Red Crown and the Upper Egyptian White Crown can be visualised as goddesses protecting the pharaoh. In a more aggressive way the Pyramid Texts proclaim the pharaoh as indestructible with power of life and death over the gods of Upper and Lower Egypt.

4 *Living king* = *deified through ritual*

At his coronation the pharaoh is considered to undergo purification by HORUS and THOTH who pour signs of life and dominion over him. The jubilee festival ('Heb Sed') is a renewal of the king's divinity and vitality. So strong is the king's godhead that rituals are performed before statues of a living monarch which are viewed as independent deities – in the first courtyard of Luxor

Pharaoh in 'nemes' headcloth and ceremonial beard protected by Wadjet. Statue of Thutmose III, Dyn. XVIII, Kunsthistorisches Museum, Vienna.

Temple at Thebes is a statue of Ramesses II put up during his reign (Dynasty XIX) and worshipped as 'RA of the rulers'.

5 *Dead king* = *deified as royal ancestor*

The god THOTH is seen in temple reliefs writing the name of the reigning pharaoh on the leaves of a sacred tree which bears the names of all the king's ancestors recognised as legitimate holders of kingship. These ancestors are honoured by the ruling monarch who might order the carving of a Kinglist where the cartouches of previous pharaohs receive incense, sacred liquid and offerings from the hands of the current occupier of the throne. Rulers condemned by subsequent pharaohs as unworthy to have governed – e.g. Queen Hatshepsut or Akhenaten (Dynasty XVIII) – are absent from this panorama of sacred kingship. The actions of some kings remembered with pride lead to their stepping out of the crowd of ancestors to be awarded special deification honours: Senwosret III (Dynasty XII) is held in high esteem for his domination of Nubia and honoured by Thutmose III (Dynasty XVIII) around 400 years later with a chapel (now in Turin) at el-Lessiya on the banks of the Nubian Nile. Similarly, Amenhotep I (Dynasty XVIII) is regarded as a patron deity by the workers on the royal tombs for making the first endowments founding their select community whose tombs and village ruins can be seen today at Deir el-Medina in western Thebes.

6 *Deceased king* = OSIRIS

This idea is first evident in the Pyramid Era where the king is seen in the Afterlife as having an existence correspondent with the god. On death every pharaoh ceases to maintain the role of HORUS on the throne of Egypt and transmutes to a life incorporating both being in the boat of the sun-god and, as Osiris, taking up the kingship of the Underworld.

The Old Kingdom gives us the first insight into how the divinity of the pharaoh is seen never to diminish as a result of physical death. The god–king is given the role of judge in the domain of RA and is suitably equated with SIA, personifying intellect. A cataclysm in Egypt will occur if the king is barred from becoming one of the company of sky-gods in the Hereafter. To emphasise a continuing possession of divinity the king (called 'god older than the oldest') is imagined to be imbued with sufficient magical force to hunt and eat the powers and intelligence of every other god. (See also AMUN section titled 'Amun and the pharaoh'; ATEN; GEB; HATHOR section titled 'Hathor and the pharaoh'; ISIS section titled 'Mother of Horus'; Seth section titled 'God of royalty', SOULS OF PE AND NEKHEN, STAR-GODS.)

Ptah

Statuette from the Tomb of Tutankhamun, Dyn. XVIII, Cairo Museum.

Creator-god of Memphis.

The usual iconography of Ptah is already established in embryo by Dynasty I on a calcite bowl from Tarkhan: the anthropomorphic god is smooth-headed, dressed in a high-collared garment with a tassel, and stands in an open kiosk holding a sceptre of dominion. Throughout Egyptian civilisation Ptah, deviating hardly at all from his earliest appearance, is unmistakable on tomb or temple walls: his head enveloped in a tightly fitting skull cap, that leaves only his face and ears to view, and his forearms emerging from the linen wrap that moulds itself closely to his form, permitting no differentiation of his limbs. The tassel from his collar is shown in profile, sometimes taking the form of the counterpoise of a necklace. His hands hold the 'was' – sceptre of dominion,

which combines at its upper terminal the 'ankh' sign (= life) and the 'djed' column (= stability). From the Middle Kingdom onwards Ptah is given a straight beard.

The name of the god (strangely not written with a distinguishing emblem or normal hieroglyphic determinative of 'divinity' until the New Kingdom) has given rise to suggestions of foreign origins in the west, but its most probable etymology is the root-word of later verbs meaning 'to sculpture' (his role as craftsman-deity?). The god's name was continually being honoured by incorporation in the names of kings and officials, e.g. in Dynasty XIX Merneptah (beloved of Ptah), Siptah (son of Ptah) and Ptahmose (Ptah is born).

In the early mortuary literature carved on the walls of Old Kingdom pyramids, Ptah scarcely gets a mention – and then only in connection with Werkaf, the butler of HORUS who happened also to be an 'elder of the palace of Ptah'. This might be explained by jealousy on the part of the priestly formulators of the inscriptions who were the main adherents of the Sun-Cult of RA at Heliopolis. On the other hand, it does not seem that Ptah had much of a role to play in the funerary cult or in the Underworld. It was the composite deity Ptah-SOKAR who had more prominence in the Afterlife (see SOKAR). However, in the life-restoring ceremony of 'opening the mouth' performed on the mummified corpse and statues of the deceased, it is the god Ptah (represented at the tomb side by his setem-priest) who is conceived as having hallowed the ritual by enacting it upon the mouths of the gods when he created them and their statues. He uses a metal chisel for the rite, suggesting his role as craftsman–god.

Although associated pre-eminently with Memphis, Ptah is a universal deity found on all major sites in Egypt and Nubia. At Thebes he had a presence in the precinct of AMUN at Karnak since at least the Middle Kingdom, more or less as that god's equivalent in Northern Egypt. The pharaoh Thutmose III (Dynasty XVIII) found the wooden and brick built sanctuary of Ptah at Karnak in a dilapidated condition and took pride in renewing it in sandstone. It was continually embellished into the Graeco-Roman period and, although its main female deity was HATHOR, it preserves one of the finest representations in black granite of Ptah's consort SAKHMET. Beyond the first cataract of the Nile Ptah was worshipped in particular at Gerf Husein and in the Great Temple of Ramesses II (Dynasty XIX) at Abu Simbel.

1 *Ptah and creation*

A remarkably metaphysical concept of how the god (coalescing with TATENEN)

brought the cosmos into being survives – miraculously – on a basalt slab in the British Museum that was used as a millstone in post-pharaonic Egypt. It is usually referred to as the Shabaqo Stone after the Sudanese king (Dynasty XXV) who ordered it to be inscribed and set up in the temple of Ptah at Memphis. It is a copy of a patently much older document whose origins (on linguistic evidence) lay in the Pyramid Age. The hieroglyphs give an account of creation formulated by Ptah's priesthood, doubtless in an attempt to eclipse intellectually the cosmogonical beliefs surrounding the sun-god creator ATUM of nearby Heliopolis. Ptah 'father of the gods' gives birth to the sun-god and his ENNEAD thereby subordinating them genealogically to himself. In the Memphite theology Ptah, self-created, thinks about the cosmos and speaks it into existence: Atum and the Ennead are conceived as the teeth and lips of Ptah, created by his heart (= seat of intellect) and his tongue (= command to action). In this cosmology Ptah is compounded with the god NUN, primeval matter, to become Ptah-Nun the 'father who begot Atum'; in the Ptolemaic period he is explained as self-generated out of Nun. He is, at the same time, a bisexual creative being in the form of Ptah-Naunet, the 'mother who bore Atum'. According to the Memphite doctrine life comes to everything from Ptah's heart and tongue – gods are born, towns are founded with shrines containing images of wood, clay and stone as bodies for the spirit (or 'ka') of every god to enter.

2 *Ptah at Memphis*

The founding of the 'white walls' or Memphis, administrative capital of Egypt, took place at or shortly after the unification of the northern and southern kingdoms, c.3000 BC. If Ptah 'lord of Ankhtawy' was not by that time already the pre-eminent deity in the district, it was not long before he had assumed all rival cults into his own being, after which only Ptah's epithets possibly witness another god's original independence. Two titles of Ptah, however, seem to be specifically descriptive of him alone.

PTAH 'RES INEBEF'=PTAH WHO IS
SOUTH OF HIS WALL

This must be a reference to the boundary wall enclosing the precinct in the temple of Ptah at Memphis. Hints of earlier structures are archaeologically attested at Memphis (modern Mit Rahina) where current excavations are also gradually presenting a fuller picture of the site, but the temple of Ptah is mainly known at present from the colossal statuary set up in it during the reign of Ramesses (Dynasty XIX). It was, in fact, Ptah's inseparable connection with the capital city that led to the modern European word for the whole country being 'Egypt': one of his temples was called 'Hut-ka-Ptah' or 'mansion of the spirit of Ptah' and was clearly the centre of a thriving community. Greeks coming into contact with the capital took this term to apply to the whole city, rendering it as 'Aiguptos', a word then applied both to the river Nile, as in Homer's Odyssey, and to the land of Egypt.

PTAH 'NEFER-HER' = PTAH BEAUTIFUL
OF FACE

This epithet explains the idea of the splendour of Ptah's divinity in the only area of his anatomy, other than his forearms, to be recognisable outside his garments. His flesh was envisaged as consisting of gold. This becomes a frequent title of Ptah in temple inscriptions, such as in his chapel at Abydos, and occurs also in love songs where the god is requested to bring the company of the desired lady to her admirer for the night.

Another title of Ptah was 'khery bakef' or 'he who is under his moringa tree'. This refers to an original Memphite tree-god absorbed into Ptah by the time that the epithet becomes current in the Middle Kingdom. The moringa tree, of which one in particular must have been tended in the temple precinct, grows extensively in Egypt producing nuts for ben oil.

In the temple of the god at Memphis resided the sacred bull which was the intermediary between Ptah and mankind (see APIS). Also at Memphis and Thebes Ptah's consort was the lioness SAKHMET. Completing the sacred triad was the god NEFERTUM, son of Sakhmet, but there is no direct evidence to link him with Ptah. A son of Ptah, however, existed as the deified architect of King Djoser, IMHOTEP.

3 *Ptah god of craftsmen*

The god was thought to have created skills in design and sculpture. In the Old Kingdom the high priest of Ptah had a title which conveyed the notion of a deity who was the smith and sculptor of mankind and the arts: 'wer kherep hemut' or 'supreme leader of craftsmanship'. How the god attracted this speciality is not certain but it may be to do with the vicinity of the Turah limestone quarries to his sanctuary at Memphis, producing the raw material for the artisans to carve.

Ptah was seen as a craftsman fashioning royalty. He moulds the body of Ramesses II (Dynasty XIX) out of electrum, and his limbs out of copper and iron. On the human level skilled artisans took Ptah as their patron god. There is interesting evidence of this from the community of workmen at Deir el-Medina in western Thebes, responsible for cutting out and decorating the tombs in the Valley of the Kings. Their patron deity is also seen as a god who ordains their individual destiny. Stelae carved by these craftsmen show Ptah seated in a kiosk being addressed by the dedicant – the god is encouraged to take notice of their prayers by the representation of human ears on the stela. In fact, one of Ptah's titles at Thebes is 'mesedjer sedjem' or the 'ear which hears'. The role of Ptah as 'lord of truth' comes across clearly on one of these stelae dedicated by Neferabu who – we lack full details – at one time made a false oath in Ptah's name. As a result Ptah caused Neferabu to 'see darkness by day', i.e. made him blind, and he now seeks the god's forgiveness, an unusually frank admission of guilt on the part of an Ancient Egyptian (see also MERETSEGER).

One particular group of craftsmen appear to symbolise physically the god Ptah as divine artisan. These are the dwarves who figure in workshop scenes normally as jewellers in Old Kingdom mastaba-tombs at Saqqara which overlooked the god's capital from the desert escarpment. In the Late Period it seems that it was Ptah who was considered to be represented in figurines and on magical stelae called 'cippi' as a big-bellied dwarf, probably deriving this form from the association with the craftsmen-dwarves. Supplementary evidence comes from the Greek historian Herodotus (fifth century BC) who mentions that on his visit to Memphis he saw statues in the temple of Hephaistos (i.e. the Greek smith-god identified with Ptah) in the shape of 'pataeci'. These, he goes on to explain, are the pygmy-like figures which decorate Phoenician triremes.

Q

Qadesh

Middle Eastern goddess of sacred ecstasy and sexual pleasure, adopted in the New Kingdom by the Egyptians into a triad with the gods MIN and RESHEP. Her name, probably meaning the 'holy', gives no clue to her origins but she seems to be a manifestation of the sensuousness inherent in the goddesses ASTARTE and ANAT.

Qadesh rides naked on the back of a lion and holds out symbols of eroticism and fertility to her companions – lotuses for Min and snakes or papyrus plants for Reshep. In the Levant the cult of Qadesh, like that of ASTARTE, involved her acolytes simulating the sacred marriage of the goddess with Reshep. This sexuality displayed by Qadesh naturally led to an identification between her and HATHOR the Egyptian goddess of Love.

Qadesh on lion flanked by Min and Reshep. Stela of Kaha, Dyn. XIX, British Museum.

R

Ra

Creator sun-god of Heliopolis.

Ra is the quintessence of all manifestations of the sun-god, permeating the three realms of the sky, earth and Underworld. Hence many deities enhance their own divinity by coalescing with this aspect of the sun-god, e.g. KHNUM-Ra, AMUN-Ra.

His main cult centre was at Heliopolis (Greek for 'sun-city'), now all but disappeared through depredations or below the suburbs of modern Cairo. The sun-temple area was called 'Iunu' by the Ancient Egyptians ('On' in biblical literature) and was written by a hieroglyph representing a column, clearly the ancient cult image on the site.

The physical manifestation of Ra is most commonly a falcon wearing the fiery disk of the sun on its head. The disk is surrounded by the body of the cobra-goddess, 'coiled one', symbolising the god's power of delivering instant death. In the Underworld his form is that of a ram-headed god. He is called 'sacred ram in the west' or, indicating his life-giving

Ra in the Underworld. Tomb of Sety I, Dyn. XIX.

properties, 'ram in charge of his harem'. In literature the sun-god is occasionally described as an ageing king whose flesh is gold, whose bones are silver and whose hair is lapis lazuli.

Inscriptional evidence for the cult of the sun-god is found in the name of the first pharaoh of Dynasty II – 'Raneb' or 'Ra is lord'. Architectural symbolism in the form of both the stepped and true pyramid – stairway to the sun-god and image of the 'high sand' at Heliopolis on which the creator-god stood to form the cosmos – provides continuing evidence of sun worship during Dynasties III and IV. Courtiers of Dynasty IV proclaim their office of 'great seer' or high priest of Heliopolis.

1 *Ra and the monarchy*

The real burgeoning of Ra's cult comes with the ruling family of Dynasty V who, as the Westcar Papyrus relates, were sons of Ra himself begotten of the wife of the high priest of Heliopolis. An element of the royal titulary is now introduced by the hieroglyph of a pintail duck and a sun disk, meaning 'son of Ra'. The name of the sun-god now continually occurs in the names of kings – Sahura (Dynasty V), Menkheperra (Dynasty XVIII), Ramesses (Dynasty XIX) – and also in private names, e.g. Rekhmira (or 'wise like Ra'). In Dynasty V the kings devoted a large proportion of the state's resources to building sun-temples – structures, open to the rays of the sun, surrounding the solar emblem of the 'benben', the first place of creation and prototype of the more slender obelisk. The king is said to belong to the two obelisks of Ra on earth, and fulfils this symbolism architecturally by erecting two obelisks before the pylon of a temple, e.g. as originally before Luxor temple in the reign of Ramesses II (Dynasty XIX) – the western obelisk now being in Paris.

The Pyramid Texts which were first carved on the burial chamber of King Unas, last ruler of Dynasty V, provide a panorama, of the Hereafter as imagined by the Heliopolitan priesthood. The monarch ascends to the sky to join the entourage of his father the sun-god on a stairway of sunshine. Ra's supremacy was the basis of the pharaoh's own security and power, governing Egypt in accordance with the universal order created by Ra. Deviation from the sun-god's dictates rendered a monarch unworthy of the divine kingship. However, such condemnation could only be posthumous as when Queen Hatshepsut (Dynasty XVIII) in the Speos Artemidos, a rock-cut chapel in Middle Egypt, calls the foreign Hyksos kings rulers 'without Ra'.

2 *Ra as creator*

Emphasis is placed on Ra's coming into being at the beginning of time. The god emerges out of the primeval waters on the mound called the 'benben'. This imagery is that of 'Ra of Bakhu' – the eastern mountains above which the sun rises at dawn. Ra is also visualised as a child rising out of the primordial lotus flower. For the acts of creation he coalesces with his other forms ATUM and KHEPRI (see also BENU). Hence in the Pyramid Texts we find Ra-Atum as father of the king and in the Book of the Dead we meet Ra-HARAKHTI-Atum-HORUS-Khepri. Ra is sometimes called the 'weeper' which refers to his creation of mankind, explained by means of a play on words: the sun-god wept and from the tear (Egyptian 'remy') that fell to earth, there sprang man (Egyptian 'remet'). He also ordered the cycle of the three seasons of the Egyptian year revolving around the annual

Ra as creator-god emerges from primeval lotus. Statue from the Tomb of Tutankhamun, Dyn. XVIII, Cairo Museum.

inundation of the Nile which he had instituted. The Book of the Dead has a passage of extreme interest concerning the self-mutilation of Ra: the sun-god 'cuts' his phallus (possibly meaning circumcision) from which drops of blood fall to form two intellectual personifications, 'HU' and 'SIA', or 'authority' and 'mind'.

3 *Ra in the Underworld*

The Egyptians gradually evolved a concept of synthesis between the chthonic god OSIRIS and the solar deity Ra. The composition known as the 'Litany of Ra', found on the walls of Theban royal tombs, describes how Ra visits his own forms in the caverns in the Underworld (seventy-four figures of the sun-god can be counted in the tomb of Thutmose III). Underlying this complexity, however, is the statement, made unequivocally, that there is only one divinity involved, 'Ra in Osiris, Osiris in Ra'. So Ra becomes 'ruler of the Underworld' or 'lord of life in the western horizon', i.e. the entrance into the Netherworld, in the mountain of

Hawk-headed sun-god Ra-Harakhti. Stela of Djed-Khonsu-Iufankh, Dyn. XXI, Louvre Museum.

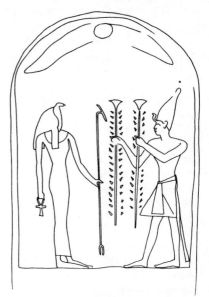

Renenutet receives papyrus plants from Thutmose IV. Stela from Deir el-Medina, Dyn. XIX.

Manu. As he passes Underworld deities he illuminates their caverns and coffins, bringing them into full existence for the moment. They then return into the 'state of death' described in hymns to Ra as existing at night in Egypt when the sun has entered the Underworld. All rebels against his authority are executed and his arch-enemy defeated (see APOPHIS). To travel in the Underworld Ra sails in the night boat called 'mesektet': he is in the form of a ram-headed god, 'flesh of Ra', and encircled by MEHEN. His morning boat to sail across the sky above Egypt is called 'mandjet'. The concept of the sun requiring a boat for its celestial journeys goes back to the Old Kingdom where Ra is dubbed 'great reed-floater'.

For Ra-HARAKHTI see under HORUS section titled 'Horus as sun-god'; for Eye of Ra see under HATHOR and SAKHMET.

Renenutet

Cobra-goddess, guardian of the pharaoh.

The iconography of Renenutet, found on walls or in statue form from the New Kingdom onwards, can be the hooded cobra rising up in anger or, anthropomorphically, an enthroned goddess. Her name suggests the idea of 'nursing' or 'raising' a child. Emphasising this role as the embodiment of divine motherhood, Renenutet can be represented as a woman (or a female with a cobra head) suckling a child. In the Pyramid Age it is Renenutet's protection of the ruler that is paramount. Her tutelary nature is referred to when the king ascends to the sky in the Hereafter to claim his heritage as a powerful monarch: Renenutet coalesces with his Uraeus (see WADJET) to provide the invincible flame that leaps from the cobra's mouth. Renenutet as a snake also has a gaze which vanquishes all enemies; but it can be a beneficial force, nurturing the crops and providing the fruits of the harvest to the Egyptians. Under this aspect she can be associated with the god OSIRIS in his form of the agricultural deity NEPER and this, by extension, links her to the pharaoh's responsibility for the cycle of good harvests.

Renenutet represents the magical power inherent in the linen garment worn by the king – in the Afterlife even the gods are said to fear this woven material. Other connections between Renenutet and linen can be found in texts from the temples of Dendera, where she is described as furnishing mummy bandages, and of Edfu, where she is called 'mistress of the robes'.

In later Egyptian thought Renenutet becomes a goddess controlling human destiny. Renenutet looks into time and apportions the length of a man's life. Together with the goddess MESKHENET she urges forward the unborn child into birth and fosters the will to live. She personifies also the prosperity than can result from the experiences and chance of life itself, a role not unlike that of the god SHAY. Another side to Renenutet is her identification with MAAT, the goddess of cosmic order and truth – e.g. in the Litany of RA found on the walls of some tombs in the Valley of the Kings a mummiform Renenutet with a cobra head is labelled the 'Lady of Justification'.

There is evidence of a cult to Renenutet existing from the Middle Kingdom onwards in the Faiyum – a region of immense fertility which could fittingly be associated with this goddess. Here she is closely allied to the Faiyum's divine protector, the crocodile-god SOBEK. Village chapels in the Faiyum illustrate the point that the worship of Renenutet had taken hold in the hearts of agricultural workers who were for the most part excluded from the ceremonies in the temples. Festivals in honour of Renenutet were held in the last month of the winter-spring season (called Peret) when all the seed had been sown, and in the first month of the spring-summer season (Shemu) when the rich harvest began to ripen.

Some tombs on the west bank at Thebes (for instance, the tomb of Nakht, Dynasty XVIII) show scenes of harvesting, winnowing and threshing where an emblem is displayed over the crop. This might be interpreted as the crescent of the new moon and as symbolising the offering of the first fruits of the harvest to Renenutet at the beginning of the month in which her festival fell. The possibility cannot be discounted, however, that the emblem is a device for warding off pests which might devour the grain. Renenutet is called 'mistress of the threshing floor', a practical role ascribed to her, in addition to the overall task of ensuring the continual fruitfulness of the Egyptian soil, and is drawn from the imagery of the snake eating mice and rats which threaten the crops.

In the Graeco-Roman period the name Renenutet is modified in Egyptian giving rise to the name of the goddess rendered in Greek texts as Thermouthis or Hermouthis. It is now that Renenutet assimilates into ISIS – an identification made easier by the close similarity of the two goddesses in pharaonic tradition, e.g. the association with Osiris and the iconography of a nursing mother. Also in an exceptional reference in the Book of the Dead Renenutet has a liaison with ATUM in primeval time and is then credited with giving birth to HORUS who is pre-eminently the son of Isis. A number of hymns from the Faiyum written in the first century BC exemplify the merging of Renenutet and Isis, an amalgamation in keeping with the Graeco-Roman concept of universal fertility goddesses such as Panthea or Bona Fortuna.

The following tabulation illustrates how in the last centuries of Ancient Egyptian religion Renenutet and the associated deities that make the sacred triad complete are equated with divinities whose cults are of more widespread appeal:

	Greek name in Faiyumic Hymns	Egyptian Equivalent	Manifestation of
mother =	Hermouthis	Renenutet	Isis
father =	Sekonopis	Sobek	Osiris
son =	Ankhoes	Horus	Horus

Reshep

A war-god whose origins are Syrian, brought into the Egyptian pantheon in Dynasty XVIII.

Reshep's characteristic stance is brandishing a mace or axe over his head. His beard is Syrian in style and he normally wears the Upper Egyptian crown adorned with a gazelle head in front and a ribbon behind. The gazelle connects Reshep iconographically with the god SETH but it is the Theban war-god MONTU with whom

Stela of Amenemopet from Bethshan, c.1300 BC.

Reshep has the greatest affinity. His martial temperament makes him an ideal royal deity, especially in an era boasting of the military and sporting prowess of its monarchs. A good example of this comes from the stela of Amenhotep II (Dynasty XVIII) set up near the Sphinx at Giza where Reshep and the goddess ASTARTE are described as rejoicing at the crown prince's diligence in looking after his horses. Perhaps not too much stress should be placed on some of the Egyptian epithets which he receives, such as 'Lord of the Sky' or 'Lord of Eternity', but his status in the New Kingdom was high – a region on the east bank of the Nile even being named the 'Valley of Reshep'. He appears on Theban stelae alongside the Egyptian god MIN and the Syrian goddess QADESH.

Reshep becomes (possibly because of Syrian enclaves among the Egyptian population) an approachable deity who can grant success to those praying to him. Also his force for destruction of royal enemies in battle can be turned against diseases affecting ordinary people. For instance, Reshep and his wife Itum are called upon in a magical spell to overpower the 'akha' demon causing abdominal pains. As a deity combining the polarities of life and death, he is known both in Egypt and the Near East as Reshep-Shulman.

S

Sakhmet

 Lioness-goddess of Memphis.

Her name simply means the 'powerful' and is extremely apt in view of the destructive aspect of her character. She is shown with the body of a lady and the head of a lioness. Sometimes the linen dress she wears exhibits a rosette pattern over each nipple, an ancient leonine motif that can be traced to observation of the shoulder-knot hairs on lions.

She is a daughter of the sun-god RA and became regarded as the consort of PTAH of

Gilded wooden statue, Dyn. XVIII, Cairo Museum.

Memphis, where she subsumed (certainly by the New Kingdom) local cults as 'mistress of Ankhtawy' (= 'life of the Two Lands', a name for Memphis). One of these cults seems to have led to her title, found on a stela in the Serapeum at Saqqara, 'lady of the Acacia'. Since there was a degree of correspondence between Sakhmet and BASTET, her son was taken to be the same as that of the cat-goddess; namely, NEFERTUM the lotus-god.

A superbly carved limestone fragment from the valley temple of Sneferu (Dynasty IV) at Dahshur shows the monarch's head closely juxtaposed to the muzzle of a lioness-deity (presumably Sakhmet) as if to symbolise Sneferu breathing in the divine life-force emanating from the goddess's mouth. This would be in line with a statement in the Pyramid Texts to the effect that Sakhmet conceived the king. Certainly, under Sahura of Dynasty V the goddess received a shrine at Abusir.

A corresponding relationship was made between Sakhmet of Memphis and the goddess MUT, wife of AMUN at Thebes, a fusion facilitated by the fact that both goddesses could manifest themselves under leonine forms. Hundreds of statues of Sakhmet were set up in the reign of Amenhotep III (Dynasty XVIII) in the precinct of Mut's temple (known as 'Isheru') south of the Great Temple of Amun at Karnak. Their quantity is attributable to their ritual purpose in receiving offerings as part of the Litany of Ra, each statue being so honoured on one particular day of the year. Sakhmet's black granite statues either show her seated holding the sign of life ('ankh') in her hand or standing with a sceptre in the shape of the papyrus, heraldic plant of North Egypt. Inscriptions on these statues emphasise her warlike aspect, e.g. 'smiter of the Nubians'.

1 *The savagery of Sakhmet*

The goddess is adopted by the pharaohs as a symbol of their own unvanquishable heroism in battle. She breathes fire against the king's enemies, such as in the Battle of Kadesh when she is visualised on the horses of Ramesses II (Dynasty XIX), her flames scorching the bodies of enemy soldiers. The wrath of the pharaoh towards those who rebel against his rule is compared by a Middle Kingdom treatise on kingship to the rage of Sakhmet. In a passage intended to flatter the pharaoh in the story of Sinuhe, it is said that the fear of the king pervades foreign countries like Sakhmet in a year of pestilence. Her title 'lady of bright red linen', which on the surface is a reference to the colour of her homeland of Lower Egypt, carries, from her warlike nature, the secondary force of meaning the blood-soaked garments of her enemies.

One myth in particular reveals the bloodthirsty side of Sakhmet. It is found in a number of versions in royal tombs at Thebes and on the outer gilded shrine which covered the sarcophagus of Tutankhamun (Dynasty XVIII). It involves also the goddess HATHOR in her vengeful aspect. The two goddesses are both 'Eyes of RA', agents of his punishment. There was a temple to Sakhmet-Hathor at Kom el-Hisn in the western Delta, and in his temple at Abydos Sety I (Dynasty XIX) is suckled by Hathor whose title is 'mistress of the mansion of Sakhmet'. In this myth the sun-god Ra fears that mankind plots against him. The gods urge him to call down retribution on men by sending his avenging Eye down to Egypt as Hathor. As the goddess slays men, leaving them in pools of blood in the deserts where they fled, she transforms into the 'powerful'. During the night the god Ra, trying to avert a total massacre of the human race by the goddess who clearly has become unstoppable in her bloodlust, orders his high priest at Heliopolis to obtain red ochre from Elephantine and grind it with beer mash. Seven thousand jars of red beer are spread over the land of Egypt. In the morning Sakhmet returns to finish her task of destroying the human race, drinks what she assumes is blood and goes away intoxicated, unable to complete her slaughter.

2 *Sakhmet as healer*

Spells exist that regard plagues as brought by the 'messengers' of Sakhmet. On the assumption that the goddess could ward off pestilence as well as bring it, the Egyptians adopted Sakhmet 'lady of life' as a beneficial force in their attempts to counteract illness. Her priesthood seems to have had a prophylactic role in medicine. The priest ('waeb Sakhmet') being present to recite prayers to the goddess was as integral a part of the treatment as the practicalities performed by the physician (the 'sunu'). In the Old Kingdom the priests of Sakhmet are an organised phyle and from a slightly later date in its extant copy the Ebers Papyrus attributes to these priests a detailed knowledge of the heart.

Sarapis Anthropomorphic god of combined Egyptian and Hellenistic attributes created during the early Ptolemaic period.

Although there is an account by the Roman historian Tacitus (AD 55–120) propounding that Sarapis's origins lay in Asia Minor, the land of Egypt itself probably provided the essential ingredients of this hybrid deity.

Bronze bust from Arsinoë, *c.* AD 200, Berlin Museum.

The Egyptian roots of the god can be summarised as:

OSIRIS + APIS = Osorapis = Sarapis

The cult of Osorapis, i.e. the sacred bull of Memphis worshipped in this form after its death, existed prior to Ptolemy I Soter's coming to the throne. The nature of Osorapis, involving the concepts of life after death and agricultural fecundity, seems to have attracted the early Ptolemies as being the quintessence of the myriad of Egyptian deities, and as the aspects most easily fused with Greek gods.

The Hellenistic elements in Sarapis predominate in his nature and iconography. The following Greek deities all contribute to the god's 'personality':

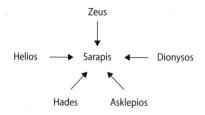

From Zeus and Helios he draws the aspects of sovereignty and sun-god, from Dionysos fertility in nature and from Hades and Asklepios links with the Afterlife and healing.

The major cult centre of Sarapis was at Alexandria but like his given consort ISIS, temples to Sarapis were widespread in the Mediterranean world in the Graeco-Roman era.

Satis

Goddess guarding the southern frontier and Lower Nubia, killing enemies of the king by her arrows. She is a lady wearing the conical white crown of Upper Egypt adorned with antelope horns or plumes.

Her name in Egyptian, Satjit, later Satet, is found on jars from the subterranean

Ptolemaic relief.

galleries of the Step Pyramid at Saqqara (Dynasty III), and she is described in the Pyramid Texts as cleansing the king by means of four unguent jars from Elephantine. This early writing of her name uses the hieroglyph of a shoulder-knot tie in a linen garment, but from the Middle Kingdom the sign is that of an animal skin pierced by an arrow.

She is associated with the annual Nile inundation and as 'Mistress of Elephantine' is the consort of KHNUM and, by inference, mother of ANUKIS. An early liaison between Satis and Theban MONTU is known.

Sebiumeker Anthropomorphic god of procreation in the Meroitic pantheon. His main centre of worship is in the temple complex at Musawwarat el-Sufra in the desert east of the sixth cataract of the Nile (see APEDEMAK).

Sefkhet-Abwy

Goddess of writing and temple libraries.

Her name means the seven-horned and she wears on her head the symbol of a seven-pointed star below an indented arc which could represent a bow.

She first appears during the reign of Thutmose III (Dynasty XVIII) and seems little more than a version of SESHAT.

Her role is to be present at the temple foundation ceremony of 'stretching the cord' where the monarch measures out the extent of the precinct. The goddess also figures among the deities responsible for writing the name of the pharaoh on the leaves of the sacred tree.

Sepa

Centipede-god from Heliopolis with powers to prevent snake bites. He can also be represented with the head of a donkey or as a mummiform deity sporting two short horns.

Serket

Scorpion-goddess.

Her name – also rendered as Selkis – is an abbreviation of the phrase 'Serket hetyt' meaning 'she who causes the throat to breathe', clearly euphemistic inasmuch as the scorpion can be a threat to life. For magical reasons her name until the New Kingdom is not followed by the hieroglyphic determinative of a full scorpion.

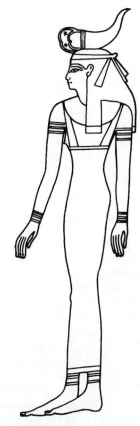

Tomb of Nefertari, Dyn. XIX.

Serket is usually represented as a lady whose head is surmounted by a scorpion with its tail raised ready to sting. The earliest reference to her entry into the Egyptian pantheon occurs in Dynasty I on the stela of Merika from Saqqara.

In the Pyramid Age she has a protective role around the throne of the king. Contemporaneously she is called the mother of NEHEBU-KAU. However, her most important role seems to be connected with the funerary cult. Her epithet, 'lady of the beautiful house' refers to her association with the embalmer's tent. She is one of the tutelary goddesses on each side of the canopic chest containing the mummified viscera of the deceased, in four jars. Her responsibility is to protect Qebehsenuef, god guarding the intestines (see SONS OF HORUS). Serket's help is required in the Underworld where, according to the Middle Kingdom coffin composition known as the Book of the Two Ways, she watches over a dangerous twist in the pathway. She is also credited with binding the hostile snake APOPHIS. It was possible (although rarely found) for the destructive power of Serket to be visualised in a form other than the scorpion: in a Dynasty XXI Mythological Papyrus the goddess called 'Serket the great, the divine mother' is represented as female-bodied, armed with knives, having a lioness-head plus a crocodile-head projecting from her back. Similarly, in royal tomb Underworld scenes she can be shown as a rearing serpent.

Serket has powers that can be used among the living for healing venomous bites although she is strangely absent from the majority of spells concerned with scorpion stings (see ISIS). From the titles 'kherep Serket' (first found in Dynasty I) which means 'sceptre of Serket' and 'sa Serket' (first occurrence Dynasty V) meaning 'protection of Serket', there is evidence that Serket was patroness of 'magician-medics' dealing with poisonous bites.

Seshat

 Senior goddess of writing, 'foremost in the library'.

Her emblem which emanates from a headband is obscure: a seven-pointed star or rosette above which is a bow-like symbol. She wears a long panther-skin robe.

As early as Dynasty II she assists the monarch Khasekhemwy in hammering boundary poles into the ground for the ceremony of 'stretching the cord'. This is a crucial part of a temple foundation ritual involving measuring out its ground plan.

Temple of Dendera, Ptolemaic period.

In the Old Kingdom Seshat has the responsibility of recording herds of cattle, sheep, goats and donkeys seized as booty by King Sahura (Dynasty V) from Libyan tribes. This scene at Abusir becomes a prototype, since we find Seshat recording names and tribute of foreign captives in the temple of Senwosret I (Dynasty XII) at el-Lisht.

In New Kingdom temples such as Karnak or Abydos Seshat records the royal jubilees. She holds a notched palm branch (the sign for 'years') which terminates in a tadpole (the number 100,000) sitting on the symbol for eternity. It is by this incalculably large number that one must multiply the jubilee festivals represented by the ritual pavilions suspended on the tip of the branch, to give the number to be celebrated by the monarch whose name she commemorates on the leaves of the persea tree – an infinity of kingship.

Seth holding the heraldic plant of Upper Egypt. Statue of Senwosret I, Dyn. XII, Cairo Museum.

Seth

God of chaotic forces who commands both veneration and hostility.

The complicated character of Seth is not solved by an acceptable etymology of his name, rendered in hieroglyphs as 'Setekh', 'Setesh', 'Suty' or 'Sutekh'.

The creature of Seth, probably a heraldic composite animal, is a quadruped with a gently curving muzzle, two appendages jutting out from the top of its head and an erect tail terminating in a short bifurcation. It appears on the macehead of King Scorpion at the end of the Predynastic Era. The god himself can take on the complete form of this creature or be shown in human form but with the animal's head.

An early tradition of the violence associated with Seth is in the emphasis that at his birth in Upper Egypt he tore himself savagely from his mother NUT. The site of his birth was the Ombos–Naqada region where his major southern sanctuary was built. In the Pyramid Texts the strength of the pharaoh is called 'Seth of Nubet' the ancient name for the site of his Upper Egyptian temple. The similarity of this name to the Egyptian word for 'gold' led to the reinterpretation of part of the pharaoh's titulary from 'golden HORUS' into 'Horus over the one of Nubet', i.e. Seth. His birthday was always regarded as an ominous event and unlucky day in the Egyptian calendar. As a god associated with foreign countries, he has consorts coming from the Semitic pantheon – ASTARTE and ANAT. The Egyptian goddess linked with him is his sister NEPHTHYS.

1 *God of royalty*

Despite the 'bad press' usually accruing to Seth in Egyptian texts, it is clear that his cult was always held in high esteem in the north-east Delta and in Upper Egypt around the district of Ombos–Naqada. His adherents also came from the upper levels of Egyptian society. In Dynasty II the ruler cult, centred around HORUS since the unification of Egypt in 3000 BC, underwent a drastic transformation during the reign of Peribsen. Instead of surmounting the 'serekh' proclaiming his throne name with the hawk-god, Peribsen chose to be heralded by the creature of Seth. His successor Khasekhemwy combined the two deities on the 'serekh' perhaps to symbolise a reconciliation between the rival cults. However, in the same reign Seth loses even this shared honour and never regains it. Nevertheless the name and cult of Seth are vigorously brought to the fore with royal support on a number of occasions:

Dynasty XII

Side panels on the thrones of statues of Senwosret I show Seth opposite Horus, separated by the emblem of the unification.

Dynasty XVIII

Thutmose III calls himself 'beloved of Seth'.

Dynasty XIX

This ruling family had its ancestral home in the Delta where Seth worship was prominent. Two of its kings have the name 'Sety' or 'Sethite'. Ramesses II fights at Kadesh on the river Orontes like Seth who is 'BAAL on the battlefield'. In the same reign Seth is equated with another foreign god in the treaty which the pharaoh made with his former enemies the Hittites: the document is sealed on a silver tablet engraved with an image of Seth 'lord of the sky' = storm-god of Hatti.

Dynasty XX

The pharaoh Setnakht ('Seth is mighty') is called KHEPRI-Seth, vanquisher of rebels against royal authority.

2 *Seth as an enemy*

From the time of the Pyramid Texts the legend of Seth as OSIRIS's murderer and HORUS's antagonist was common currency. References to the viciousness of the struggle for the throne of Egypt mention how Seth's foreleg and testicles are torn off by Horus. The god is condemned to carry Osiris on his shoulders eternally and the heads of Seth's followers are offered to the king. However, in the papyrus documenting the culmination of the contest between Horus and Seth it is clear that initially Seth has very powerful supporters: the sun-god prefers the claim of Seth because Seth is the elder. Seth's violent temper shows through when the gods become sympathetic to the case presented by ISIS – he threatens to slay one god a day with his sceptre (4,500 lbs in weight) if the goddess is not barred from the proceedings. Eventually Seth loses his right to the throne of Egypt but remains in favour with the sun-god. (For Seth the killer, see Osiris; for the details of the fighting and trial, see Isis and Horus.) Because of the upheaval and confusion Seth can cause he was identified by the Greeks with their rebel-god Typhon.

3 *Seth in the solar boat and in the Underworld*

After the tribunal of gods awarded the throne of Egypt to HORUS, the sun-god RA announced that Seth would live with him as his son to speak out as thunder from the sky. In the Book of the Dead Seth 'lord of the northern sky' is held responsible for storms and cloudiness, a notion which we also find in a historical document: having concluded a diplomatic marriage with the daughter of the Hittite king, Ramesses II (Dynasty XIX) appeals to Seth to remove the obstacles of rain, cold and snow which are delaying the princess in Lebanon en route to Egypt. Seth makes the skies clear and the weather warm.

There is a point of peril for the sun-god Ra as he sinks into the western horizon. APOPHIS the snake attempts to swallow the sun but Seth in the prow of the sun-boat fetters and spears the coiled serpent. This imagery is borrowed by the pharaoh Ramesses III (Dynasty XX) to describe his destruction of the Sea Peoples commemorated on the northern wall of his mortuary temple at Medinet Habu in western Thebes. Because Seth prevails over the sun-god's arch-enemy he receives the title 'great of strength in the barque of millions'.

For the Underworld of the private Egyptian Seth was a terror to be avoided. In the Middle and New Kingdom funerary literature Seth is said to seize the deceased's soul, swallow putrefaction and generally inhabit dark and gloomy quarters. His coterie are goats which were slaughtered in OSIRIS's town of Busiris in the Delta so that their blood would fertilise the earth.

4 Animals linked to Seth

Certain creatures became symbolically sacrificed in temples as an act of triumph over Seth. One such animal, the desert oryx, is frequently represented with the pharaoh about to cut its throat. In the earliest literature the red ox, standing for Seth, is offered up as a sacrifice. Conversely the pig becomes an abomination and not admitted as part of the sacrificial ritual in the cult of HORUS: in the Book of the Dead the sun-god instructs Horus to look at a black boar (= Seth), which causes such a violent sensation in the god that he loses consciousness. The pig remained taboo in his cult from that time on.

The hippopotamus which has a benign role in Egyptian religion (see TAWERET)

can be a destructive phenomenon leaving in its wake upturned papyrus skiffs and trampled stalks of barley. As such it is Seth and has to be slaughtered. The royal hippopotamus hunt, symbolising the victory of Horus over Seth, is found already occurring in Dynasty I. Mastaba-tombs of courtiers in the Old Kingdom use the theme of hunting hippopotamuses on their walls to recreate life for the deceased as he would have remembered it, but even in this depiction of a 'sport' there would still be Sethian undertones. On the walls of Edfu temple the priests had Seth's annihilation as a hippopotamus carved, and would symbolically eat a hippopotamus cake to leave no doubt of his non-existence (see Horus).

Other symbols of Seth include the crocodile into which the god had been transformed by GEB after the murder of Osiris. From the last centuries of Egyptian civilisation the Papyrus Jumilhac gives an aetiological myth on how the panther received its markings: ANUBIS branded Seth, who had changed into a panther, with iron. From the Middle Kingdom a creature called the 'hiu' is also a manifestation of Seth: it is a braying donkey or a snake with an ass's head. In Ptolemaic hieroglyphs the donkey is shown as killed by a knife in its back. The ritual of strangling a goose is also taken to be the symbol of Seth's destruction: a master butcher called Khenmu, living in the Pyramid Age, has some mysterious phrases among his titles which seem to refer to this rite when he describes himself as opening the 'darkness' by throttling the 'desert bird'.

Shay

God personifying destiny.

Shay exists both as a concept and as a divinity. In the New Kingdom funerary papyrus of the royal scribe Ani, Shay appears in the Weighing of the Heart scene (see ASSESSOR GODS) as anthropomorphic. In the New Kingdom book of moral and religious precepts known as the Instructions of Amenemopet, one passage stresses the futility of pursuing riches by pointing out that no one can ignore Shay, i.e. what is fated. The god, as a personification of the span of years, and prosperity that a person can expect to enjoy, comes out clearly in inscriptions from the reign of Akhenaten (Dynasty XVIII) where either the king or the god ATEN is described as 'the Shay who gives life'.

The god frequently appears mentioned beside goddesses who have some affinity with his role – RENENUTET, MESKHENET and Shepset, a benign minor goddess favoured at Memphis. Shay coalesces in the Graeco-Roman period with Agathodaimon, the popular serpent-god of fortune at Alexandria.

Shed

A god whose name is conventionally translated as 'saviour' and whose role is that of a protector of mankind against dangerous desert animals.

Close scrutiny of the context in which Shed's name appears on New Kingdom stelae and papyri as well as a Ptolemaic cippus (see HARPOKRATES) indicates that the name had the meaning of 'Reciter' with the magical sense of 'Enchanter'.

Shed is shown as a youth wearing a side lock, holding some of the creatures he dominates such as snakes and oryx and standing on the backs of crocodiles, his power as a hunter defined by the quiver on his back. Sometimes he is depicted in a chariot pulled by griffons. He is closely associated with HORUS particularly under that god's form of Harpokrates who offers similar amuletic protection against wild beasts.

Shed was extremely popular in the New Kingdom, especially among the community of artisans at Deir el-Medina.

Shesmetet A leonine goddess, probably a manifestation of SAKHMET. Shesmetet gives birth to the king according to the Pyramid Texts and with the 'democratisation' of Egyptian belief becomes the mother of the deceased in funerary papyri. In a spell to be recited on the last day of the year the name of Shesmetet is invoked as a magical force against demons of slaughter. There is a clue to the exotic origins of this goddess in her epithet 'Lady of Punt', i.e. the incense-region near the coast of modern Eritrea.

Shezmu

Bloodthirsty god of wine and unguent-oil presses.

Shezmu is a deity with a dual personality who can both exhibit cruelty and provide benefits. These contrasts are apparent as early as the Pyramid Era and coexist down to the Roman period. He is normally envisaged as anthropomorphic but in the later period of Egyptian civilisation a lion-iconography of this god becomes more popular.

In the spell in the Old Kingdom pyramids where the king absorbs extra divine strength by eating certain deities and powerful beings, it is Shezmu as butcher who cuts them up and cooks them for the monarch on the evening hearth stones. Also in the Pyramid Texts he brings the king grape juice for wine production. There is evidence from a bowl found near the Step Pyramid that at this time Shezmu already had a priesthood. By the Middle Kingdom his cult had become well established in the Faiyum.

From the Coffin Texts there is the vivid image of an Underworld demon who squeezes out heads like grapes and who lassoes sinners for the slaughter-block. A Mythological Papyrus (Dynasty XXI) depicts this vengeful aspect of the wine-press god by showing two hawk deities twisting the net of the wine press which contains three human heads instead of grapes and explains to the Egyptian mind the red glow of the sky after sunset.

There is a definite preference from the New Kingdom to concentrate on the beneficial role of Shezmu as producer of fragrant oils and perfumes. Hieroglyphs on the sarcophagus of Ankhnesneferibra (Dynasty XXVI), the Divine Adoratrice of AMUN, in the British Museum describe the god as manufacturer of prize quality oil of RA. Temples like Edfu and Dendera, where architecturally we can still see the production and storage rooms for cult unguents, emphasise Shezmu as 'master of the perfumery'.

Shu

 The god of sunlight and air.

Shu takes a human form wearing a plume (the hieroglyph of his name) on his head and with his arms raised supporting the sky-goddess NUT whom he holds apart from her consort the earth-god GEB.

He is one of the first two deities created by ATUM the sun-god of Heliopolis.

Headrest from the Tomb of Tutankhamun, Dyn. XVIII, Cairo Museum.

His birth, like that of his sister–wife TEFNUT, was from the semen of Atum; as an alternative explanation involving a play on words, Shu originated from the mucus which Atum sneezed from his nostrils.

In the Pyramid Texts the bones of Shu, probably the clouds in the sky, are used by the king in his ascent to heaven. The lakes of Shu (perhaps the mist that gathers over the Nile) purify the monarch.

Shu as a god of sunshine is first attested in the Old Kingdom where he is responsible for bringing RA and the king into life every day. The pharaoh Akhenaten over a thousand years later emphasises this theme by describing Shu as dwelling in the sun's disk (see ATEN).

The role of Shu as air-god gives rise to his identification with some head-rests which then provide the user with a circulating oxygen supply forever.

In the Underworld Shu is a dangerous god leading a band of torturers and executioners and whose slaughtering-block is a great peril for the deceased. But he can also be a protection against the annihilating snake-god APOPHIS. In a similar way on earth, the power of the poisons of Shu are conjured up in magical spells to ward off the threat to a person's internal organs from Akhu or Samana (malevolent demons of Middle Eastern origin).

Sia

The god personifying the perceptive mind.

Sia was created from blood dripping from the phallus of RA, the sun-god. In the Old Kingdom Sia is visualised at the right side of Ra and responsible for carrying the sacred papyrus whose contents embody intellectual achievement. On the walls of tombs in the Valley of the Kings Sia travels in the boat of the sun-god.

Probably Sia is equatable with the intellectual energies of the heart of PTAH in the Memphite theology, resulting in the creative command of Ptah's tongue (see HU).

Sobek

 Crocodile-god symbolic of pharaonic might.

Sobek makes his debut in Old Kingdom religious texts where he is called 'Rager' and is said to be the son of NEITH.

He can be completely crocodile in shape with a crown of plumes, or partly anthropomorphic. The adroitness of the crocodile to snatch and destroy made it an admirable manifestation of royal prowess. A fine dyad statue dating to the reign of Amenhotep III (Dynasty XVIII) in Luxor Museum from Sobek's sanctuary at 'Sumenu' illustrates the close relationship between the god and the monarch.

The haunts of crocodiles, swamps and river banks, became employed in titles of Sobek. He is also 'lord of Bakhu', mountain

of the horizon where he is alleged to have a temple made of carnelian. His temples in Egypt were widespread. The Faiyum was particularly sacred to him and he was linked to specific sites in it, e.g. Sobek of Shedet. The Greek communities continued to venerate him, sometimes as Sobek, sometimes as 'Suchos', calling one town 'Crocodilopolis' in his honour. In Upper Egypt the last temple before Aswan at Kom-Ombo was sacred in its eastern sector to Sobek, his consort HATHOR and their child KHONSU.

Sokar

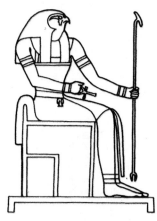 Hawk-god of the Memphite necropolis.

The essential iconography of Sokar is a low mound above which the head of the sparrow-hawk rests on a boat. The god can also be pictured in human form with the hawk's head, often in an elaborate crown of two horns, two cobras, a conical 'atef' centre and a sun disk.

One of the Pyramid Texts possibly gives the etymology of the god's name: OSIRIS said – as a cry of help – to his wife

Bronze statuette, *c.*200 BC, British Museum.

Sokar holding 'sign of life' and sceptre of dominion. Temple of Sety I, Abydos, Dyn. XIX.

and sister, 'Sy-k-ri' or 'hurry to me', becoming the name of the god Sokar with whom he has funerary affinities. From the Old Kingdom it seems that Sokar was seen as a manifestation of Osiris slain by SETH in Nedyet (= Abydos, thus extending the god's presence from an environment centred around Memphis into Upper Egypt). Equally possible, however, is an explanation of the god's name connecting him with a ritual of the fertility of the earth: SESHAT in the temple of Sety I at Abydos calls Sokar 'cutter', from his holding the mattock to break into the first clod of Nile silt.

In the Old Kingdom Sokar amalgamates with PTAH – this fusion as Ptah-Sokar (always in that order) is mentioned in the sixth-dynasty autobiography on the façade of the tomb of Harkhuf at Aswan. As a result Sokar takes SAKHMET as his consort. It is not until the New Kingdom, however, that Ptah-Sokar is visually represented – normally hawk-headed. In addition, by the Middle Kingdom, prayers are addressed to the tripartite deity Ptah-Sokar-Osiris.

Sokar's funerary role seems only to develop as a result of his connection with Osiris. It is suggested that his own personality was originally a god of craftsmen rather than of the necropolis. In the Pyramid Age Sokar is manufacturer of the royal bones and in the Book of the Dead he fashions the silver bowls for the deceased to use as foot-basins. From the idea of moulding objects as an artisan Sokar becomes associated with the mixing of aromatic substances to provide the unguents so important in Egyptian ritual. His craftsman image made the identification with Ptah, also a god of artisans, occur as a smooth transition.

His funerary aspect, however, is of extreme importance. As Sokar of 'Rosetau' or 'mouth of the passages' (i.e. into the Underworld) he was the patron deity of the necropolis to the west of Memphis. He is 'lord of the mysterious region' and is prominent in the decoration of Theban royal tombs, e.g. Amenhotep II (Dynasty XVIII) where Sokar's head emerges from a pyramidial mound as 'he who is on his sand'. This emphasises him, like Osiris, as a resurrected god of the dead, of unrestricted movement and power as his epithet 'great god with his two wings opened' indicates. The ultimate statement of Sokar as a funerary deity is the superbly wrought silver coffin in the form of the god, discovered among the royal burials at Tanis (Dynasty XXII).

The festival of Sokar was celebrated on a considerable scale especially in western Thebes where reliefs on the walls of the mortuary temple of Ramesses III (Dynasty XX) at Medinet Habu show that it almost rivalled the New Year Festival of Opet. The essence of the Sokar Festival was the continuity of the cult of the divine king bound up with the resurrection of the god. Sokar was conveyed in an elaborate boat known as the 'henu', united with his other forms of Osiris, Wenen-nofer and Ptah.

Sons of Horus   The four gods responsible for protecting the embalmed internal organs of the deceased.

During the mummification process at least as early as Dynasty IV, the viscera were removed, dried out in natron and

Sokar 'lord of the mysterious region.' Tomb of Thutmose III, Dyn. XVIII.

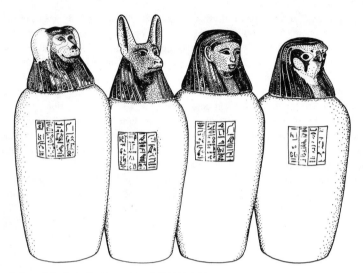

Canopic jars of the lady Neskhons, Dyn. XXI, British Museum.

wrapped in linen packages. The organs were placed in containers – known modernly for a completely unrelated reason (i.e. the resemblance to a late local god of Canopus in the Delta) as Canopic jars. The stoppers for the jars were in the shape of the deceased's own head until the end of Dynasty XVIII, e.g. the wooden stopper of King Nebhepetre Mentuhotep (Dynasty XI), the calcite ones of Tutankhamun and the limestone ones of Horemheb (Dynasty XVIII). The iconography of the jar stoppers then developed into one human and three animal-headed deities. In two-dimensional representations these gods are shown mummiform to the shoulders, e.g. in the vignette in the Book of the Dead which shows them standing on a blue lotus before OSIRIS in the Hall of the Two Truths. Each Son of Horus was protected in turn on the outside of the chest into which the jars were placed by a greater power in the form of a goddess:

Son of Horus		*Form*	*Tutelary Goddess*	*Organ*
Imsety		Human	ISIS	Liver
Hapy		Baboon	NEPHTHYS	Lungs
Duamutef		Jackal	NEITH	Stomach
Qebehsenuef		Hawk	SERKET	Intestines

The earliest textual references to these gods can be found in the Pyramid Texts where they are called the 'friends of the King'. They assist the monarch with rope and wooden ladders for his ascension into the eastern sky. The connection of the deities with HORUS goes back to the Old Kingdom in these texts where they are described not only as his 'children' but also his 'souls'. In the Middle Kingdom Coffin Texts the role of each god towards the deceased is given in terms of a play on words of their names, e.g. Duamutef (literally 'he who praises his mother') is told by Horus to 'worship' the deceased, while Qebehsenuef ('he who cools his brother') 'refreshes' the dead person. They also have a cosmic association in that they bring the king his name as a star in the sky. Later in the New Kingdom they are found in the northern sky beyond the Great Bear as members of the Council (the 'seven blessed ones') set up by ANUBIS as a magical protection around the coffin of Osiris.

Sopedu

Gilded wooden standard from the Tomb of Tutankhamun, Dyn. XVIII, Cairo Museum.

A border-patrol god in his role of 'lord of the east', depicted either as a crouching falcon or Bedouin warrier wearing a crown of tall plumes.

However, in the Pyramid Texts it is the astral nature of Sopedu which is stressed. The king impregnates the goddess ISIS in her aspect of the star Sirius (SOTHIS), herald of the Nile inundation. The result of this union is HORUS-Sopedu, a natural coalescence of two hawk deities. More evidence of Sopedu as a stellar deity occurs in the equation of the god with the teeth of the king when the latter has become a STAR-GOD. This notion emphasies the king's invincibility since Sopedu is 'sharp of teeth' himself, a vivid epithet of a bird of prey.

The eastern desert is part of Sopedu's domain and he also protects Egyptian interests in the turquoise mines of the Sinai peninsula where inscriptions bear witness to his worship at Serabit el-Khadim.

His main cult centre is in the north-east Delta at Saft el-Henna.

Sothis

Goddess personifying the star Sirius (Dog-star), herald of the annual Nile inundation by its bright appearance in the dawn sky in July ('Heliacal rising').

The Egyptian name of this goddess is 'Sopdet' from which derives the Greek version Sothis, normally used in Egyptology. She is visualised as a lady with a star on her head.

Perhaps as early as Dynasty I Sothis is called 'bringer of the New Year and the Nile flood' – the agricultural calender

Late Period bronze statuette, British Museum.

the following equation possible:

$$\underbrace{\text{Sothis} \quad \text{Orion}}_{\text{SOPEDU}} = \underbrace{\text{ISIS} \quad \text{OSIRIS}}_{\text{HORUS}}$$

In the Lamentations of Isis and NEPHTHYS (a fourth century BC papyrus) Isis asserts that she is Sothis who will unswervingly follow Osiris in his manifestation as Orion in heaven. In the Late Period the cult of Isis-Sothis results in less autonomy for the star-goddess and Hellenistic interpretations of this dual-deity – such as the iconography of a goddess riding upon the back of a dog – alienate Sothis even further from her pharaonic origins.

Souls of Pe and Nekhen

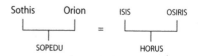 Gods symbolising the Predynastic rulers of the northern and southern kingdoms of Egypt, regarded as protective ancestors of the living monarch.

> The 'Bau' (souls) of Pe have the heads of falcons
>
> Pe or Buto = the capital of the Delta kingdom
>
> The 'Bau' of Nekhen have the heads of jackals Nekhen or Hierakonpolis = ancient capital of Upper Egypt.

The gods are upholders of the divine kingship rightfully inherited by the ruler in his manifestation as the god HORUS. In the Pyramid Texts the 'Bau' of Pe show their outrage at the murder of OSIRIS, symbolically the pharaoh's father, by tearing their flesh and tugging at their sidelocks. They feed the flames of the royal anger at the killing by urging the vengeance of Horus against Osiris's slayer. The ascent of the king into the sky is

began with the rise of the river Nile. Sothis therefore became associated – like the constellation ORION – with the prosperity resulting from the fertile silt left by the receding waters.

In the Pyramid Texts, where there is strong evidence of an early Egyptian astral cult, the king unites with his sister Sothis who gives birth to the Morningstar. She is also the king's guide in the celestial Field of Rushes. In later funerary texts of deceased courtiers Sothis has become 'mother' and 'nurse'.

Because Sothis and Orion are astral symbols that augur abundant crops, the aspects of fecundity and agriculture that exists in the Osirian cycle of myth made

Tomb of Sety I, Dyn. XIX.

facilitated by the provison of a gold ladder from the 'Bau' of Pe and Nekhen.

The link between the monarch and the 'Bau' of Pe seems to be the strongest, perhaps because the town of Pe was given to Horus (i.e. the king) by the sun-god RA as a recompense for the injury sustained to his eye in the struggle for the throne.

Temple reliefs of rituals include the the shrine of the god being carried on poles which rest on the shoulders of the 'Bau' of Pe and Nekhen. In scenes which emphasise the renewal of royal power the gods escort the king into the temple.

To a lesser extent they figure in funerary practices. It has been shown that the 'dance of the Muu' performed at the tombside conjures up the presence of the 'Bau' of Pe. In the Valley of the Kings the iconography of the 'Bau' shows them on one knee with one arm raised in the air, usually quite close to a depiction of the monarch himself, an attitude indicative of their readiness to hammer their lawful descendant's enemies.

Star-gods   Deities called the 'Imperishable Ones' who personify the ever-visible circumpolar stars in the north of the sky.

In the Old Kingdom the evidence of an early astral cult is encapsulated in statements regarding the king's diverse role in the Hereafter. As the Morning-star the pharaoh is assigned by ATUM to the 'wise' Imperishable Ones. The king accompanies these deities in the role of a guide. They prepare the fire for the cauldrons of those gods whose magic the king acquires by consuming them (see PHARAOH section titled Deceased king = OSIRIS).

A clear attempt is made to combine the ideas of a stellar existence for the monarch with the dominant solar theology. The sun-god travels across the celestial ocean with the Imperishable Ones (including the king) in his boat. In a New Kingdom royal tomb, a painting of Gate 10 of the Underworld shows twelve oar-carrying gods who are Imperishable Ones described as coming out of the primeval waters with RA. Likewise, the growth of the Underworld cult is responsible for the stars being labelled 'followers of Osiris'.

A more elaborate conceptualisation of the night sky evolved with its division into 'decans' – thirty-six star-gods or constellations moving by boat in 10-day periods across the firmament. Also the ceilings of royal tombs give the whole vista of the night sky visualised as groups of star-gods. Some constellations appear, e.g. as a falcon-headed deity driving along a bull and others are headed by a combined hippopotamus and crocodile goddess. But beyond the identification of SOTHIS (Sirius), ORION and the four 'spirits of the north' who comprise the 'foreleg of SETH' (i.e. our Great Bear), there is immense uncertainty in identifying the Egyptian constellations by their equivalent modern names.

T

Ta-Bitjet

 Scorpion-goddess called wife of HORUS in a number of magico-medical spells against poisonous bites. The power of the spell stems from the conjuration of the blood that flowed when Horus took her virginity upon an ebony bed.

Tasenetnofret

A goddess whose name means 'the good (or beautiful) sister', consort of Haroeris (see HORUS section titled 'The struggle for the throne of Egypt') and mother of PANEBTAWY in the western sanctuary of Kom-Ombo temple.

She is only a colourless manifestation of HATHOR in the role of divine wife.

Tatenen

God symbolising the emergence of the fertile Nile sil from the receding waters of the inundation.

His name means 'exalted earth' and he was originally an independent deity at Memphis. Tatenen is represented anthropomorphically with a distinct crown comprised of two plumes upon rams' horns. As a chthonic god of vegetation he can be painted with a green face and limbs.

However, by the Old Kingdom he has become amalgamated with the god PTAH and is viewed as a manifestation of Ptah as creator-god. In this role of primordial deity he is found in the important credo of the creation of the world according to the Memphite theologians as formulated on the Shabaqo Stone (see Ptah). How he came to represent the idea of cosmogony

is the subject of a number of speculations:

(a) Tatenen is the counterpart at Memphis of the notion of the 'high sand' or primeval mound or 'benben' put forward by the priests of Heliopolis.

(b) Tatenen is the arable land reclaimed at Memphis from papyrus swamps through irrigation projects.

(c) The god is a specific stretch of land at Memphis, submerged by the annual flood and then rising out of the Nile.

(d) Tatenen is a personification of Egypt and an aspect of the earth-god GEB.

The god as creator receives the title 'father of the gods' and can be regarded as a bisexual deity – a papyrus in Berlin Museum calls him 'fashioner and mother who gave birth to all the gods'. He has a protective role towards the royal dead, guarding their path through the Underworld – Ramesses III (Dynasty XX) is shown on the walls of the tomb of his young son Amunhirkhopshef in the Valley of the Queens inviting the god to look after the dead prince.

Taweret

Hippopotamus-goddess, protectress of women in childbirth.

Her name means 'the great one', rendered into Greek as Thoueris. According to Plutarch (AD 40–120) Taweret was the concubine of the god SETH but deserted him for HORUS'S side in the dispute over the Egyptian throne. This episode perhaps reflected the differentiation between the beneficent Taweret and the male hippopotamus as a manifestation of Seth,

Late Period glazed composition amulet, British Museum.

fulsome belly. Vases moulded into the form of the goddess had a perforation at one of her nipples so that milk, magically endowed by being in the effigy of Taweret, could be poured out to accompany a spell. In magical texts the goddess can be referred to as the 'reret' or 'sow', benign and protective towards the child Horus, and so invoked on behalf of children poisoned by scorpion stings.

Her antecedents can be traced back to the Pyramid Era in the form of IPY. Her popularity throughout the Middle and New Kingdoms is not restricted to commoners: she is shown in graffiti on pylon VIII of Karnak temple at Thebes, an area from which the general populace were excluded. There are also fine statues dedicated to her by high officials such as Pabes, high steward of Nitokris, Divine Adoratrice of AMUN (Dynasty XXVI).

Taweret becomes a cosmic goddess in her title 'mistress of the horizon' which emphasises her as the pharaonic constellation of the Hippopotamus, placed by the Egyptians in the northern hemisphere of the sky. An excellent painting of the goddess in this astronomical role is on the ceiling of the sarcophagus chamber in the tomb of Sety I (Dynasty XIX) in the Valley of the Kings.

a destructive force for boats on the Nile, and in the corn fields adjoining its habitat of the Nile marshes.

Her iconography is composite: the head of a hippopotamus, the legs and arms of a lion, the tail of a crocodile and human breasts. This ferocious appearance deters malevolent forces from harming women at the time of labour and childbirth. Taweret often rests one arm on the 'sa'-amulet which indicates 'protection'.

Her well-disposed nature made Taweret a great favourite with ordinary Egyptians. Charms of glazed composition in the shape of the goddess, with suspension loops, were manufactured on a large scale to be worn by pregnant women. In these figurines her association with childbirth is emphasised by the goddess's own

Tayet

Goddess of weaving.

The most crucial role that Tayet plays is provider of woven cloth for embalming. In the letter which the pharaoh Senwosret I (Dynasty XII) sends to Sinuhe, an ex-harem official, inviting him back to Egypt after a long sojourn abroad, there is a fine passage evoking the rituals of the funerary cult: after Sinuhe's death there will be a night of unguents and 'wrappings from the hand of Tayet'. This refers to the mummy bandages of the embalmers that keep the corpse intact. In the Old Kingdom a prayer was addressed to the goddess to guard the king's head and gather his bones. Tayet also weaves the curtain (embroidered by the god PTAH) which hangs in the tent of purification where the ritual of embalmment is carried out.

In daily life, linen bandages were used sparingly for medical complaints. One spell that has come down to us had to be recited over threads of fabric: it was to prevent a haemorrhage and its consequent defilement of the purity of the 'land of Tayet', i.e. the bandages.

Tefnut

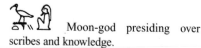 Primeval goddess personifying moisture.

Tefnut is the female partner of the first couple to be created by the sun-god ATUM. He 'spat out' the goddess and her name, onomatopoeically, represents this expectoration. On the walls of Ptolemaic temples Tefnut's name can be written by the symbol of a pair of lips spitting. Her connection with moisture is tenuously established from her position among deities representing cosmic elements and hints in inscriptions such as in the passage from the Pyramid Texts where the goddess creates pure water for the king's feet from her vagina (= the morning dew?).

Her brother–consort is the air-god SHU and their offspring are GEB and NUT.

As an 'Eye of RA' she appears lioness-headed. Shu can also take leonine form and the couple were worshipped as a pair of lions in the Delta at Leontopolis. Tefnut also had a sanctuary at Heliopolis, cult centre of her father Ra-Atum, called the Lower Menset. In addition, a reference in the Pyramid Texts describes her iconography as a serpent rearing up on a sceptre.

There are indications that Tefnut has an important role to play in relation to the king but references to her Old Kingdom inscriptions are rare. However, it is possible to glean that she is responsible for the pharaoh's Delta residence and constructs a pool for him.

Her relationship with her father Ra was at one time hostile, as a Demotic papyrus relates. The goddess quarrelled with the sun-god and went to Nubia. The god THOTH was sent after her as a mediator and flattered her into returning to Egypt. This framework is used by the author of the document as an opportunity to write fables told by Thoth to entertain Tefnut on her journey back.

Thoth

Moon-god presiding over scribes and knowledge.

Thoth – 'Djeheuty' in Ancient Egyptian – can be represented under two forms:

(a) Sacred ibis

The ibis that becomes associated with Thoth appears perched on a standard on slate palettes of the late Predynastic period. Certainly by the Old Kingdom the association between the bird and the god had been made: in the next life the wing of Thoth will carry the king over the celestial river if the ferryman is reluctant. Further, the king can transform into a bird whose wing feathers are those of Thoth 'mightiest of the gods'. The ibis symbol also appears early on in courtiers' tomb inscriptions, in reference to offerings being regularly left for the deceased on the Festival of Thoth.

(b) Baboon (Papio Cynocephalus)

By Dynasty I the baboon in its formal squatting posture which was to become the symbol of Thoth had

Late Period glazed composition statuette, Louvre Museum.

greeting to the rising sun by creatures of the moon-god. Certainly the baboon is, shown in Egyptian art, in such an attitude of deferential greeting, e.g. in the vignette accompanying the hymn to the sun-god. At the beginning of the Book of the Dead baboons stand on their hind legs with front paws raised in honour of RA, or, above the colossal statues of Ramesses II at Abu Simbel (Dynasty XIX), a frieze of baboons is carved to face the rising sun. It is also possible – but not provable – that the Egyptians had noticed that the hierarchy of a baboon pack mirrored to a certain extent their own society – dominant aloof male = pharaoh, select female baboons = royal harem – and therefore this animal exhibited a wisdom worthy of the god Thoth in his role as sacred repository of knowledge. In typical Egyptian fashion scribes did not concern themselves with the historical or logical development that might have led to the adoption of these creatures as sacred to Thoth but explained their association with the god by a series of puns – e.g. Thoth as the ibis (= 'hib') treads on (= 'hab') his enemies.

The god's birth was, according to one legend, unnatural in that he sprang from the head of SETH. Elsewhere, such as in the inscription of the statue of Horemheb (Dynasty XVIII) as a scribe in the Metropolitan Museum of Art, New York, Thoth is called the son of Ra.

There is a clear concept of Thoth as a conciliator among the deities because, as one text puts it, the 'peace of the gods' is in him. The skill of his words brings order to warring factions in Egypt itself. However, as early as his appearance in the Pyramid Texts there are hints that Thoth could be merciless to enemies of truth, decapitating them and cutting out their hearts. He is a staunch advocate of HORUS and is seen opposite him on temple walls in the ritual of pouring signs of life over the monarch between them.

made its appearance in glazed composition figurines from Abydos.

Thoth can be depicted as the ibis or baboon appear in nature or, in the case of the ibis, anthropomorphic with the bird's head superimposed on his shoulders. In each instance the god wears a crown representing the crescent moon supporting the full moon disk. Both his sacred creatures can be interpreted in terms of lunar symbolism. Thoth as moon-god could manifest himself as the sacred ibis whose long curved beak hints at the crescent new moon and whose black and white feathering could be seen as indicating the waxing and waning of the moon. Baboons make agitated chattering sounds at dawn and consequently this could be understood as a

1 *God of Scribes*

Thoth as 'lord of the sacred words' gave to the Egyptians the knowledge of how to write by picture symbols, hence hieroglyphs could always possess a magical force. Scribes regarded themselves as 'followers of Thoth'. They were a privileged professional class and, according to one hymn to Thoth, the eye of the baboon watched out for scribes who abused their skill by applying it to illicit self-gain.

The palette which contained their red and black ink and their pens became the symbol of their expertise. The close relationship between the scribe and Thoth is evidenced in two New Kingdom statuettes. One, in the Ashmolean Museum at Oxford, shows the official supporting the baboon of Thoth on his shoulders and the other, in the Louvre Museum, is of Nebmertuwef seated cross-legged on the ground with his papyrus roll stretched across his knees listening to the dictates of the baboon on an altar beside him.

Thoth represented to the Egyptians the embodiment of all scientific and literary attainments, being in command of all 'the sacred books in the house of life'. The 'house of life' (or 'per ankh') was a revered resource centre accessible only to scribes, containing a wealth of knowledge on papyri – all under the protection of Thoth – e.g. medical manuals, mathematical problems and instructional documents on social etiquette. The idea of Thoth transmitting wisdom, too secret for profane eyes, to a few initiates (notably to scribes in charge of temple libraries) comes across in the Middle Kingdom story set centuries before in the reign of King Khufu (Dynasty IV) about a magician called Djedi: Djedi knows the number of the secret chambers in the sanctuary of Thoth, powerful knowledge not even possessed by the pharaoh himself.

2 *Thoth in the Underworld*

The god is himself the scribe of the ENNEAD, responsible for writing letters on all important decisions or disputes. His impartiality and integrity are beyond question – hence a common assertion made by an official about his life was that he had been 'straight and true' like Thoth. It is Thoth's duty to record all the souls entering 'Duat' or the Underworld. In the Hall of the Two Truths the god is in charge of the balance, an Ancient Egyptian equivalent of the lie detector. In vignettes from the most elaborate Books of the Dead (especially those of Ani or Hunefer, royal scribes, or Anhai, a priestess, in the British Museum) Thoth, ibis-headed, appears in front of the scales in which the heart of the deceased is weighed against the feather of Truth (see ASSESSOR GODS). He holds his reed brush and palette ready to write down the result of the examination of the heart. Frequently, in his shape of a baboon he sits on top of the balance. He has the vital task of announcing to OSIRIS, ruler of the Underworld, that the deceased has led a blameless life and is 'true of voice'.

3 *Temples of Thoth*

His major cult centre was in Middle Egypt at modern el-Ashmunein. Greek visitors called it 'Hermopolis' ('Hermes-town') after the god in their pantheon most closely resembling Thoth. The full identification was with Hermes 'trismegistos' = three-times-great, a description evolving it seems from one of Thoth's epithets found in the temple of Esna: 'Djeheuty pa aa, pa aa, pa aa' = 'Thoth the great, the great, the great'. To the Ancient Egyptians it was 'Khemnu' or 'eight-town', a name referring to four pairs of primeval deities who were eclipsed in importance by the arrival of Thoth 'lord of the city of the eight'. The consort of Thoth 'bull of Khemnu' is

Ibis headed god Thoth from the Papyrus of Anhai, Dyn. XIX, British Museum.

a rarely documented goddess called Nehmataway. The site itself has only been sporadically explored in previous years but is now undergoing systematic excavation. Despite its ruined state it was a major temple under the pharaohs – Amenhotep III (Dynasty XVIII) set up a number of 30-ton baboons carved out of quartzite in honour of Thoth. Much later in the fourth century BC Petosiris, the high priest of Thoth, following the turmoil of the Persian invasion of Egypt, renovated the temple monuments and relaid the park for the sacred baboons and ibises – thousands of these mummified creatures were buried in a vast catacomb not too far from the tomb of Petosiris himself at Tuna el-Gebel. The most important event, however, that his autobiographical inscription mentions is that part of the shell of the sacred cosmic egg (probably envisaged as an ibis egg) from which the sun-god emerged at the beginning of time still existed at Hermopolis.

Thoth had temples in Nubia and in the Dakhla oasis in the western desert. He is also an important deity in Sinai, controlling the mining of turquoise – Ramesses VI (Dynasty XX) is shown praying to Thoth of Mesdyt in the temple at Serabit el-Khadim.

Tutu   A leonine god protecting individuals against diseases. In Greek texts his name is Tithoes.

His iconography is hybrid consisting of the body of a striding, winged lion, the head of a human, other heads of hawks and crocodiles projecting from the body, and the tail of a serpent. Such complex forms seem to be the attempts in Graeco-Roman Egypt to comprehend divine power in all its possible manifestations. Modern labels for the image of Tutu include 'pantheistic' or 'paniconic'.

As well as a festival in his honour held at the Temple of Esna, Tutu appears outside of the actual Nile Valley in a mud brick shrine, dated to the second century AD, in the temple complex of Ismant el-Kharab (ancient Kellis) in Dakhla Oasis in the western desert. He is accompanied by the goddess NEITH, considered to be Tutu's mother, his mother and a local goddess called Tapsais. He is also carved on the ceiling slab showing constellations of the sky in the temple at Deir el-Hagar in Dakhla Oasis.

His popular appeal can be seen in the Roman town of Karanis in the Faiyum, where he is among deities painted on the walls of private houses.

U

Underworld deities The Egyptian imagination evolved a myriad of gods and goddesses dwelling in the Netherworld. These cover the walls of tombs in the Valley of the Kings (741 can be counted on the walls of the antechamber of the tomb of Thutmose III, Dynasty XVIII), or form vignettes in the funerary papyri known as the 'Book of the Dead'. The complexity of names and epithets does not in most cases lead to an understanding of the deities' origins. Consequently, they remain mysterious but can be divided into overall categories – following the Egyptian practice of dividing the royal tombs' walls, decorated with images of the sun-god's journey through the Netherworld, into distinct compositions such as the 'Amduat' (Book of 'that which is in the Underworld'), Litany of RA, and Book of Gates.

The following are the major Underworld divinities discussed in this dictionary: AKER, APOPHIS, ASSESSOR GODS, CAVERN DEITIES, GATE DEITIES, HOURS, OSIRIS.

W

Wadjet

Cobra-goddess of Buto (Tell el-Farain) in the Nile Delta, preserver of royal authority over Northern Egypt.

Wadjet is represented as a cobra rearing up to strike with lethal force any enemy of the king. She can also appear as a lioness in her role as 'Eye of RA' (compare SAKHMET and TEFNUT).

Her name (also found in Egyptological literature as Edjo or Uto) means 'green one', a reference both to a serpent's colour and to the Delta's papyrus swamps which, according to one of the Pyramid Texts, she created.

She is the tutelary goddess of Lower Egypt and is symbolised as such by a title in the royal protocol (see PHARAOH). The major Delta shrine, the 'Per-nu', is under her protection. Wadjet is in harmony with her southern counterpart NEKHBET – in temples or tombs she can frequently be seen with the full body or just the wings of the vulture-goddess of Upper Egypt.

Wadjet as royal cobra. Gold coffin of Tutankhamun, Dyn. XVIII, Cairo Museum.

In the legend of the upbringing of the young HORUS in Khemmis in the Delta it is Wadjet who is his nurse leading to a later identification with ISIS. Along with several other leonine deities she is given the relatively undistinguished role of mother to the god NEFERTUM.

The royal Uraeus

The symbol of sovereignty backed up by a superhuman force of destruction is the cobra worn on the royal head-dress or crown. According to a Pyramid Text the god GEB awarded the cobra to the king as legitimate holder of the throne of Egypt. This emblem is Wadjet rising up in anger about to spit flames in defence of the monarch. The imagery ('iaret' in Egyptian) lies behind the Greek word for 'serpent', normally used in its Latinised form of Uraeus. In war the Uraeus on the king's brow destroys his enemies with her fiery breath as in the inscriptions, e.g. describing Thutmose III (Dynasty XVIII) at the battle of Megiddo and Ramesses II (Dynasty XVIII) at Kadesh.

The sun-god RA also wears the Uraeus which envelops his solar disk within its coils, here Wadjet is Ra's agent of annihilation, especially of the hostile snakes of the Underworld which might threaten the sun-god on his nightly journey.

So closely is the Uraeus identified with kingship that when Akhenaten (Dynasty XVIII) adopted the device that reduced the iconography of the sun-god to abstract essentials, the cobra-goddess was retained on the solar disk, emphasising the god ATEN to be overall sovereign.

Wadj Wer Fertility-god personifying under this name (which means Great Green) either the Mediterranean sea off the north coast of Egypt or the major lagoons of the Nile Delta itself, i.e. Lake Mariut, Idku, Burullus and Mazala. As early as the Old Kingdom this deity is shown in a relief from the pyramid site of Abusir. He proceeds among the fecundity figures, carrying an offering-loaf on a mat and with symbols of life (the 'ankh' sign) suspended from his arm. Under his androgynous form with an emphasised breast and a belly indicative of pregnancy, Wadj Wer is clearly associated with pro-creation and prosperity. Water signs are carved across his body suggesting the rich fishing in the Delta lakes.

Temple of Sety I, Abydos, Dyn. XIX.

Weneg

A son of the sun-god RA found in Old Kingdom texts. He seems to represent the cosmic order, rather like Ra's daughter MAAT, by supporting the sky and so keeping the forces of chaos from crashing down onto the earth. He is also a judge of other gods, probably administer-ing the cosmic laws of Ra.

Wepwawet

Jackal-god of Upper Egypt, champion of the monarch.

His name means 'opener of the ways', applicable both in a secular context in asso-ciation with royal conquests and as a funer-ary concept referring to the Underworld.

The archaeological evidence of slate palettes suggests that his origins lie in the south of Egypt among the rulers of the late Predynastic period. He is represented on one of the four standards preceding the conquering monarch on the monument of Narmer, the uniter of Upper and Lower

Egypt, *c*.3000 BC. However, by the Old Kingdom Wepwawet is seen as a god of Lower Egypt as well – indeed a pyramid inscription locates his place of birth as in the 'Per-nu', the shrine of the northern goddess WADJET. Elsewhere he is described as 'emerging from a tamarisk bush'.

In front of Wepwawet 'who is on his standard' is a symbol called the 'shed-shed' which is a bolster-like protruber-ance. According to the Pyramid Texts it is on this mysterious emblem that the monarch ascends to the sky. It has been suggested that the 'shedshed' sign repre-sents the royal placenta and that Wepwawet stands for the king himself as the legitimate first-born heir – the 'opener of the ways' from the womb.

On the Shabaqo Stone in the British Museum, a Dynasty XXV copy of an orig-inal papyrus dating to the Pyramid Age, Wepwawet is unequivocally identified with HORUS. This link extends naturally to the pharaoh himself. On a fragment of a relief from Sinai, Wepwawet's 'shedshed' symbol leads King Semerkhet (Dynasty III) as he crushes all opponents threatening the routes to the turquoise mines of Wadi Maghara. Here Wepwawet is 'opener of the ways' in a strategic sense. He is prominent in royal rituals symbolising the unification of the Egyptian state. In the pharaoh Nyuserra's jubilee festival celebrations (Dynasty V), carved in his sun-temple at Abu Gurob, Wepwawet's shrine is entered by the king in the ritual of dedicating the 'field', i.e. the land of Egypt.

In a funerary context it is the adze of Wepwawet that is used to 'split open' the king's mouth in the ceremony of vivification performed at the time of burial. In non-royal mortuary texts Wepwawet is 'opener of the ways' in the sense of guiding the deceased onto a good path in the Underworld. At Abydos, as we learn from the Middle Kingdom stela of Ikhernofret, there was a 'procession of Wepwawet' that began the mysteries of his 'father' OSIRIS. Wepwawet, in the enactment of the ritual drama, warded off the enemy attacks upon the 'neshmet'-boat of the god. Very rarely Wepwawet is seen as the sun-god. In the Pyramid Texts he is called RA who has 'gone up from his horizon', possibly with the idea of being the 'opener' of the sky to the light of dawn. Also, according to the thankful dedicator of a stela in the Ramesside period, it is Wepwawet-Ra 'lord of awe' who saved him from being devoured by a crocodile.

Wepwawet as 'lord of Zauty' had ancient connections with the region of Assiut. The later Greek interpretation of Wepwawet as a wolf led to his sacred town being named 'Lycopolis' or 'Wolf-City'.

Weret-Hekau

Cobra or lioness Goddess, guardian of the pharaoh.

Her name means 'Great of Magic' – which as an epithet frequently follows the names of major goddesses such as HATHOR, ISIS, MUT, PAKHET or SAKHMET. In the Pyramid Texts, the title 'Great of Magic' is also given to the Crowns of Upper and Lower Egypt.

As an independent deity, Weret-Hekau occurs in reliefs and inscriptions of the New Kingdom. On the Eighth Pylon of the Temple of AMUN at Karnak, Weret-Hekau with the head of a lioness accompanies the pharaoh Thutmose III (Dynasty XVIII) in the procession of the sacred boat carried on the priests' shoulders. The most beautiful representations of the lioness goddess are on the interior northern wall of the Great Hypostyle Hall at Karnak where she presents the pharaoh Sety I (Dynasty XIX) with the symbol of the jubilee festival (see PHARAOH section titled 'Living king = deified through ritual'). On the small Golden shrine discovered in the tomb of Tutankhamun (Dynasty XVIII) the name of the pharaoh, and that of his queen Ankhesenamun, is often linked to Weret-Hekau, sometimes called 'Mistress of the Palace'. In the shrine itself was an amulet showing Weret-Hekau as a cobra-goddess, with a human head and arms, suckling Tutankhamun. Her closeness to royalty is particularly stressed on the inscription on the dyad statue of the pharaoh Horemheb (Dynasty XVIII) and his queen Mutnodjmet, now in Turin Museum. The inscription describes how during Horemheb's coronation ceremony in the Temple of Karnak, Weret-Hekau embraces the new pharaoh and establishes herself as the Uraeus on his brow. In the Graeco-Roman Era Weret-Hekau participates in the mourning rituals depicted on the walls of the OSIRIS chapel on the roof of the Temple of Philae.

Wosret

Goddess of Thebes whose name means 'the powerful'. Possibly she was the earliest consort of AMUN at Karnak, preceding MUT. Certainly Middle Kingdom pharaohs of Theban origins take her name as an element in their own – Sen-Wosret or 'man belonging to Wosret'.

Y

Yamm Tyrannical god of the sea, who occurs as an enemy of BAAL in cuneiform texts from Ugarit in Syria, found in a fragmentary papyrus which seems to hint that his exorbitant demands for tribute from the other deities were eventually thwarted by the goddess ASTARTE.

Select further reading

General interpretations of deities and religion

Assmann, J. (2001) *The Search for God in Ancient Egypt*, Cornell University Press: Ithaca, NY and London.

Dunand, F. and Zivie-Coche, C. (2004) *Gods and Men in Egypt 3000* BCE *to 395* CE, Cornell University Press: Ithaca, NY and London.

Hart, G. (2003) *Egyptian Myths*, The British Museum Press: London.

Hornung, E. (1983) *Conceptions of God in Ancient Egypt*, Routledge & Kegan Paul: London.

Meeks, D. and Favard-Meeks, C. (1997) *Daily Life of the Egyptian Gods*, John Murray: London.

O'Connor, D. and Silverman, D.P. (eds) (1995) *Ancient Egyptian Kingship*, E.J. Brill: Leiden.

Quirke, S. (1992) *Ancient Egyptian Religion*, The British Museum Press: London.

Robins, G. (1993) *Women in Ancient Egypt*, The British Museum Press: London.

Sauneron, S. (2000) *The Priests of Ancient Egypt*, Cornell University Press: Ithaca, NY and London.

Shafer, B.E. (ed.) (1991) *Religion in Ancient Egypt: Gods, Myths, and Personal Practice*, Routledge: London.

—— (1998) *Temples of Ancient Egypt*, I.B. Tauris: London and New York.

Taylor, J.H. (2001) *Death and the Afterlife in Ancient Egypt*, The British Museum Press: London.

Wilkinson, R.H. (2003) *The Complete Gods and Goddesses of Ancient Egypt*, Thames & Hudson: London.

Special studies on Egyptian deities

Allen, J.P. (1988) *Genesis in Egypt: the Philosophy of Ancient Egyptian Creation Accounts*, Yale University: New Haven, CT.

Assmann, J. (1995) *Egyptian Solar Religion in the New Kingdom: Re, Amun and the Crisis of Polytheism*, Kegan Paul International: London.

Gwyn Griffiths, J. (1960) *The Conflict of Horus and Seth*, Liverpool University Press: Liverpool.

—— (1980) *The Origins of Osiris and his Cult*, E.J. Brill: Leiden.

Hornung, E. (1999) *The Ancient Egyptian Books of the Afterlife*, Cornell University Press: Ithaca, NY and London.

—— (2001) *Akhenaten and the Religion of Light*, Cornell University Press: Ithaca, NY and London.

Otto, E. (1968) *Egyptian Art and the Cults of Osiris and Amun*, Thames & Hudson: London.

Quirke, S. (2001) *The Cult of Ra: Sun Worship in Ancient Egypt*, Thames & Hudson: London.

Translations of Ancient Egyptian Texts

Allen, T.G. (1974) *The Book of the Dead*, University of Chicago Press: Chicago.

Borghouts, J.F. (1978) *Ancient Egyptian Magical Texts*, E.J. Brill: Leiden.

Fairman, H.W. (1974) *The Triumph of Horus*, B.T. Batsford: London.

Faulkner, R.O. (1969) *The Ancient Egyptian Pyramid Texts*, Oxford University Press: Oxford.

—— (1973) *The Ancient Egyptian Coffin Texts I: Spells 1–354*, Aris & Phillips: Warminster.

—— (1977) *The Ancient Egyptian Coffin Texts II: Spells 355–787*, Aris & Phillips: Warminster.

—— (1978) *The Ancient Egyptian Coffin Texts III: Spells 788–1185*, Aris & Phillips: Warminster.

Foster, J.L. (1995) *Hymns, Prayers, and Songs: an Anthology of Ancient Egyptian Lyric Poetry*, Scholars Press: Atlanta, GA.

Lichteim, M. (1973) *Ancient Egyptian Literature I: Old and Middle Kingdoms*, University of California Press: Berkeley and Los Angeles, CA and London.

—— (1976) *Ancient Egyptian Literature II: the New Kingdom*, University of California Press: Berkeley and Los Angeles, CA and London.

—— (1980) *Ancient Egyptian Literature III: the Late Period*, University of California Press: Berkeley and Los Angeles, CA and London.

Murnane, W.J. (1995) *Texts from the Amarna Period in Egypt*, Scholars Press: Atlanta, GA.

Parkinson, R.B. (1997) *The Tale of Sinuhe and Other Ancient Egyptian Poems 1940–1640* BC, Oxford University Press: Oxford.

Piankoff, A. (1954) *The Tomb of Ramesses VI*, Pantheon Books: New York.

Simpson, W.K. (ed.) (2003) *The Literature of Ancient Egypt*, Yale University Press: New Haven, CT and London.

Translations of Classical Authors

Gwyn Griffiths, J. (1970) *Plutarch's De Iside et Osiride*, University of Wales Press: Swansea.

—— (1975) *Apuleius of Madauros: the Isis-Book (Metamorphoses, Book XI)*, E.J. Brill: Leiden.

Murphy, E. (1990) *The Antiquities of Egypt: a Translation with Notes of Book I of the Library of History of Diodorus Siculus*, Transaction Publishers: New Brunswick, NJ and London.

Waterfield, R. (1998) *Herodotus: the Histories*, Oxford University Press: Oxford.

Ancient Egyptian Deities and Later Perceptions

Assmann, J. (1999) *Moses the Egyptian: the Memory of Egypt in Western Monotheism*, Harvard University Press: Cambridge, MA and London.

Fowden, G. (1993) *The Egyptian Hermes: a Historical Approach to the Late Pagan Mind*, Princeton University Press: Princeton, NJ.

Hornung, E. (2001) *The Secret Lore of Egypt and its Impact on the West*, Cornell University Press: Ithaca, NY and London.

Iversen, E. (1993) *The Myth of Egypt and its Hieroglyphs in European Tradition*, Princeton University Press: Princeton, NJ.

Historical, Geographical, Social and Artistic Background

Assmann, J. (2002) *The Mind of Egypt: History and Meaning in the Time of the Pharaohs*, Harvard University Press: Cambridge, MA and London.

Baines, J. and Malek, J. (1980) *Atlas of Ancient Egypt*, Phaidon: Oxford.

Donadoni, D. (ed.) (1997) *The Egyptians*, University of Chicago Press: Chicago, IL and London.

Hornung, E. (1999) *History of Ancient Egypt*, Edinburgh University Press: Edinburgh.

Robins, G. (1997) *The Art of Ancient Egypt*, British Museum Press: London.

Schulz, R. and Seidel, M. (eds) (1998) *Egypt: the World of the Pharaohs*, Konemann: Cologne.

Shaw, I. (ed.) (2000) *The Oxford History of Ancient Egypt*, Oxford University Press: Oxford.

Siliotti, A. (1994) *Egypt: Splendours of an Ancient Civilization*, Thames & Hudson: London.

Concordance of divine names

Amonrasonther see 'Amun-Ra, King of the gods' under AMUN

Anhur see ONURIS

Apep see APOPHIS

Aphrodite, Greek goddess see 'Goddess of love, music and dance' under HATHOR

Apollo, Greek god see HORUS

Arsaphes see HERYSHAF

Artemis, Greek goddess see BASTET, PAKHET

Athene, Greek goddess see NEITH

Buchis see MONTU

Duamutef see SONS OF HORUS

Dunanwy/Dunawy see ANTI

Edjo see WADJET

Ernutet see RENENUTET

Great Green see WADJ WER

Great Honker see GENGEN WER

Hapy see SONS OF HORUS

Harakhti see under HORUS

Harendotes see under HORUS

Harmachis see under HORUS

Haroeris see 'The struggle for the throne of Egypt' under HORUS

Harpokrates see under HORUS

Harsiese see 'Horus the son of Isis: Harsiese' under HORUS

Harsomtus see under HORUS

Hauhet see OGDOAD

Helios, Greek god see RA

Hephaistos, Greek god see PTAH

Herakles, Greek god see HERYSHAF

Hermes, Greek god see THOTH

Imouthes see IMHOTEP

Imsety see SONS OF HORUS

Kamutef see 'Amun as creator' under AMUN

Kauket see OGDOAD

Kek see OGDOAD

Kematef see 'Amun as creator' under AMUN

Khentamentiu see OSIRIS, ANUBIS

Kneph see 'Amun as creator' under AMUN

Menhyt see KHNUM

Naunet see OGDOAD

Nemty see ANTI

Onnophris see 'Osiris in the Middle and New Kingdoms' under OSIRIS

Osorapis see APIS, SARAPIS

Pan, Greek god see MIN

Phoenix see BENU

Quebehsenuef see SONS OF HORUS

Raettawy see MONTU

Rhea, Greek goddess see NUT

Ruty 'The Twin Lions' i.e. SHU and TEFNUT

Selkis see SERKET

Sopdet see SOTHIS

Sphinx at Giza see HARMACHIS, HAURUN

Suchos see SOBEK

Sutekh see SETH

Thermouthis see RENENUTET

Thoueris see TAWERET

Tithoes see TUTU

Typhon, Greek god see SETH

Uraeus see WADJET

Yun-Mutef see 'Horus and the King' under HORUS

Wenen-Nofer see 'Osiris in the Middle and New Kingdoms' under OSIRIS